Hell
and
High
Water

Hell
and
High
Water

The Battle to Save
the Daily *New Orleans
Times-Picayune*

By Rebecca Theim

PELICAN PUBLISHING COMPANY
GRETNA 2013

ISBN: 9781455618811
E-book ISBN: 9781455618828

Printed in the United States of America

Published by Pelican Publishing Company, Inc.
1000 Burmaster Street, Gretna, Louisiana 70053

For Jessica, who I hope someday appreciates what it means . . .

"I owe my exalted position in life to two great American institutions—nepotism and monopoly."
— Unnamed Southern newspaper publisher, quoted in a section of the 2012 Berkshire Hathaway Shareholders' Letter concerning the continuing financial allure of US newspapers

"News is what somebody, somewhere wants to suppress; all the rest is advertising."
— Alfred Charles William Harmsworth, 1st Viscount Northcliffe, British newspaper and publishing magnate, who upon his death in 1922 left three months' pay to each of his 6,000 employees

Table of Contents

Preface

Although I no longer remember many of the details of the six magical, maddening, exhilarating, and exasperating years I spent in New Orleans and at the *Times-Picayune,* I still recall, with an intensity that startles me, the precise hour I knew an important chapter in my life would unfold there. After a number of visits — most involving the New Orleans native who would eventually become my fiancé, and then in relatively rapid succession, *Times-Picayune* colleague, husband, and former husband — I badgered editors at the newspaper to hire me. It took fifteen months, but the newspaper finally brought me to town for formal interviews. At their conclusion, I wandered back to the French Quarter and bought a good-luck talisman: a brass charm of a tiny drunk hanging on a Bourbon Street lamp post. It was the perfect homage to my future home, an appropriately quirky — some may say twisted — testament to my belief that I had found my Xanadu, and if I could only get this job, I would never, ever leave.

I did get the job, but I did eventually leave. And although I have lost jewelry far more valuable than that charm, I somehow managed to hold on to it, and still wear it, nineteen years later.

I have often wondered why New Orleans held such an allure for me, but there's never been a ready answer. As Louisiana-native Cheryl Wagner observed in her 2009 post-Hurricane Katrina memoir, *Plenty Enough Suck to Go Around,* "New Orleans . . . has evolved into the place where Southerners send their laidback people who can't or won't get with the program — their artists, gay relatives, eternal optimists, funny hat wearers, weirdoes and

9

intellectuals. Many of us are in New Orleans for a reason: to escape the fundamentalist Other South but still get to live near where we're from."[1] No one has ever accused me of being laidback, or an eternal optimist, and I don't wear funny hats, but aside from that, there's some truth to Wagner's observation for me. I first visited New Orleans as a sixteen-year-old high school student participating in an athletic competition held in conjunction with the annual Sugar Bowl football game, one of New Orleans's more raucous weekends each year. A group of us was chaperoned by an impeccably mannered and appointed mother from tony, old-moneyed Mountain Brook, Alabama, whose children would never be among the misfit Southerners compelled to flee to the Big Easy. I finagled my way into an outing to the French Quarter with the seventeen- and eighteen-year-olds in our group. For a kid from white bread Huntsville, Alabama — home of NASA and US Army Missile Command installations that build rockets and space ships, and employ eminently practical pocket-protector-clad-engineers (including my long-retired father) — I could have just about as easily been visiting Mars. The music, the food, the decadence, the decay — I was captivated. Ten years later, I got to move there.

I realize my perspective is not a particularly unique one, but my time in New Orleans, in hindsight, seems to have sometimes bordered on the mystical. It was, however, also painful — part of that stage in each of our lives when we learn that things aren't going to turn out exactly as we had thought. After a year of kicking political patronage butt at Louis Armstrong New Orleans International Airport, I was promoted at age twenty-seven — far too early, I later came to understand — to cover New Orleans City Hall. I had enjoyed almost free rein exposing the influence peddling and political shenanigans commonplace at the airport (the federal money that flowed to it meant it was one of the only public institutions in the very poor city that offered the mayor opportunities to reward his friends and supporters with lucrative contracts). But when I got to City Hall, I ran into roadblocks and frustrations at the byzantine institution. Some of my difficulties were, no doubt, related to my relative inexperience, but I also encountered sacred cows in the form of politicians I felt strongly I had proved were up to no good, but whom the newspaper seemed intent on protecting. I understood the phenomenon intellectually, but I couldn't reconcile it emotionally or psychologically. So when my marriage also painfully failed, I left New Orleans for a graduate school program that would pave the way to a different career in a different city.

Although I made periodic visits to New Orleans in the years after my departure and stayed in touch with a handful of the friends I made while I was there, I didn't really reconnect with the city and the newspaper in any profound way until May 23, 2012. Late that evening, the *New York Times* broke a story on its website that the *Times-Picayune's* owner, New York-based Advance Publications, would put the publication at the center of a radical experiment in metropolitan newspaper journalism. The 175-year-old *Times-Picayune*, which had never missed a day of printed publication until Hurricane Katrina stilled its presses for three days in the summer of 2005, would no longer be published daily. Instead, its website, NOLA.com, would become the daily medium of conveying its reportage. As a result, hundreds of employees, contractors, and freelancers would lose their jobs, including one-half of those who worked in the newsroom.

Much of the remainder of this book chronicles the more than four-month battle the community waged to save the daily *Times-Picayune*. The irony has not been lost on me or others that I was able to become so deeply involved in the effort—from my current home near Las Vegas, some 1,500 miles away—largely because of the Internet and social media the newspaper is now striving frenziedly to harness. Although I had been digitally savvy since my graduate studies, and subsequently worked for three companies with significant Internet divisions, I never would have predicted how much could actually be accomplished from so far away via

Facebook, websites, Twitter, and phone calls. Our activities are detailed in chapter ten of this book.

But most important, the September 2012 weekend provided chastened employees the "community group hug"—as now-former veteran *Times-Picayune* political columnist Stephanie Grace characterized it—they desperately needed in the face of the startlingly callous and inept reorganization carried out by the newspaper and Advance. Editor Jim Amoss, new publisher Ricky Mathews, director of state news and sports James O'Byrne, and former online editor Lynn Cunningham (also former colleagues of mine at the newspaper) never responded to my requests for interviews for this book. Steven Newhouse, chairman of Advance.net, the company's digital arm, declined my request for an interview, contending in a May 2013 email that my "account of events that you were so personally and actively involved in, is not credible." Ashton Phelps, Jr., the newspaper's veteran publisher who announced his retirement shortly before the changes were implemented, also declined to be interviewed.

Many other newsroom managers and "content producers"—known as "staff writers" back in the day I worked at the newspaper—who continue to work in the new organization declined to comment, many out of their fear of retribution. Two agreed to be interviewed, and then thought better of being quoted by name when tensions reignited after New Orleans billionaire businessman John Georges acquired the *Baton Rouge Advocate* in the spring of 2013 and promptly poached some of the *Times-Picayune*'s top talent. Because receiving severance required that they sign a legal agreement that prohibited them from making "any materially disparaging statements" about the company, some former employees agreed to talk to me only if I did not reveal their identities.

I know at least three people previously employed by the *Times-Picayune* who have varying levels of discomfort bordering on disdain over the way I suddenly reappeared, eighteen years after leaving the newspaper and the city, and became so fervently involved in what was very much an organic and grassroots battle in a community historically famous for its aversion to carpetbagging grandstanders. I'm sure there are others who view me as opportunistic, particularly those who worked so tirelessly in the aftermath of Hurricane Katrina and have witnessed the financial deterioration of their once-immensely profitable newspaper, despite its continuing journalistic excellence. All I can say in response is I get that. While my heart never left New Orleans, I physically departed and built a new life elsewhere, and I wasn't nearly as good as I should or could have been at staying connected.

While my attention and love were somewhat renewed by Katrina—when I realized that this beloved place that I thought would *always* exist may not recover—my passion for the battle over the daily *Times-Picayune* emanated from life experiences I had far away, and which began several years before Katrina, which I discuss in chapter one.

Because it certainly appeared that executives at the newspaper and Advance weren't going to make any extra effort to lessen the emotional and psychological blow they were delivering to so many, I almost instinctively stepped in to the breach created by the painful news. At the time, no one could have predicted all that would occur after publication of that initial *New York Times* story. And although we lost the intended battle, I like to think we won a war—at least of sorts. As my former editor, friend, and now retired (before his time) veteran *Times-Picayune* editor and reporter Bruce Nolan said at our September 29, 2012, farewell commemoration to the daily *Times-Picayune*, the outpouring of local, national, and even international support was "the most astonishing thing I've ever seen." He wasn't alone in his amazement.

—August 4, 2013

Acknowledgements

Whenever someone sets out to write a book that involves a cast of characters like the ones who work, have worked for, and/or love the *Times-Picayune* of New Orleans, one thing she won't be is bored. Add to that troupe an extraordinary cause that renewed friendships that had been diminished by distance and time while simultaneously unraveling ones that had been celebrated daily just a little over a year ago—and you have quite the story to recount.

I'm one of the lucky ones in that I have renewed far more friendships than were strained or shattered by this odyssey. This book simply would not have been possible without the support of those individuals. The biggest thanks goes to the scores of employees, past and present, of the *Times-Picayune*, who until October 1, 2012—except the three days during which the presses were stilled by 2005's Hurricane Katrina—chronicled life daily for 175 years in one of America's most unique and beloved cities.

Second on that list is Kit Wohl, who was an early supporter of dashTHIRTYdash, the charity that raised money for the employees who lost their jobs and raised awareness about the changes coming to the newspaper. Kit and I became friends while I was still working for the *Times-Picayune*. We reconnected nearly two decades later via Facebook but grew close only during this saga. She encouraged me to write this book and provided wise counsel every step of the way. Recognizing that first books are seldom money makers, she and her husband, Billy, opened their home in the Lower Garden District to me during many past (and likely future) trips to New Orleans. I will never be able to repay Kit and Billy for their support.

Jed Horne, former metro editor at the *Picayune* and an accomplished author himself, provided insightful recommendations on how to make early drafts of this book more compelling and clear. Ron Thibodeaux, Chris Cooper, Jonathan Eig, Millie Ball, and Sheila Grissett, all former *Times-Picayune* colleagues of mine, provided early advice or thoughtful comments after reading drafts of the manuscript. Although his bosses weren't happy about it, longtime *Times-Picayune* environmental reporter and author Mark Schleifstein stepped up and was the most-senior employee who still works for the newspaper or its owner, Advance Publications, to speak to me on the record. I'm grateful for his willingness to do so. Other employees who remain at the newspaper also talked to me, but only on background, and I'm grateful for their reflections and recollections. To the must-remain-anonymous former *Times-Picayune* staffer who supplied a treasure trove of company memos, letters, and other documents that allowed me to flesh out critical moves by the newspaper in the past several years: thank you. Your apparent pack rat tendencies paid off this time.

Thomas Maier, author of 1997's *Newhouse: All the Glitter, Power, & Glory of America's Richest Media Empire & the Secretive Man Behind It*, also graciously provided his insight and suggestions. I jump-started this manuscript with an online class through MediaBistro.com and benefited from careful reading and suggestions by instructor Leslie Sharpe and my classmates, notably freelance writer Laura Kaufman. News media consumer analyst Ken Doctor made time in his busy schedule to review a critical chapter on the business side of the newspaper industry and confirm my assertions. Attorney James Gregorio got me through the apparently always-maddening book contract negotiation. Pelican Publishing Editor in Chief Nina Kooij was an early believer in the story and resolute that it be told by a

New Orleans publisher, while editor Katy Doll did a superb job with the manuscript.

The alternative media in several markets in which Advance owns newspapers provided invaluable coverage of the dismantling of their communities' daily newspapers, reportage that the newspapers themselves were predictably unwilling to do. Kevin Allman, editor of New Orleans' alternative weekly *Gambit*, provided the definitive coverage of the saga as it unfolded in the Crescent City, uncovering and chronicling many of the most heartbreaking and infuriating episodes. The reporting of Rob Holbert, co-publisher and managing editor of the Mobile, Alabama, alternative bi-weekly, *Lagniappe*, filled in critical blanks about Advance Publications' conduct in that market, particularly in relation to a revealing civil lawsuit brought against the Advance-owned *Press-Register* newspaper by its former publisher in 2009, and Advance which this book discusses. To learn what was going on with the *Birmingham News*, I relied on the work of the alt-weekly the *Weld for Birmingham*, and Wade Kwon, who maintains the Media of Birmingham blog. Ed Griffin-Nolan with the *Syracuse New Times* chronicled that community's loss of hundreds of years of reporting, editing, and photographic experience as a result of the changes there, while Aaron Mesh at Portland's alternative weekly, *Willamette Week*, documented the early phase of the latest Advance newspaper to go "digital-first," the *Oregonian*. In the trade press, Dean Starkman and Ryan Chittum of the *Columbia Journalism Review* critically looked at assertions by *Times-Picayune* owner Advance Publications and NOLA Media Group, and found their forthrightness lacking, at best, while former *American Journalism Review* editorial assistant Michaelle Bond penned notable feature articles, including a profile of *Times-Picayune* editor Jim Amoss. Reporting by Andrew Beaujon at Poynter.com and media blogger Jim Romenesko also kept the issue front and center. Dean's, Ryan's, Michaelle's, Andrew's, and Jim's work is reflected throughout the pages of this book. The chapter about Hurricane

Katrina draws on powerful reports former *Times-Picayune* staff writer Brian Thevenot wrote for the *American Journalism Review.* And beyond the alternative media, there was, of course, David Carr, media reporter of the *New York Times,* who broke the story and kept it in the spotlight long after the initial shocking changes. His work is cited literally on the first and final pages of this book and on many pages in between. Within the industry itself, Susan Kantor at the Alliance for Audited Media provided ready access to the organization's voluminous data and answered numerous substantive and mundane questions.

I hired three former newsroom staffers to help with this book's creation and completion. Former *Times-Picayune* designer and illustrator Ryan Smith took on the job of designing a cover for the book. Former veteran Suburban Desk editor Dennis Persica gave the book a thorough read for factual errors, inconsistencies, or other problems. Former NOLA.com copy editor Cathy Hughes gave portions of the manuscript a careful copy editing.

I would never have had the idea to write a book without dashTHIRTYdash and the cast of volunteers who created a proper send-off for the daily *Times-Picayune* and its staff. They include civic activist Babs Bryant Johnson (my first, most dedicated, and most passionate lieutenant). Fellow alum Sheila Grissett and her daughter, Erin McAlister, did yeoman's work before, during, and after the commemoration activities held the final weekend of the newspaper's daily publication. They were assisted by a legion of newspaper alumni, including: Millie Ball, Brenda Bell, Chris Bynum, Edwin Curry, Stephanie Grace, Mary Heffron Arno, Susan Larson, Sharon Litwin, Renee Peck (and her husband, Stewart), Katy Read, and Suzanne Stouse; NOLA.com | *Times-Picayune* food editor Judy Walker; local communications maven Cheron Brylski; and retired philanthropy whiz Jackie Sullivan. Dozens of businesses and additional individuals contributed venues, food, and entertainment to the efforts. They are detailed in chapter ten, "Black, White & Read All Over."

The community support was what touched so many and would never have been ignited and then sustained without the passion and time of philanthropist Anne Milling, attorney Kim Lieder Abramson, freelance writer Michael Tisserand, and community activist Anne Rolfes. Former *Times-Picayune* managing editor Dan Shea, who is now general manager and chief operating officer of the *Advocate* newspaper, and his wife, former *Times-Picayune* assistant city editor and InsideOut editor Stephanie Stokes, not only provided information and perspective that informed my manuscript, but they were the single largest individual contributors to dashTHIRTYdash. Long after most people have directed their charitable giving elsewhere, Dan and Stephanie recognize that getting a job in journalism is incredibly tough these days and have continued to match select donations that aid former employees—many of whom are at an age at which getting a new job is not an easy accomplishment, regardless of the field. Thanks also to fifty-six friends, relatives, supporters, and lovers of the *Times-Picayune* who contributed to a crowdfunding effort I launched to finance completion of the book and its early promotion.

I never could have dedicated the time and energy to this endeavor without the flexibility and support of my employer, Las Vegas-based marketing communications agency R&R Partners. Special call-outs to president, chief collaboration officer, and partner Mary Ann Mele, and to my boss, corporate vice president of public relations Peter O'Neill.

And then there are the two people who bore the brunt of my obsession: my husband, George Molnar, and our daughter, Jessica. They haven't understood what it means to miss New Orleans in the way that I do, but they did their best to stand by me during this endeavor.

Hell
and
High
Water

CHAPTER I

"This Isn't the Death of a Newspaper. This Is a Drive-by Shooting."

Veteran editor Jim Amoss was perhaps the only person in the *Times-Picayune* newsroom to suspect that the evening of May 23, 2012, would be particularly inauspicious in the history of the 175-year-old newspaper. About 10:30 p.m. local time, a story by *New York Times* popular media reporter David Carr—who unsuccessfully had sought comment from Amoss earlier that evening—went live on the newspaper's "Media Decoder" blog. Carr's report was explosive for employees and anyone who loved New Orleans, its celebrated newspaper, or who followed the long-struggling newspaper industry. It detailed how the newspaper's New York-based owner, Advance Publications, would put the *Times-Picayune* at the center of a bold experiment in US journalism: New Orleans would become the largest American city without a daily newspaper. The daily *T-P* would be replaced with a three-day-a-week publication and a beefed-up NOLA.com, the newspaper's website that was routinely criticized by Internet experts and Joe Everyman alike as badly organized, aesthetically unappealing, and difficult to navigate. The story reported that the newspaper faced deep staff cuts, and that longtime co-managing editors Peter Kovacs and Dan Shea—the two most powerful people in the newsroom after Amoss—would lose their jobs as a result of the changes. The only significant error in Carr's report was that Amoss also would leave the newspaper after overseeing the transition.[1]

Newsroom employees had grown increasingly apprehensive in the past two months, ever since the announcement that veteran

23

publisher, Ashton Phelps, Jr., would retire and be replaced by Ricky Mathews, publisher of the Advance-owned *Mobile (Ala.) Press-Register* and president of the company's Alabama Media Group, which also oversaw Advance's two other newspapers in that state. Although Phelps had insisted the decision to retire was his alone, his departure would be the first time since 1918 that a Phelps would not be publisher of the newspaper.

Anxiety had mounted in recent weeks as senior editors began disappearing from the newsroom—first for hours, then for days—a phenomenon sardonically labeled the "Rapture" by those excluded from the ominously secretive gatherings. Amoss and Phelps were the only local newsroom executives who initially knew about the coming changes, but Amoss had steadily expanded the inner circle of editors entrusted with knowledge of the coming changes. The group eventually included features editor Mark Lorando, online editor Lynn Cunningham, sports editor Doug Tatum, NOLA.com editor James O'Byrne, and online news desk editor Paula Devlin. City editor Gordon Russell was the last to join the meetings, which began in late April or early May during the annual New Orleans Jazz and Heritage Festival. All participants were required to sign confidentiality agreements and were sworn to secrecy, with Russell forbidden to talk even to Shea or Kovacs about what was going on. "I went to Peter and said, 'One guy here has to tell me the truth,'" Shea recalled in March 2013, "and [Peter] responded, 'I'm out. I'm not part of this. Even Gordon won't tell me what's going on.'"[2]

As the harsh news detailed in Carr's report spread through the region in the early hours of May 24, 2012, the newspaper's employees were scared, confused—and angry. "Some gathered for an impromptu porch party, checking the Internet on a laptop, smoking cigars, killing a case of Coors Light," wrote Kevin Allman, editor of the city's alternative weekly, *Gambit*, who trailed Carr by only a few hours in confirming and posting a story on his publication's website about the coming changes. "Others went to [local watering hole] Wit's Inn in Mid-City for a wee-hours bacchanal. A few others tied one on with city editor Gordon Russell at his Uptown home."[3]

Over the course of the next several months, Allman became the often-confidential mouthpiece of the newspaper's rank-and-file, a main source of information as the newspaper's brass closed ranks and shared little with the staff or the inquiring news media. "I had to find this out by Twitter," one reporter told Allman the night the news broke. "Do I go in to the office tomorrow? Do I even have a job to go in to tomorrow? I don't know. No one has called me. No one has said anything."[4]

Outside the newspaper, rumors also had been buzzing. Uptown doyenne Anne Milling, wife of retired Whitney Bank president and 1993 King of Carnival R. "King" Milling, fielded two calls from reporters the day before the *New York Times'* story broke, asking whether she had heard anything about major changes coming to the newspaper, including it becoming a less-than-daily publication. A longtime member of Phelps's *Times-Picayune* community advisory board and past winner of the newspaper's annual philanthropic "Loving Cup" award, Milling was a natural source for reporters to contact regarding issues about the management or future of the newspaper. The possibility sounded so ludicrous, however, that she dismissed it out of hand. A freelancer called *New Orleans Magazine* associate publisher and editor in chief Errol Laborde with a similar rumor. "It sounded so sensational that I didn't pay much attention to it," Laborde recalled in a March 2013 interview.[5]

When Milling saw the *New York Times'*s story the next morning, she immediately called her more digitally savvy friend, New Orleans public relations consultant Diana Pinckley, who walked her through the process of buying her first internet domain. "At eight o'clock that morning, I sent an email to the newspaper's leadership: 'I just bought the URL, "Save the Picayune." We're going to go down fighting. Lots of love, Anne,'" she recalled in March 2013.[6] Within hours, and with the help of Pinckley, "Save the Picayune" also had a Facebook page and Twitter feed, each of which attracted hundreds of followers in the first few days.

In response to the *New York Times* story, NOLA.com posted a story about 8:30 a.m. While laying out the newspaper's new structure in broad-brush strokes, the article and a morning staff memo from Phelps acknowledged that newspaper managers were very much still crafting plans and seemed to admit they had been caught flat-footed by the *Times*'s reporting. The NOLA.com report confirmed that the *Times-Picayune* in the not-too-distant future would be published in newsprint form only three times a week: Wednesdays, Fridays, and Sundays, the three days in highest demand by the publication's advertisers, and that new focus would be placed on the website and the company's mobile efforts. The story, which carried no byline, closed by conceding that "the transition will be difficult."

At the time, *Times-Picayune* pressman Cass DeLatte was only a couple of weeks away from receiving his twenty-five-year anniversary watch at the annual luncheon hosted by Phelps to commemorate the milestone in employees' careers. DeLatte's father, a thirty-eight-year pressroom veteran who died while still working at the newspaper, had gotten his son the job right out of high school. DeLatte's wife, Lisa, was selecting new cabinets for a much-anticipated remodeling of the kitchen in her family's modest Metairie home the morning NOLA.com posted its story. A clerk at the cabinet store asked her what she and her husband planned to do about the coming layoffs at the newspaper. "I called Cass, hoping to God that it was just a bad rumor. But it wasn't."[7]

As employees streamed into work in the downtown newsroom and the newspaper's bureaus the morning after Carr's story broke, the mood was characterized as funereal. Molly's at the Market, a longtime French Quarter bar popular with the city's news media, put out the word that *T-P* employees would drink for free after 10 p.m. Amoss hastily scheduled what would be three understandably tense staff meetings throughout the day. "The most extraordinary moment was when Jim said, with a sense of disgust, that there were a lot of things wrong with the *New York Times* story," Shea recalled about the morning staff meeting held downtown. "The only thing that was wrong was that he was leaving."

That staff meeting also was marked by a devastating soliloquy by Bruce Nolan, a forty-one-year veteran who had written the front-page story in late March about Phelps's coming retirement. Nolan's remarks were particularly notable—and momentous—because of his longstanding friendship with Amoss (the two graduated from New Orleans's Jesuit High School together), his role as periodic Phelps speechwriter, and his reputation as an even-tempered, deeply religious, family man not prone to openly criticizing the company. But that changed in this meeting. "I think everyone here thinks this doesn't feel like the old *Times-Picayune*," said Nolan, his voice slightly quivering and almost cracking near the end of his remarks, a recording of which was surreptitiously released to the *New York Times* and posted on its website. "Over the last week, there was a sense of anxiety and dread, a sense of disrespect, a sense that people were being kept in the dark about terribly important things, and that shouldn't have happened," he said. Harking back to the tumultuous 1980 merger of the *Times-Picayune* and its then-sister paper, the *States-Item,* and the way then-new publisher Phelps Jr. shared that news with employees, Nolan remembered, "People had the feeling that they had been told what could be told, and that things would work themselves out, either for good or for ill, but that there had been a sense of respect, and a sense that people's dignity had been honored." He went on:

> And I didn't see that this week. . . . To read in the *New York Times* this morning that a forty-year career, in my case, is ending this way . . . that wasn't right . . . So, we'll go all go forward, and we'll watch each other's backs and we'll do what we need to do, and we'll just bring this to as graceful an end as we can, but it's gonna be tough. And I wish we had done it differently.[8]

At the end of the hearty applause that followed Nolan's statement, a stunned Amoss responded simply: "I fully recognize that this is not what you call a graceful end, or a graceful transition. It's a rough, traumatic one. And I wish it weren't so."[9]

In the span of that four-minute-and-eighteen-second rebuke, Nolan was transformed in the eyes of his colleagues from an editor and reporter deeply loyal to the newspaper and its managers to the "People's Reporter," a hero of the rank-and-file. "I wish [the recording] hadn't gotten out, but I'm happy to stand behind it," he recalled almost ten months later. "I was dimly aware that I had a certain standing, both with Jim, and by virtue of my time there. Someone needed to tell them that the people who poured themselves out during Katrina—for themselves, for the city, for the organization, and had created an industry legend—deserved to be treated better than this."

Nolan said Amoss later approached him and told him, "'I want you to know that I get it.' His message to me was 'message received,' and that there would be no blowback," Nolan remembered.[10] Nearly three weeks later, Nolan was informed that he was one of the more than two hundred *Times-Picayune* employees who would lose their jobs as a result of the changes.

As devoid of specific information as Amoss's meetings were, at least he held them. Employees on the first floor, where the newspaper's business-side employees worked, were told nothing except to read Phelps's memo. Pressroom and packaging employees, the latter who assembled and prepared the newspaper for home delivery and transport to newsstands and boxes, were treated similarly. "By the time I got to work, everyone was talking about it, but managers and supervisors—silence," recalled one veteran production employee who requested anonymity over the employee's concerns about continuing severance payments.

After Amoss's initial staff meetings and the corresponding vague announcement that changes were on the way, it became clear that the newspaper's management was either unwilling or simply unprepared to provide meaningful information about what would happen, and when. Mike Marshall, editor of the *Press-Register*, which also was forced by the *New York Times'* story to announce that it, too, was making the "digital-first" leap, told industry news site Poynter.org the next day that "the rollout of these changes wasn't supposed to have occurred for a couple of [more] months."[11] That remark was astonishing in and of itself, in that it revealed that executives expected a secret of this magnitude to keep for months in organizations staffed by people who specialized in uncovering information and persuading reluctant individuals to share sensitive information. Even NOLA Media Group stalwart O'Byrne, who was then editor of NOLA.com, later admitted at an industry conference that the newspaper's management was "arrogant to think we could keep a secret in a newsroom."[12]

This level of secret-keeping extended to the uppermost echelons of the newspaper's management and ultimately would destroy professional relationships that had endured essentially for entire careers. For close to three decades, Kovacs had overseen the logistics and practicalities of running the newsroom, assuming a no-nonsense, often brusque manner that got the job done and allowed Amoss the luxury of remaining somewhat detached from the oftentimes messy and imperfect work of producing a daily newspaper. Kovacs waited all day for some word from Amoss, his boss, and the man with whom he had spoken nearly every weekday for more than twenty-nine years. When no conversation had occurred by day's end, and Kovacs was left with no sign as to whether the *New York Times'*s report of his impending termination was true, he stuck his head in Amoss's office as he prepared to leave work about 6:30 p.m., several employees close to Kovacs recounted. "You know what I don't get?" Kovacs asked Amoss. "How little your reputation means to you." Although Kovacs declined to talk about the episode, it must have been particularly painful for him because he had spent his entire professional life at

Advance newspapers, starting his career at the *Birmingham News* before accepting a job with the *Times-Picayune* in 1983.

Only a few hours after the news broke, former *Times-Picayune* reporter Steve Ritea, now a senior communications official with the University of California at Los Angeles, created the "Friends of the *Times-Picayune* Editorial Staff" Facebook group, a private, by-invitation-only page specifically for employees, alumni, and newspaper supporters. Although the irony was lost on no one that social media would become an important weapon in the attempts to save a print outlet from a digitally driven death, the "Friends Page" nonetheless became the central communications channel for rallying support and efficiently and quickly relaying news and information to newspaper employees, alumni, and supporters. My involvement in the saga began on the Friends Page, whose membership quickly swelled to more than 1,600, including former employees throughout the country, journalists covering the developments, New Orleans community and civic activists, and scores of people who simply loved the newspaper. The group was and continues as a digital watering hole sans the cocktails, an online gathering spot analogous to the real-life Molly's at the Market.[13] By not providing meaningful information in the weeks after the initial announcement, the *Times-Picayune*'s and Advance's executives created an information vacuum that fueled growth of the Friends Page and made it a central information conduit for most rank-and-file employees and their supporters. As a result, Advance and the newspaper's brass unwittingly legitimized and fueled one of the most effective tools its detractors would deploy in the coming months.

Because I now lived 1,500 miles away, near Las Vegas, I was at a decided disadvantage in providing significant help. Although only a few confirmed details were available at this point, everyone expected the full picture—whenever it was revealed—to be ugly. Beyond confirming that the paper would be reduced to a thrice-weekly print schedule, both the memo that morning from Phelps and the NOLA.com story quoting incoming publisher Mathews confirmed that some employees would be asked to stay, but that "a reduction in the size of the workforce" was inevitable.

Although hardly a rare utterance during the country's Great Recession and the economy's glacial recovery, that phrase is what got my attention. Since leaving the *Picayune* in 1994, I had lost my job twice in economically driven downsizings, and a third time after I disagreed too often and too stridently with executives over the handling of wholesale layoffs at that company. I knew how psychologically and economically devastating a job loss inevitably was, particularly later in one's professional life. The situation was going to be exacerbated in New Orleans because so many of the *Times-Picayune*'s employees had spent all or most of their careers at the place—and had built full lives in the community. Add to that the state of the US newspaper business—almost 165,000 jobs had been eliminated at the country's daily and weekly newspapers in the past decade, including nearly 16,000 in the newsrooms of the nation's daily newspapers. This meant that even if a *Times-Picayune* employee was committed to staying in the business and chose to relocate to find a new newspaper job, a successful job search likely would be difficult.

Long after I had left, I heard about friends at my first newspaper, the Tribune Company-owned *South Florida Sun-Sentinel*, grappling with buyouts and layoffs, and then witnessed the same thing at the company's flagship *Chicago Tribune* a few years later, when I moved to that city after leaving the *Times-Picayune*. However, unlike at the *Sun-Sentinel*, and to a lesser extent, at the *Chicago Tribune*, employees remained at the *Picayune*—often for much or all of their working lives. As this drama unfolded, it occurred to me that scores of people I had worked with were still employed there, eighteen years later. Not until that moment did I consciously consider how extraordinary that was in 2012—in any business, but certainly in the battered newspaper industry. And although I hoped the daily *Times-Picayune* could be saved, I held out little hope, mainly because of the severe steps being taken by so many newspaper companies desperate to return to the lucrative profit margins of the past, but also because Advance had never been an organization that made decisions lightly or reversed them easily—if ever.

Although my physical distance from New Orleans limited what I was able to do, I could spend every free moment on the Facebook page, cheerleading, sharing information I heard, and trying to prepare people for the worst. My one concession toward the idea that the Newhouses could be persuaded to go a different route was an online petition I created "to implore Advance and the Newhouses to maintain the publishing frequency and proud legacy of the *Times-Picayune*." It was the type of thing I could do from afar, and the petition ultimately attracted almost 10,000 signatures. In a play to attract news media coverage—the one thing I hoped might weaken the Newhouses' resolve or lessen the severity of whatever they had planned—I joined with several Facebook friends to recruit famous signatories with ties to either New Orleans or the news business. We ultimately secured signatures from New Orleans resident and national political pundit James Carville; "Doonesbury" cartoonist Garry Trudeau; NPR and ABC News political commentator and New Orleans native Cokie Roberts; native New Orleanian and *Moneyball* and *Liar's Poker* best-selling author Michael Lewis; "Prairie Home Companion's" Garrison Keillor; broadcast journalist Linda Ellerbee; *Interview with a Vampire* author and former New Orleanian Anne Rice; and musician Branford Marsalis.

Others began considering the idea that if Advance no longer wanted to publish a daily newspaper in New Orleans, it might be willing to sell the *Times-Picayune* to someone who did. The day after Amoss's May 24 staff meeting, New Orleans clarinetist Evan Christopher sent an open letter to legendary billionaire investor Warren Buffett, inquiring about his possible interest in the *Times-Picayune*. Buffett the year before had identified small- and medium-sized US newspapers as a business sector in which his Berkshire

Hathaway, Inc., would invest, and the company had purchased sixty-five newspapers over a two-year period. "Naturally I've been following the *Times-Pic* situation with interest," Buffett promptly responded to Christopher. "I don't know any of the facts on their profitability, but was really surprised when they made the announcement. It seems to me that three days a week is simply unsustainable over the longer term . . . New Orleans seems to me to be a very strongly defined community and I believe the *Times-Pic* has high penetration. Therefore, I'm puzzled as to why the economics don't work on a seven-day basis." But Buffett closed his letter by reiterating what many already knew: the Newhouses rarely sell their business assets.[14]

A couple of days later, Tom Benson—billionaire owner of the New Orleans Saints NFL team, New Orleans Pelicans NBA team, and FOX New Orleans TV station, and a former *Times-Picayune* paper boy and avowed fan of the newspaper—sent a letter to Steven Newhouse. In it, Benson noted that a city that hosts Super Bowls, Final Four Championships, Bowl Championship Series, and All-Star games should have a daily newspaper. "I understand the need to embrace the evolving technology that comes with the digital media," Benson wrote. "However, I see on a daily basis the need to have a vibrant newspaper in the hands of those that have made it a daily habit to . . . read from cover-to-cover. I proudly count myself in that number and have for much of my life. Our city needs and deserves the *Times-Picayune* to remain a daily newspaper."[15]

Benson also threw his support behind the *Times-Picayune* Citizens' Group, a coalition quickly arranged by Milling that read like a "Who's Who" of New Orleans's business, political, cultural, and social elite. Besides Benson, and Milling's husband, the group included a number of past kings of Carnival; several fellow Loving Cup winners; best-selling author, New Orleans native, and *States-Item* alum Walter Isaacson; Carville, and his fellow national political pundit wife, Mary Matalin; New Orleans

Archbishop Gregory M. Aymond; the presidents of Tulane and Xavier universities and the University of New Orleans; Charles Rice, president and CEO of Entergy New Orleans Inc., the region's utility; Ralph Brennan, of New Orleans's famed restaurant family; actor Wendell Pierce, star of the HBO show *Treme*, about life in post-Katrina New Orleans; and scores of other business, civic, and cultural leaders and organizations. This influential alliance sent two strongly worded letters — the second to twenty-two members of the extended Newhouse family — and reportedly lined up two prospective buyers for the newspaper.

"New Orleans will be hosting the Super Bowl, we'll be hosting . . . the NBA All-Star Game, [it will be] our 10-year anniversary since Katrina, it's our 300th year anniversary [as a] city," Greg Rusovich, chairman of the Regional Coalition of Business Councils, told WWL-TV on June 4, 2013, the day Milling's first letter was publicly released. Rusovich also suggested that the powerful signatories might be willing to protest with their wallets through advertising and subscription boycotts. "We've got to have a daily newspaper," he declared.[16]

Alex Rawls, creator of the New Orleans music and culture site My Spilt Milk, one of the many local digital outlets that rose to prominence in the wake of the changes at the *Picayune*, drew an analogy between Advance's ham-fisted approach and the post-Hurricane Katrina phenomenon of treating New Orleans like a giant sociological testing ground:

> What upsets me most is that once again New Orleanians are the guinea pigs for an experiment. Since Katrina, we are America's petri dish. Want to test theories on education? New Orleans is broken — go there. Want to test theories on public housing? New Orleans' projects have been emptied — go there. Now Newhouse wants to test its ideas about 21st Century publishing on us, and in each case, the realities of our lives are taken for granted. Our children are test subjects, our poor are simply a demographic in mixed income neighborhoods, and we're potential clicks for a

publishing house . . . The people who will lose their jobs are not abstract entities or job titles; they have families and car payments and lives . . . For Newhouse to dismiss our lives and the impacts the decision will have so summarily is a profoundly hostile act that will not be forgotten.[17]

The *New Orleans Levee* newspaper, a satirical publication founded exactly a year after the 2005 post-Katrina failure of the levees, has its own brand of fun with the issue. First up was a faux edition of the *Times-Picayune* with a front-page banner headline, "Drew Brees signs contract . . . two days ago!" poking fun at the

A front page of the *Times-Picayune,* as imagined by the *New Orleans Levee,* the Crescent City's answer to the *Onion,* in a world where important news would have to wait to be published under the *Times-Picayune's* three-day-a-week publishing schedule. *Image courtesy of the* New Orleans Levee.

newspaper's upcoming thrice weekly publication schedule and what it would mean for major stories such as the then-long-anticipated contract renewal of the New Orleans Saints's beloved quarterback.[18] The mock front page went viral throughout New Orleans and across social media. Another front page story featured an image of an iPad serving as a poor substitute for a newspaper underneath a pile of crawfish.

Late in the afternoon of the same day that Milling's first letter was released, a handful of volunteers led by freelance writer and former *Gambit* editor Michael Tisserand, and Anne Rolfes, founding director of the environmental health and justice organization Louisiana Bucket Brigade, organized a proletariat-style rally at New Orleans's Rock 'n' Bowl music hall and bowling alley that attracted more than three hundred people to protest Advance's plans. Gathered in the parking lot on one of the most oppressive afternoons of the year, attendees enjoyed gratis musical entertainment by legendary pianist Allen Toussaint; jazz trumpeter, singer, and composer Kermit Ruffins (also a regular on *Treme*); roots rock band the Iguanas; and others. In true New Orleans fashion, the crowds came donning costumes (including Joan of Arc accompanied by her knight, known as "the Bastard of New Orleans"), carrying signs, and sporting pressman-style hats, fashioned out of *Times-Picayune* newspapers.

Rock 'n' Bowl owner John Blancher, who regularly credits both the Virgin Mary and the *Times-Picayune* for his business success, vividly recalled how a story in the newspaper in early 1989 took his fledgling bowling alley from hosting about sixty games on a weekend night to six hundred the following weekend, *Gambit's* Allman reported. Rolfes, who wore a custom T-shirt emblazoned with "Print or Sell," asserted, "This is the start of a long, hot summer for Steven Newhouse," while Tisserand fired up the crowd by proclaiming, "This is not a part-time city; we don't deserve a part-time paper." Retired longtime *Times-Picayune* columnist Angus Lind quoted veteran newspaper photographer

Pianist Allen Toussaint entertains attendees at the Save the Picayune Rally in early June 2005 at Rock 'n' Bowl.

John McCusker in quipping, "This isn't the death of a newspaper. It's a drive-by shooting."

Amid the revelry and resolve, however, nerves were frayed. As the event got underway, current employees disregarded their fears of retribution by the newspaper's management and began showing up. "I can't work for those people after this," one confidentially complained to Allman, while another disclosed that he had a letter of resignation he was tempted to release at the rally.[19] Bill Grady, a former reporter at the newspaper who had taken an early retirement in 2007, had a beer thrown on him by an attendee who took umbrage with caustic comments Grady had made earlier on the Friends Facebook page.

The event was a ready-made media circus and its allure didn't disappoint: It attracted coverage by three of the city's four commercial TV stations, the *New York Times*, National Public Radio, the *Atlantic*'s website, Al Jazeera English, several independent local video production companies, most of the city's alternative media, and the *Times-Picayune* itself. "It is incredible so many people love the newspaper," Mathews told WWL-TV in a statement. But "a three-day publishing model puts the paper in the best position to survive and serve the public." He also squelched any plans that would rely on Advance selling the newspaper to someone interested in keeping it a daily: "The owners are clear. The *Times-Picayune* is not for sale."[20]

CHAPTER II

"I Knew We Were in Trouble as Soon as I Heard about Ashton."

To understand why the changes at the *Times-Picayune* were greeted with such shock and disbelief, one need go no further than Ashton Phelps, Jr. A tall, imposing man with a comb-over of thinning white hair, a patrician drawl distinct to Uptown New Orleans, and a gangly gait and chronically untucked shirttail that belie his stature within the community, he was the latest of five generations of Phelps men to hold leadership roles with the newspaper. After graduating from the elite Metairie Park Country Day School, Yale University, and Tulane Law School, Phelps joined his father at the *Times-Picayune* in the late 1970s.[1]

Both men had followed their fathers, grandfathers, and great-grandfathers into the executive offices of the newspaper, and the younger Phelps knew his father was a formidable act to follow. Ashton Sr. was a larger-than-life character who actually sported the stereotypical Southern gentleman's garb and accoutrements of white linen suits and cigars. Although the local Nicholson family had been affiliated with the newspaper since 1842 and came to own it through marriage in 1878,[2] the white-shoe, old-moneyed Phelps family was so publicly identified with the publication that most New Orleanians assumed they instead actually owned it. So, it caused a stir when Nicholson Publishing Co. sold the newspaper and its then-sibling, the *States-Item*, to New York "carpetbagger" and media magnate Samuel Irving "S.I." Newhouse, Sr., in 1962.

Newhouse was a seventh-grade drop-out whose introduction to the newspaper business came at seventeen, when the New Jersey lawyer and city magistrate for whom he worked accepted the money-losing *Bayonne Times* as payment for a bad debt, and directed Newhouse to "take care of the paper until we get rid of it." Newhouse instead turned it into a moneymaker, and ultimately bought the newspaper from his then-employer, the first of many he would acquire.[3] By the time a newspaper broker working for Newhouse in the early 1960s suggested that he consider buying the then-two New Orleans newspapers, Newhouse already had a national reputation for identifying potentially financially lucrative family-owned newspapers and paying top dollar to entice sometimes-fractious families to sell. With a price tag of $42 million (roughly $314.5 million in today's dollars), the acquisition of the *Times-Picayune* and the *States-Item* was, at the time, the "biggest deal in U.S. journalism history . . . more than three times what the Louisiana territory had cost the US," *Time* magazine noted.[4]

Far from being uncomfortable with the nepotistic practices prevalent at the *Times-Picayune*, Newhouse had a longstanding reputation of employing scores of relatives within the ranks of his company, and promoted Phelps Sr. to the post of publisher in 1967.[5] That regard for family — both in a literal and figurative business sense — was personified at the August 1979 memorial service for Sam Newhouse at New York's historic Temple Emanu-El. "My friend referred to his group of newspapers as a family, and that is how we felt — as a family," Phelps Sr. told the congregation in the service's first eulogy.[6] Upon Sam Newhouse's death, his son Donald assumed leadership of the company's newspapers, and four months later, in December 1979, Phelps Jr. assumed the role of president and publisher of the *Times-Picayune* from his father.

If he felt any hesitancy in acting boldly in the lingering shadow of his father (who remained chairman of the company until his death in 1983), Phelps Jr. didn't show it. Seven months after being named to his new role, he merged the *Times-Picayune* and the *States-Item*, which shared business operations but were fiercely competitive editorially.[7] In sharp contrast to what would become common practice at consolidating newspapers across the country,

Phelps continued a long-running staffing policy at the newspaper: He laid off no one as a result of the merger. Instead, he deployed a chunk of the newly combined workforce to establish five suburban bureaus that spanned both banks of the Mississippi River, the north and south shores of massive Lake Pontchartrain, and extended thirty miles west into the region's River Parishes toward the state capital of Baton Rouge, and fifty miles south into the wetlands of St. Bernard and Plaquemines parishes.

Those bureaus, in turn, filled five zoned editions widely credited with deterring fledgling suburban competition and solidifying the *Times-Picayune's* monopoly grip on the region. Phelps also created the twice-weekly community news sections, which were filled with community-specific "softer news" about civic, religious, recreational, and educational notables and happenings. Originally called "Our Town," and later the "Picayune" sections (as they are still called today), they were distributed to both newspaper subscribers, with their daily subscription, and non-subscribers, for free each Wednesday and Sunday. "For decades, the local 'Picayune' sections built bonds with readers—and provided advertisers a vehicle for blanketing homes regardless of newspaper readership," the *Times-Picayune* and its companion NOLA.com website noted in a March 2012 article. "As circulation and advertising revenues among US newspapers began to fall dramatically with the onset of the digital revolution in the mid-2000s, *The Times-Picayune's* community news sections proved key to sustaining revenues by helping print advertisers reach non-subscribing households in the region."[8] The strategy worked. "Three out of four people [in New Orleans see] the paper each week, whether they get it at home, buy it at a newspaper box or pick it up somewhere, like a barber shop, beauty parlor, bar or coffee shop," veteran business journalist Micheline Maynard observed in May 2012. "Obviously, that figure doesn't translate directly to sales . . . but it would seem to denote just how important the *Times-Pic* is."[9] An astounding 85.8 percent of the New Orleans market read either the newspaper or its website, NOLA.com, the highest ratio in the country, according to a 2009 report by syndicated market analytics company the Media Audit.[10]

New Orleans is a special place among America's great cities, known equally for its idiosyncratic way of life; long, multicultural history; full-throated embrace of revelry; and the colorful escapades and scandals of its politicians and institutions. While reportedly wildly profitable for most of its contemporary history, the *Times-Picayune* was, for decades, regarded as a horrible publication. In 1974, it was named among the ten worst US newspapers by *[MORE]*,[11] a popular journalism review published in the 1970s whose alumni included TV news broadcasting veteran Brit Hume and the late journalist, screenwriter, and film director Nora Ephron. In calling out the *Times-Picayune*, *[MORE]* wrote:

> Once well-nigh universally acknowledged to be the worst big-city daily in the South, this bloated, sluggish, myopic giant of the Delta morn is showing signs of becoming merely bad . . . You can still find a five-column Sears ad on the op-ed page and Jane Fonda vilified on the editorial page. A page-one salute to President Nixon signed by publisher Ashton Phelps. Ads that look like news stories. News stories that read like ads. Pitiful Washington coverage. No investigative reporting at all.[12]

That abysmal record steadily began to change under Phelps Jr. and former editor Charlie Ferguson, and then Jim Amoss, who, like Phelps Jr., had spent his entire career at the company and was named editor in 1989.

During their shared tenure, Phelps and Amoss oversaw some of the most important editorial chapters in the newspaper's history. These included coverage of the political ascendancy and descent back into ignominy of former Knights of the Ku Klux Klan Grand Wizard David Duke; the newspaper's subsequent 1993 series, "Together, Apart: the Myth of Race," which exhaustively examined race and racism in New Orleans's complex ethnic and socioeconomic tapestry (and which Phelps in 2003 labeled "the most significant work we've ever done"[13]); its "Oceans of Trouble" series that documented the decline of the world's fisheries and captured the 1997 Pulitzer Prize Gold Medal for Public Service; the prescient 2002 "Washing Away" five-part series that explored what would likely happen to South Louisiana when the next major hurricane hit; and the internationally lauded (and double-Pulitzer Prize-winning) coverage of the aftermath of 2005's Hurricane Katrina.

During Phelps's and Amoss's thirty-eight-year professional association, the *Times-Picayune* won all four of its Pulitzer Prizes (which included a 1997 award for political cartooning by the newspaper's former editorial cartoonist Walt Handelsman), and most of journalism's other big prizes, including the Selden Ring Award for Investigative Reporting, granted by the University of Southern California's Annenberg School for Communication and Journalism; the George Polk Award in Journalism, conferred by Long Island University; the John B. Oakes Award, presented by Columbia University's School of Journalism; and the Scripps Howard Edward J. Meeman Award. The latter two were for exemplary environmental reporting, a specialty for which the *Times-Picayune* became widely recognized, in large part because of the exhaustive, yet nuanced work of its longtime environmental reporter, Mark Schleifstein. The newspaper went from "being a joke in . . . journalism circles to being a darling," Carol Felsenthal observed in her 1998 book about the Newhouse media dynasty, *Citizen Newhouse: Portrait of a Media Merchant*,[14] and became regarded as one of the country's preeminent regional newspapers.

It's unclear, however, which Phelps oversaw the local implementation of what would become an important operational aspect of being a Newhouse newspaper: The "Pledge." The Pledge was an extraordinary and unusual job security pact that simultaneously helped to keep organized labor at bay and to retain non-unionized employees by guaranteeing their jobs at the twenty-some-odd daily papers owned by Advance Publications, Newhouse's newspaper arm. "The Newhouse Pledge was so well-known throughout the newspaper industry that it was almost considered legendary," according to a lawsuit brought in Mobile, Alabama circuit court in 2009 that centered on the Pledge. "In fact, it has been touted by the Newhouse Family as the hallmark of the Newhouse Newspapers and the reason for employee loyalty."[15]

Almost everyone who has worked at a Newhouse newspaper in the past forty years is at least aware of the Pledge, although none interviewed for this book could pinpoint its actual incarnation. Donald Newhouse, the son of Advance founder Sam Newhouse, testified in April 2011 when the Mobile suit finally came to trial that he had written it more than three decades earlier.[16] "The Pledge certainly predates my time at the company," said an executive who spent more than thirty years with the organization and spoke to me for this book on the condition of anonymity. "I would have to assume its origins were with the Newhouse family." A staple of both employee handbooks and the *Times-Picayune* annual employee meetings, an iteration of it from the early 1990s read: "For all Permanent Employees: No one will lose his or her employment because of technological changes or economic conditions so long as the newspaper continues to publish and you are willing to retrain for another job, if necessary."[17]

Sam Newhouse had a lifelong antipathy toward organized labor, and his career was marked by vitriolic and protracted battles with unions from Oregon to New York, including a particularly nasty six-year battle in Portland from 1959-65 during which his cousin, who was production manager of the *Oregonian* at the time, was injured by a shotgun blast.

"I refuse to stand by passively and allow any union to 'bust' me," he wrote in *A Memo to My Children*,[18] a thin, self-published memoir that is apparently the only personally penned record of his life and career. Several authors and reporters who have studied Sam Newhouse's life and career noted that his hostility toward organized labor ran so deep that he undoubtedly was at least the Pledge's early architect, if not its actual author. "S.I. Newhouse was as violently opposed to organized labor as a newspaper publisher could be," Richard Meeker, publisher of Portland, Oregon's, alternative weekly, *Willamette Week*, and author of 1983's *Newspaperman: S.I. Newhouse and the Business of News*, told me. "He allowed some lax, sloppy practices by his employees in an effort to avoid [the] hostility between employees and managers"[19] that could foment organized labor. Aaron Mesh, Meeker's *Willamette Week* reporter who has covered the wrenching changes of "digital first" at the *Oregonian*, reported in late June 2013 that the Pledge actually originated in Portland as a response to the city's protracted and violent labor strike and Advance's determination to permanently extinguish any threat of a union resurgence there. It then "soon spread to other Advance newspapers," Mesh wrote.[20] Some *Times-Picayune* employees recall Phelps's annual employee presentations to them traditionally ended with a declaration of the company's dislike of unions followed by a recitation of the Pledge. "The 'Newhouse Pledge,' far from being a gracious offer from the uber-rich Newhouses to their employees, was really nothing more than an attempt to keep out unions," Rob Holbert, co-publisher/managing editor of Mobile, Alabama's, alternative biweekly *Lagniappe,* wrote in an article about the Mobile circuit court trial in which Donald Newhouse testified.[21]

On June 23, 2008, Phelps distributed a memo to *Times-Picayune* employees that talked about the mounting and seemingly intractable business challenges afflicting the US newspaper industry. While never explicitly acknowledging that the Pledge had been revised, the memo added several phrases in the version Phelps was communicating, as noted in bold-faced text below:

> No **permanent, non-union** employee will lose his or her employment because of technological changes or economic conditions so long as you perform your work in a responsible,

productive manner, without misconduct, you have completed your probationary period, the newspaper continues to publish **daily its current newsprint product** and you are willing to retrain for another job, if necessary.[22]

Phelps went on to say "The Pledge was never intended to apply to weekly publications or to distribution of content over the Internet. The Pledge's protection is tied to the daily publication of the *Times-Picayune's* current newsprint product—not the functions you perform individually . . . The Pledge does not apply to situations in which our newspaper ceases to publish daily our current newsprint product." Phelps felt the need to reiterate the revised language in another memo to employees distributed a mere six months later.[23]

In retrospect, these changes to the Pledge make it clear that Advance began contemplating a less-than-daily publication schedule for at least some of its roughly two dozen daily newspapers sometime before June 2008, which paved the way for the workforce reductions previously prohibited by the Pledge, but which would occur once the Advance newspaper at issue no longer printed daily.

Although the changes to the Pledge didn't cause much stir among *Times-Picayune* employees, language in another memo Phelps issued in November 2011 did. "Looking ahead to 2012, current projections for business again look very tough," the memo began. "I will be making some announcements before the end of the year and will make those to everyone as soon as I am able to."[24] Two months later, Phelps announced the seemingly good news that the company would reimburse wages employees had forgone for unpaid furloughs they were required to take in 2011, but then added, "We have put in place a 2012 budget for the company which doesn't require any further company-wide announcements at this time. However, I feel obliged to report that with the serious challenges ahead of us, we may need to make additional changes to our operations in 2012. I certainly hope that 2012 turns out better than we can currently project."[25]

Journalists, whether by training or temperament, tend toward paranoia and conspiracy theories, so this ominous language, coupled with Phelps's unexpected retirement announcement in March 2012, only three months into the newspaper's yearlong 175th anniversary commemoration, led many to begin fearing the worst. Phelps declined to be interviewed for this book, but the *Times-Picayune* article announcing his coming retirement, written by veteran reporter Bruce Nolan, seemed forthright. In it, Phelps insisted that, while difficult, "this is one hundred percent my decision." A subsequent unbylined article in late May 2012 said Phelps first talked to the Newhouses in August 2011 about his desire, at age sixty-six, to reduce "the day-to-day stress" of being the newspaper's "full-time lead operator." In February 2012, Advance asked Phelps to stay, but he declined, having already started looking forward to his retirement, the report said. Phelps's successor would be Ricky Mathews, the Alabama native and longtime Gulf Coast resident, who was publisher of the *Press-Register* and president of Advance's Alabama Media Group.

Change, however, can be difficult, especially in a community as provincial and tradition-bound as New Orleans, a reality the story tacitly acknowledged. "The change will be a milestone for New Orleans," the March 2012 report noted. Mathews's ascendancy "will mark the first time in 133 years the 175-year-old newspaper, with its civic, cultural and social voice, has not been led by a [native] New Orleanian."[26] The story announcing Phelps's retirement and Mathews's appointment went to great lengths to highlight a bond between New Orleans and the newspaper's new publisher, noting that Mathews spent time in New Orleans while growing up in nearby Gulfport, Mississippi. It also pointed out that he had been past publisher of the *Sun-Herald* in neighboring Biloxi, which had shared the 2006 Pulitzer Prize Public Service Gold Medal for coverage of Hurricane Katrina and its aftermath with the *Times-*

Picayune. However, the differences between Phelps and Mathews were stark. In addition to their disparate pedigrees (Mathews was born in Birmingham, raised on Mississippi's Gulf Coast, and earned undergraduate and MBA degrees from Southern Mississippi University), the two men also shared passionate but contrasting leisure interests: Phelps is an avid, lifelong tennis player, while Mathews prefers hunting and fishing. Phelps is a longtime member of the Krewe of Rex, the pre-eminent, old-line New Orleans Mardi Gras organization that selects the King of Carnival each year, and of the Boston Club, one of the oldest elite men's clubs in the country. For his part, Mathews, a fitness fanatic, favored rubbing elbows with governors and serving on state boards addressing issues ranging from coastal erosion to the BP clean-up. (He counted Mississippi's Haley Barbour and Alabama's Bob Riley as friends.)

Less immediately apparent in New Orleans was Mathews's penchant for a level of self-promotion that simply was not part of Phelps's psyche. For example, during Mathews's twenty-nine month *Press-Register* tenure, the newspaper averaged more than one story every month that either featured or was written by him, most which included photographs of Mathews.[27] An employee at the *Sun-Herald* said such grandstanding also was commonplace there.

The announcement of Phelps's retirement rattled no one more than the newspaper's employees. In the seven years since Katrina had ravaged New Orleans, little had been predictable beyond the continuity of their employer's leadership and its commitment to publishing a daily newspaper. Now, that stability, like Louisiana's critical and protective marshlands, appeared to be dangerously eroding.

It is impossible to understand contemporary New Orleans and the *Times-Picayune* without having some appreciation for the magnitude of the tragedy that was Katrina. Although few observers will soon forget the searing images that emanated from the shattered region, the equally carefree representations of Mardi Gras, the Super Bowl, and Final Four championships the city has since hosted make it easier to forget how truly imperiled New Orleans was. The Central Business District, French Quarter, West Bank of the Mississippi River, and historic neighborhoods located on the geographic high ground—referred to by locals since the storm as the "Sliver by the River"—were relatively undamaged. However, vast expanses of New Orleans were inundated by floodwaters. Approximately 80 percent of the city flooded, making Katrina the largest residential disaster in US history. The final death toll from the storm and its aftermath was 1,836, including 1,577 from Louisiana. (In contrast, Hurricane Sandy, which struck far more populous communities in twenty-four East Coast states in October 2012, claimed about 113 American lives.[28]) More than one million Gulf Coast residents were displaced by Katrina, and as many as 600,000 households were still dislocated a month later. In New Orleans alone, 134,000 housing units—70 percent of all occupied residences—suffered storm and/or flood damage.[29] Roughly one-third of *Times-Picayune* employees were among those whose homes were seriously damaged or destroyed. "Like our readers, we're also the ones to whom the events happened, at once narrator and subject," Amoss reflected in a speech given to the American Bar Association almost six months after the storm. "The intersection of these two roles has been excruciating. In the course of a single day, our way of life and sense of order were wiped out."[30]

In a powerful account about the first days after the storm published in the *American Journalism Review*, then-*Times-Picayune* staff writer Brian Thevenot recalled a conversation with an exhausted and crying editorial page editor Terri Troncale about the city's questionable viability after such a devastating blow. "I just don't see how you can have a newspaper without a market," Troncale told Thevenot, who immediately realized that "in the flurry of work, it hadn't even occurred to me that Katrina may have destroyed my newspaper, that the *Picayune* might fold or become a shell of its former self."[31] As the months unfolded, Troncale's fears seemed to materialize: the city's population fell by nearly 64 percent—from 437,186 to 158,353 in the year after Katrina.[32]

Historical circulation figures provided by the Alliance for Audited Media (an industry auditing organization previously known as the Audit Bureau of Circulations) supported the notion that a combination of Phelps's suburban strategy, New Orleans's tradition-bound ways, and the newspaper's steady improvement in quality likely helped it avoid the same steep decline many other US metropolitan newspapers experienced in the twenty-five years before Katrina. The newspaper's 1980 daily, average circulation was nearly 281,000, a number that remained somewhat steady through 1999. (The *Times-Picayune*'s average daily circulation, however, fell more than 5 percent between 1999 and March 2005, the last figures available before the storm, slightly more than overall daily newspaper circulation declined nationally during the same time period.) The *Times-Picayune*'s circulation then plunged nearly 30 percent in the twenty-seven months after Katrina, while national circulation fell by less than 5 percent. Between 2007 and 2012, the *Times-Picayune*'s circulation dropped more than another 25 percent, while national circulation between 2007 and 2011 (the most recent year for which figures were available) declined about 12 percent.

The newspaper's continued, sharp decline post-Katrina was no doubt propelled by the region's smaller population, but it also gives credence to the company's arguments that the Internet hurt the *Times-Picayune* in the same way it wounded newspapers across the country. New Orleans's recovering post-Katrina population is also younger, better-educated, and more tech-savvy, which could at least partially explain the continuing circulation decline of the print product.

Advance is a privately held company and releases very little financial or operational data. After its local management team had acknowledged that the *Times-Picayune* historically has been profitable (which both Amoss and Steven Newhouse, chairman of Advance.net, confirmed to news media as late as August 2012), the newspaper did release limited financial data to the *Wall Street Journal* in September 2012, presumably in an attempt to illustrate how dramatically its business fortunes had reversed. Mathews provided figures to the *Journal* that indicated that the *Times-Picayune*'s print ad sales had fallen by more than 42 percent since 2009, including a 10 percent annual decline through August 2012. "With a 10 percent revenue decline this year, it could be not profitable real quick, unless you drastically cut costs," Mathews told the *Journal*.[33]

Most newspapers began giving away their content for free as soon as they built websites to complement their print products beginning in the mid-1990s, and planned to primarily support their digital operations as they had financed their print products — through advertising. That approach, however, conditioned readers to expect journalism for free that was far from free to produce. As a result, readers defected from print to the web, which steadily chipped away at both circulation and advertising revenues. "Even a valuable product . . . can self-destruct from a faulty business strategy," billionaire investor Warren Buffett, noted in the 2012 shareholders' letter of his Berkshire Hathaway, Inc., a significant section of which was devoted to the company's new newspaper holdings. "How could this lead to anything other than a sharp and steady drop in sales of the printed product? Falling circulation, moreover, makes a paper less essential to advertisers."[34]

The plethora of free content on the web also created more advertising competition for newspapers than they had ever faced for their print products. As search engines such as Google and Yahoo became popular and dominant, websites began offering search-related advertising at an even lower cost. In the span of only a few years, newspapers were forced to trade "print advertising dollars for Internet dimes, and then Internet dimes for search engine pennies," as the industry saying goes. This means that while print advertising revenues earned by US newspapers have fallen almost every year since 2001, they still exceeded online advertising revenue by more than five-fold in 2012, with $18.9 billion generated by print advertising and $3.4 billion from digital advertising, according to the annual review by the Newspaper Association of America.[35] Between 2011 and 2012, print advertising revenues dropped by nearly 9 percent, while online advertising revenues grew about 6 percent—but on a far smaller base. For its part, the *Times-Picayune* collected $64.7 million in print advertising revenues in 2011, but only $5.7 million via NOLA.com, according to estimates that advertising intelligence firm Kantar Media provided to *Advertising Age*.[36] (Kantar declined to release corresponding 2012 figures for this book.)

As the Internet grew, more readers turned to online iterations of publications, and away from their print counterparts, or to new, digital-only outlets. The severity and length of the Great Recession only exacerbated print newspapers' declines. Circulation declines led to continued decreases in advertising revenue, and given that US newspapers have historically generated 70 percent to 80 percent of their revenues through advertising, such a financial model was simply unsustainable. The 2013 edition of the annual "State of the News Media" report issued by the Pew Research Center's Project for Excellence in Journalism concluded that for every $1 in digital ads US newspapers gained in 2012, they lost $16 in print advertising revenue, a number that had worsened from $10 only a year earlier.[37]

Although Amoss did not respond to two requests for an interview for this book, he underscored this point in a June 2012 front-page commentary about the coming changes at the newspaper:

That downward trend [in national advertising revenue] has

been matched by continual print circulation declines and sharp increases in the cost of printing and delivering the paper to readers' doorsteps seven days a week . . . Meanwhile, the world around us has turned upside down. Readers no longer want today's news tomorrow. They want it now.[38]

Because of its privately held status, only the Newhouse family and an inner circle of trusted lieutenants know exactly how commercially successful Advance has been over the years, but it has historically been regarded by industry watchers and newspaper analysts as among the country's most profitable newspaper chains. "Typical for the Newhouse papers are profit margins of 25 or even 30 percent," Felsenthal noted in *Citizen Newhouse*. *Forbes* magazine in 1998 described Advance Publications as "a fat cash cow."[39] These assumptions extended to the individual property level. For example, the Mobile, Alabama, *Press-Register* was nicknamed the "Cash Register" because of its reputed extraordinary financial returns. In the six years I was a staff writer with the *Times-Picayune* (from 1988 until 1994), it was informally, but unquestionably, assumed that the newspaper was wildly profitable.

That widely held perception, coupled with the employment security offered by the Pledge, meant Advance employees generally did not fear for their jobs, even after other newspaper chains initiated layoffs as their profit margins narrowed and then oftentimes disappeared altogether in the early years of the twenty-first century. "I know plenty of former newspaper employees who once thought they had job security," former *Press-Register* reporter Mark Holan wrote in a 2009 article for Poynter.org about the Pledge. "They figured they'd never be laid off because their companies raked in so much money that they could weather cyclical economic downturns. At newspapers owned by Advance Publications, many workers based that feeling on something firmer than water cooler talk. Their employment stability was promised in writing, right on the first page of the employee handbook."[40]

However, as the *Times-Picayune* continued to be buffeted by both the stubborn aftereffects of Katrina and the rise of the Internet, changes occurred that gave even the most oblivious employees pause. Immediately after Katrina, the newspaper began by folding its stand-alone, six-day-a-week business section into its inside pages, although it did continue publishing a freestanding Sunday business section until the newspaper went to three days a week on October 1, 2012. Advance then closed its Washington, D.C.-based Newhouse News Service (NNS) after the November 2008 presidential election. NNS employed about two dozen staffers who provided US Capitol coverage to the chain's newspapers, and to other subscribers.[41] (To cover Louisiana-relevant news emanating from Congress and the US government, the *Times-Picayune* retained NNS correspondent Bruce Alpert, who continues to work for the newspaper and NOLA.com, and hired fellow NNS correspondent Jonathan Tilove, who was laid off as part of the 2012 changes.)

The *Times-Picayune* and other Advance newspapers then announced the company's pension plan would be frozen, effective May 2009, and Advance's contributions to its employees' guaranteed monthly retirement income would be replaced with a modest increase to the company's existing 401(k) contribution. That change was far less-costly to the company — and far less valuable to employees. It was particularly damaging for veteran *Times-Picayune* employees who, in many instances, had spent much or all of their careers with the newspaper with the assumption that a comfortable pension would await them upon retirement.

In March 2009, Advance also announced upcoming mandatory, ten-day annual unpaid furloughs at most of its newspapers. "It is certainly a difficult day," Steven Newhouse, Sam Newhouse's grandson, told trade publication *Editor & Publisher* in announcing the changes. "We are facing unprecedented economic challenges."[42] Four months later, Advance began requiring employees to contribute to their health insurance premiums for the first time in the company's history, and increased the rates employees contributed to have their families insured. Employees were required to absorb three significant rate increases over the next two years. As a result, premiums paid by the average *Times-Picayune* employee insuring himself, and his spouse and children, increased significantly, to more than $9,600 a year. "It was 'Disaster of the Month' for a while there," former longtime columnist Stephanie Grace recalled about the triple whammy of the discontinued pension, furloughs, and escalating insurance contributions.

Through early-to-mid 2009, a small group of highly regarded, longtime *Times-Picayune* newsroom employees—including Living columnist Angus Lind, travel editor Millie Ball, civil courts reporter Susan Finch, Living section associate editor Mary Lou Atkinson, and InsideOut home and garden section editor Renée Peck—voluntarily retired, enticed—some privately said politely coerced—by a "one time only, get it while you can" offer of company-paid health insurance until they turned sixty-five, and company-paid supplemental prescription drug coverage once they became eligible for Medicare. (Because of their long tenures with the company, most were eligible for pension benefits at or close to the maximum allowable benefit.) A few months later, the company lured a larger group of employees to follow suit—including columnists Chris Rose and Lolis Eric Elie, books editor Susan Larson, police reporter Walt Philbin, and features writers Lynne Jensen and Chris Bynum—by offering buyouts equal to one year of salary and employer-paid health insurance coverage for the same period. All told, almost thirty newsroom employees accepted buyouts in 2009, while another fifty employees companywide who sought them were turned down "because we think we will need them as part of our team," Phelps said in a December 2009 memo to the staff.[43] (The company extended another buyout offer in August 2011.[44])

In February 2010, Advance delivered its biggest shock to date: it rescinded the Pledge companywide. "When *The Times-Picayune*'s Job Security Pledge was implemented over 25 years ago, the newspaper industry was thriving," Phelps wrote to employees in an August 2009 letter that announced the Pledge's revocation effective in early 2010. "Daily newspapers had significant space devoted to classified as well as display advertising, and the revenue from it. The Internet was not invented and online competition did not exist. Today, of course, is much, much different." He went on to say:

> For *The Times-Picayune* to survive this extremely serious economic crisis, we must have the flexibility to adjust our staffing levels to the circumstances facing us. Our goal is to remain a daily newspaper, printed and distributed seven days each week—we have been serving readers and advertisers in our community in this fashion for over 172 years. We believe that gaining the option of laying off employees due to economic conditions or technological change is necessary to attain this goal.[45]

"When Ashton called everyone together to say the Pledge was gone, he did it very adroitly," Nolan recalled in March 2013. "It was very much, 'This is a corporate change that I have to communicate to you. It reflects an industry that is struggling, but I continue to believe that we're in the best position in the business, and we'll continue to keep our heads above water. I've been publisher here for thirty-some-odd years, and we've never laid off a single person. There are other foot pedals to play on this organ without throwing people overboard. But I can't make you any promises.'"

Phelps wasn't overstating the seriousness of the situation. Total US newspaper advertising revenue had fallen by more than 57 percent between 2001 and 2011, according to Newspaper Association of America figures. In 2012 dollars, advertising revenues in 2012 fell below the $19.75 billion spent in 1950. "The dramatic decline in newspaper ad revenues has to be one of the most significant Schumpeterian gales of creative destruction in recent years," University of Michigan economics professor Mark J. Perry concluded in a commentary for the conservative think tank American Enterprise Institute. "And it's not over."[46] Perry noted that global market research firm IBISWorld a year earlier had included newspaper publishing as one of ten industries that may be on the verge of extinction in the United States.[47] Seemingly supporting that prediction, during the same time period, the number of daily and weekly US newspapers declined nearly 11 percent and total sector employment plummeted a staggering 41 percent nationwide, Bureau of Labor Statistics figures showed, from 404,072 to 239,375.[48] Full-time daily newspaper editorial employment fell more than 32 percent between 2000 and 2013, from 56,200 to 38,000, according to the annual census compiled by the American Society of News Editors,[49] the first time the figure has fallen below 40,000 since the employment count was created in 1978. (The 2013 number had fallen another 2,600 over the previous year, even without the participation in that year's census of at least fourteen large US newspapers, many of which had instituted deep personnel cuts during the year—including the *Times-Picayune*.[50]) Many of the country's largest newspaper chains were struggling financially, and at least a half-dozen had entered bankruptcy since 2008.

"We felt that it was the right thing to communicate to people that we could no longer afford not having the flexibility to do something if the revenue challenges continue," Steven Newhouse told the *New York Times* in a report about the Pledge's revocation. The "flexibility to do something" he mentioned would be layoffs, which previously had never taken place at any Advance newspaper. "I think the policy was meant for a time when the newspaper business had ups and downs, but was relatively stable. It was not meant for a time when our newspapers, like others, are struggling to survive."[51] Nonetheless, the Pledge's demise was the institutional equivalent of a shock to the system. "It was the end of the solemn promise," a former *Oregonian* reporter told *Willamette Week's* Mesh. "It was incredibly painful."[52]

However, the Pledge's cancellation also was likely influenced by the changes Advance already had begun at some of its newspapers. Its revocation also could have been swayed by a $7.3 million civil lawsuit brought against the company in September 2009 by Howard Bronson, the longtime former publisher of Mobile's *Press-Register*. During the trial, Bronson testified that he agreed to become the *Press-Register's* publisher at the age of fifty-five only after repeated assurance from both Donald Newhouse and his nephew, Advance executive vice president Mark Newhouse, that Bronson would be covered by the Pledge and would be free to work as long as he wished. He instead was forced to retire in 2009, at the age of seventy-two, after seventeen years in the role. Both Donald and Mark Newhouse were subpoenaed, and testified about the Pledge and its historic role within the Advance newspaper chain. In pre-trial motions regarding depositions related to the trial, Bronson's attorney, Vince Kilborn, contended that the company feared the precedent the case would set for scores of Advance daily newspaper employees previously covered by the Pledge, who had been or would be laid off after its revocation. (It was revoked between Bronson filing his suit and it coming to trial. The suit ultimately was settled out of court in April 2011 for an undisclosed sum, shortly before the jury was to hear closing arguments.[53])

Even before the Pledge was repealed, the *T-P's* ranks already had been dramatically thinned by attrition and buyouts. The news operation—including the downtown newsroom, and the newspaper's five suburban, Baton Rouge, and Washington, D.C. bureaus—employed about 265 before Katrina, a number that had fallen to between about 165 and 170 by mid-2010, according to figures the newspaper supplied to the *Columbia Journalism Review*.[54]

Throughout his career, Phelps had a reputation of opposing layoffs, reasoning that their damage to morale more than offset the value of the money saved, resulting in his thirty-two-year record of having never enforced a compulsory workforce reduction. The announcement of his retirement caused employees to wonder whether that record was about to change. "I didn't know exactly what was going to happen, and I never thought it would be as bad as it ultimately was, but I knew we were in trouble as soon as I heard about Ashton," one longtime employee said. Many newsroom employees assumed involuntary layoffs were coming, and perhaps even a sale of the newspaper, the former of which was confirmed by the startling May 23, 2012 *New York Times* story about the coming dramatic changes to the *Time-Picayune*.

Those revelations led shocked New Orleanians to respond with a somewhat hackneyed list of local customs that could not possibly continue without a daily print newspaper. For example, former longtime *Times-Picayune* columnist Chris Rose opined in an alternately poignant and comical essay published in *Oxford American* magazine that it "bordered on self-parody how many have mentioned chicory coffee — its taste, smell, and consistency — as a constant companion to the paper."[55] A local shop created a T-shirt emblazoned with the message, "Dear Editor: How will we eat crawfish Mondays, Tuesdays, Thursdays and Saturdays? — NOLA," referencing the days of the week that would no longer have print editions of the *Times-Picayune*, which often serve as the disposable tablecloth upon which the Louisiana delicacy is served. Environmental reporter Schleifstein later recounted being approached by an elderly congregant following services at their temple who told him that the lack of a daily newspaper to accompany her into the bathroom each morning had left her irregular.[56]

However, the seriousness of the loss of a daily print newspaper in a city so unique, tradition-bound, and parochial was not being exaggerated. "Despite its international undergirding and Mardi

Gras reputation, New Orleans is, in its own way, among the most provincial of all Southern cities, with a separateness embraced by the locals and misunderstood everywhere else," the *American Journalism Review* commented in a 1997 article about the improving quality and fortunes of the newspaper.[57] ("One of the charms of New Orleans is that we are ten years behind in everything, and that includes the web," a *Times-Picayune* reporter told Carr.)

"I'm a New Orleanian, by adoption, and I can attest to the uniqueness of the place," Harry Shearer — actor, comedian, musician, and voice of Principal Skinner and Mr. Burns on the *Simpsons* animated TV show — wrote in a June 2012 article that appeared in the *Columbia Journalism Review*. "Not just for the reasons visitors might think — the beads, the boobs, the music, the food — but for the most important reason of all: New Orleans is a genuine community. A strong community has intense ties to its institutions, too. That includes the [Mardi Gras] Krewe of Rex, the Catholic Church, and *The Times-Picayune*. People love them or hate them, but New Orleanians tend not to be indifferent about them."[58]

Aside from cultural considerations, a very real pragmatic concern existed about largely replacing a print publication with a website: between 40 percent and 60 percent of metropolitan New Orleans doesn't have residential broadband Internet access, according to data released in March 2012 by the Investigative Reporting Workshop at Washington, DC's American University. That meant it would be inconvenient, at best, for those residents to access NOLA.com on the four days a week the newspaper would no longer be produced in print form. The impact would be even greater for New Orleans's poor residents. Although 80 to 100 percent of wealthy, overwhelmingly white Uptown New Orleans and suburban areas such as Metairie have broadband, corresponding rates in predominantly African American neighborhoods such as the city's Lower Ninth Ward were between 0 and 40 percent, the report found.[59]

The same afternoon as Amoss's May 24, 2012 staff meetings in New Orleans, similar gatherings took place at Advance newspapers in Huntsville, Birmingham, and Mobile, Alabama, laying out identical transformations in similarly nebulous strokes. Employees in both states were told that substantial layoffs were likely, and that their newspapers would no longer be published daily. However, no dates for any changes were provided and no one was told whether he would keep or lose his job. Advance employees in both states would wait almost three more weeks before learning any additional details, including their individual fates.

CHAPTER III

– 30 –

Because so little was offered in the way of specifics at editor Jim Amoss's May 24, 2012, staff meetings, *Times-Picayune* employees had no indication whether they would still have jobs with the newspaper in the near future. Although he was rumored to have been in town for the secret, off-site meetings, Ricky Mathews had not been spotted in the building since outgoing publisher Ashton Phelps had announced his retirement in late March and introduced Mathews as his successor. As days ticked by with no announcements about coming changes or future employment prospects, tensions and emotions began to run dangerously high. Crying jags were not uncommon and some staffers were worried about the mental stability of at least a few co-workers. Newsroom staffers complained bitterly, albeit privately, that neither Amoss nor his longtime chief administrative lieutenant, online editor Lynn Cunningham, would look them in the eye. Workplace friendships that had endured for decades began to snap under the strain.

Frustrated by the lack of specifics Amoss had offered during his staff meetings, several editorial employees drafted a detailed list of questions, which they sent to him and Cunningham on June 1 covering "Transition, Employment, Benefits" and "Operations of the New Firms."[1] "We were deeply concerned about what we had heard so far, and were hoping it wasn't as bad as it had seemed, and that they had actually thought through more than it appeared that they had," one former employee involved in the drafting of the questions recalled in May 2013. "Of course, they hadn't thought through any of that stuff and still hadn't." The list of questions appeared on the website of media think tank and continuing education center the Poynter Institute the same day it was delivered to Amoss and Cunningham, who never responded. "We cared deeply about the news operation, and all of us would have preferred to stay if they could have convinced us that good journalism would remain their top priority and that they really had thought through the plan," the former employee added.

Although nothing official was communicated, employees around the same time the letter was sent began hearing that meetings, during which an individual's employment status would be disclosed, were to be held that week. Almost as quickly as that message began circulating, *Gambit's* editor Kevin Allman broke a story on the paper's website that those meetings had been cancelled and would not be rescheduled for the following week, either. "No explanation was offered, and the change was announced verbally, employee to employee, not on paper," Allman reported.[2] It was widely speculated that newspaper management wanted to avoid having its meetings coincide with Tisserand's and Rolfes's rally, which no doubt would have given the *Picayune's* anticipated grim news greater media currency and wider coverage.

The axe finally fell June 12, 2012, twenty days after Carr's *New York Times* story broke. One-third of the *Times-Picayune's* employees would lose their jobs, effective September 30, including nearly one-half of the newsroom. "Today is a painful day for many of us at the newspaper," Amoss said in a statement reported on NOLA.com. "But our goal is to serve our community well into the future. That means moving aggressively into the digital world while maintaining a substantial print presence. We have a well thought-out plan. We're committed to being the journalistic watchdog of our communities. We're committed to the high quality of journalism our readers have come to expect from us, produced by a formidable news staff. And we're committed to deploying by far the largest news-gathering team in the region."

Former *Times-Picayune* editorial staffers Steve and Laura Beatty, New Orleans freelance writer Michael Tisserand, and Loyola University mass communications professor David Zemmels created a massive sign they hung from the Broad Street overpass across the Pontchartrain Expressway adjacent to the *Times-Picayune* Howard Avenue office.

The day started uncharacteristically early for NOLA.com copy editor Cathy Hughes, who typically worked until 11 P.M. or midnight, but was asked by online editor Cunningham, her supervisor, to report to the newspaper at 7 A.M. "I was totally shocked," Hughes recalled during a March 2013 interview about hearing the news that she would be losing her job. "I cried, and I guess she didn't expect it, because she didn't have any tissue and scurried off to the restroom to bring me some of those brown hand towels." As she was leaving the meeting, Hughes noticed fliers hanging in the newsroom informing employees that counselors would be available in Human Resources, "but HR was locked up; they weren't in yet."[3] Although HR was not yet in the building, other employees did report increased security throughout the downtown office.

Amoss, Cunningham, Lorando, and sports editor Doug

Tatum—derisively dubbed "the firing squad" by some employees—were stationed throughout the various editorial departments that filled the building's third floor, and met individually in five-to-ten-minute increments with staff members to inform them of their fates. Mathews was not seen with his new subordinates, or even in the building, on the day of the announcements. As employees emerged from the executive offices where many of the meetings were held, most returned to the newsroom and an anxious throng of waiting colleagues, and signaled—with either a thumbs-up or a slash across the throat—whether they had been asked to stay or would be terminated. For friends, alumni, and supporters who were not at the newspaper's offices that day, the scene played out on the Facebook page, as recounted by alumna Renée Peck on NolaVie, the New Orleans nonprofit lifestyle and culture website she co-founded after leaving the newspaper in 2009:

> The numbers on Facebook's Friends of the *Times-Picayune* Editorial page continued to mount, hour by hour.
>
> -30-
> -30-
> -30-
> After 27, it's a -30-
>
> And thus legacy journalists signaled, succinctly and poignantly, the end of their careers, in a way that only their peers could appreciate and understand. "Thirty" is the traditional notation that a reporter writes after an article, telling editors that the story has come to an end. And so it has for 201 *Times-Picayune* employees, who were told in one-on-one meetings Tuesday that they will not be among the hires when NOLA Media Group starts up in the fall.

Visiting the Facebook page at just about any point that day was to witness a digital death march.

Among those also terminated were assistant city editor Rhonda Nabonne, who had been with the newspaper for nearly forty years, and Katy Reckdahl, who had been lauded for carving out a beat in recent years covering poverty and the large cross-section of often-overlooked New Orleanians caught in its grip (and who had given birth to her son one day before Katrina hit New Orleans in 2005). Twenty-something business reporter Ricky Thompson arrived in the newsroom that morning with a bottle of Crown Royal, which he offered to share with his boss, business editor Kim Quillen, and then with city editor Gordon Russell, with whom he had his meeting to discuss his future employment. Thompson also brought a photograph of his family to his meeting with Russell, in a comically faux attempt to invoke sympathy. It didn't work; both Thompson and Quillen were terminated. Also dismissed were scores of bureau chiefs and assistant editors, nationally syndicated political cartoonist Steve Kelley, eleven artists, and eight photographers.[5] The copy desk—any newspaper's quality control hub—was devastated. The entire HR department and library staff were eliminated (although librarian Danny Gamble was ultimately "unfired" and remained with the organization), along with nearly half of the display advertising creative department. Forty percent of the pressroom, 42 percent of the packaging center (the employees who assemble the newspaper), and nearly 42 percent of transportation were targeted.

Among those laid off was photographer John McCusker, who had spent his entire twenty-six-year professional career at the newspaper, beginning as a freelancer while completing his college degree at Loyola University New Orleans. "There are things about that day that I'll remember for the rest of my life," he recalled in March 2013. "When I went in to see Lynn [Cunningham], I had no illusions about what was going to happen. She said, 'John, we're offering you a severance,' and I replied, 'OK, fine, Lynn, I don't want to work for your f—ing company anyway.'"

St. Tammany Parish bureau chief Ron Thibodeaux, who had been with the newspaper since 1981, was scheduled to meet with

Amoss, while Thibodeaux's twenty-odd staffers would be told by Lorando whether they still had jobs. "Jim had very little to say to me," Thibodeaux remembered nine months later. "He appeared to be reading a script. He said that tough decisions had to be made and there was no place for me in the new organization." At the conclusion of the two-minute exchange, Thibodeaux had only one question. "I was Father Goose to eighteen or twenty people, and I wanted to know what was going to happen to my staff, but he wouldn't tell me. He said I'd find out with everyone else."

Longtime photo editor Doug Parker recalled a similar meeting with Amoss. Parker's termination came in the same room and in the same chair in which he had sat when Amoss promoted him to his current post eighteen years earlier. "No emotion. No apologies. Not even a thank you. Hell, he couldn't even look me in the eye," Parker remembered in March 2013. Parker's wife, photographer Kathy Anderson had accepted a buyout from the newspaper in 2009 to start her own photography business. She recalled the reaction of the couple's two high-school-aged daughters when they heard about their father's termination. "'Why should we even try to go to college?' their oldest daughter asked Anderson. 'We can't afford to go after Dad got laid off.' That was the most heartbreaking thing of all of this." At the time, Parker also was dealing with the terminal illness of his father, who he recalled asking, "'Doug, how are you going to feed your family?' Here's a World War II fighter pilot dying of cancer and he was worried about us."[6]

A longtime employee, who provided details about his meeting with Amoss on the condition that his identity would not be revealed, recalled an encounter equally devoid of empathy or emotion. "I kept waiting for an acknowledgement, but we just stared at each other," the veteran employee remembered. "I asked him if that was it, and he said yes. I shook my head, picked up my packet and left. To do that so coldly, without any acknowledgement of what people had contributed over the years, was unconscionable. There was no humanity to it."

Religion reporter Bruce Nolan was regarded by some in the newsroom as bullet-proof after his heralded statement at the May staff meeting. That proved not to be the case. His termination meeting with Russell was at least more humane than many held by other managers. "By the time I came in, he was pummeled," Nolan told the *Columbia Journalism Review* in March 2013, referring to Russell. "He was beaten up. He was very sorry; he was remorseful. He said, 'This is a terrible thing; I'm sorry this is happening to you. You know how much I love you.' We both understood we were being carried along by forces bigger than both of us. And I came out, and I walked through a corridor and into the newsroom, where everyone is standing around. It's a death march. Every face turns to me, and I draw my finger across my throat. It was stunning."[7]

The suburban bureaus and the "Picayune" community news sections, which two decades earlier had helped secure the newspaper's financial health by holding suburban competition at bay, were savaged. Two-thirds of the newspaper's East Jefferson Bureau — where I had my start at the newspaper twenty-four years earlier — was terminated, while its bureau chief, Drew Broach, was told he would be spared after September 30 — if he would return to reporting. (He did and was subsequently re-promoted back to an editing position after a rash of resignations in May 2013, including by Russell and news editor Martha Carr.)

Community news editors Annette Naake Sisco and Eva Jacob Barkoff, the latter of whom was the newspaper's first community news editor and was with the paper for twenty-eight years, were fired, along with most of the editors and reporters for every one of the five sections. Four of the five employees in the River Parishes Bureau would be laid off, along with five of eight working in the West Bank Bureau. "Half of the newsroom was terminated, prompting readers to question how the paper's — and the website's — coverage could remain comprehensive and in-depth," Rose observed in his *Oxford American* essay. "Newsroom cuts seemed random, an equal blend of new folks and 40-year veterans."

"Even those who knew we were going, [fellow managing editor] Peter [Kovacs] and me, were shocked by the scale of it," Shea recalled in March 2013.

Somewhat in contrast—and in presumed support of NOLA.com's future focus on entertainment and sports—just a few of the newspaper's sixteen sports staff members were laid off, while only three of its fifteen Living section employees were terminated.

Elsewhere in the newspaper's main offices, the layoffs were handled equally haphazardly. "My boyfriend and I were getting ready for work, and it was on WWL-TV," Patty Pitt, who had worked in the display advertising department for nearly fifteen years, recalled in May 2013. "I knew I was gone" she said, primarily because of personality conflicts she had had with Kelly Rose, then vice president and director of advertising for the *Times-Picayune*, who would be promoted to NOLA Media Group's vice president of sales less than two months later.[8] Pitt waited with eleven other employees, all of whom were women, in an office on the building's first floor. Only she and Sue Schneider, a forty-year veteran now in her sixties, met with Rose. Because Pitt's meeting was scheduled last, at 4 p.m., she departed for the walk she routinely took during her afternoon break. But at 3:15, "they came outside looking for me, they came hunting me down." When Rose broke the news that she would lose her job, Pitt couldn't help but recall that she lobbied for a buyout in 2009, which would have provided a significantly better financial deal for her and would have offered the added advantage of putting her back in the job market at forty-four, instead of forty-nine. At the time, however, "Kelly [Rose] told me 'We can't let you go. We need you,'" Pitt recalled.[9]

Confusion abounded among those asked to stay, and among those labeled as "unfired"—employees who were originally told

East Jefferson Parish Picayune section editor Eva Barkoff was the newspaper's first community news editor and worked there for twenty-eight years. When she lost her job as part of the changes, her husband Alex Barkoff, a former *Times-Picayune* photographer, purchased a billboard in her honor at one of the area's most highly trafficked intersections. *Photograph courtesy of Alex Barkoff.*

they were losing their jobs, but in the succeeding days, weeks, and months, were instead asked to remain. Few whom the newspaper hoped to retain initially were told what their jobs or who their bosses would be. "Among the more notable names leaving the paper are food writer Brett Anderson and longtime sports columnist Peter Finney," the story on the newspaper's website read. This came as news to Finney, who had joined the newspaper right out of high school a few months before the end of World War II in 1945, and had not yet had a meeting about his employment status. When the story appeared on NOLA.com, he was at home working on his latest column, *Gambit* reported. (Finney ultimately retired but agreed to continue writing his column on a freelance basis. The sixty-seven-year veteran's initial response to the reprieve? "I hope they won't expect me to twit or toot, or whatever they call it. I'm a writer, not a twitter!")

Brett Anderson, who had chronicled the post-Katrina recovery of the region's all-important seafood and restaurant businesses and was a winner of the James Beard Award — the "Oscar for food writers," as Rose described it — had already formally been granted a leave of absence by the newspaper to complete a prestigious Nieman Fellowship in journalism at Harvard University beginning that August, the program's seventy-fifth year. "I was told I'm being let go because I'm taking a Nieman Fellowship," Anderson told the *Washington Post*'s Erik Wemple, in what undoubtedly was one of the most Kafkaesque utterances in a day full of nightmarish episodes. (It also was not a situation the Nieman Foundation apparently had ever encountered. "As far as we know, in the past no one else has been laid off specifically because they received a Nieman fellowship," the foundation's communications officer Ellen Tuttle told Wemple.[10]) Anderson also sent two cryptic tweets that afternoon, one with a link to a video performance of a song titled, "I really need a goddamn job," and a second that said simply, "Turns out I picked the right song," followed by humor the next day: "Thanks for all the love in the last 24. On the day I lost my job, I could at least take solace that I was briefly a trending [Twitter] topic."[11]

Jefferson Parish education reporter Barri Bronston, a thirty-one-year veteran, drove up to the building, and saw Anderson, along with features copy editor Jerry McLeod, who was sobbing outside of the building and being comforted by food editor Judy Walker, who kept her job. "When Brett welled up, and said, 'I'm out,' I knew I was finished," Bronston recalled. "The way they treated people who worked so hard for this newspaper was so shameful."

However, in yet another bizarre twist that reportedly included behind-the-scenes lobbying by the city's influential restaurant industry and two lunch meetings in one week between Anderson and Amoss, the newspaper relented and announced Anderson's job would be waiting for him if he returned from Cambridge in the fall of 2013.[12]

Several hundred miles away, four hundred employees across Alabama were terminated at Advance's three newspapers there. A soon-to-be-laid-off staffer at the state's largest newspaper, the *Birmingham News*, penned an essay for *Weld for Birmingham*, that city's alternative weekly, about the layoffs titled "Death by 400 Cuts." The account was posted anonymously to avoid violating the non-disparagement clause contained in the agreement all laid-off employees were required to sign to receive severance:

> So many people were involved behind the scenes in creating that daily miracle delivered to your door: layout people, graphics artists, proofreaders and, of course, printers. Ramona Wells: she never got a byline, but she was a hub of information in the newsroom, able to connect your call where it needed to go. No matter how stressed I might be, when I heard Ramona answer the phone, I knew everything would be okay. Same with David Knox on the sports desk. He knew every coach and every stat, and no matter how hot things got on a sports weekend, he was always cool.
>
> Keysha Drexler started as a reporter, moved up to collecting "Classroom Clips" and that led her to an editing position. As far as I know, she was never made a full-time hire. Likewise photographer Jeff Roberts, who took assignments all over the map. He'd always ask questions about what I was writing to make sure he got the right images. Jeff got a lot of notice, but he never got a full-time position.[13]

Other notable editorial departures, reported on the MOB (Media of Birmingham) website maintained by freelance writer and blogger Wade Kwon, were business editor Jerry Underwood, photography director Walt Stricklin, veteran reporter Chuck

Dean and Washington correspondent Mary Orndorff. Two pregnant newsroom employees were laid off, Kwon reported, while a third employee was terminated in advance of a scheduled cancer operation.[14] When several employees who would remain employed by the newspaper asked what their new job titles meant, editors meeting with them said they didn't know, the *Weld of Birmingham* reported.

In that single day, four Advance newspapers became responsible for close to one-third of all jobs eliminated in 2012 at the nation's almost 1,400 daily newspapers.

That weekend, McCusker hosted a party at the Gentilly home he rebuilt after Katrina ravaged it, and he hired a brass band to

Veteran reporter Bruce Nolan, and his wife of forty years, Emily, sport a pair of the satirical T-shirts that sprung up in response to the controversial changes at the newspaper. *Photograph courtesy of Dennis Persica.*

perform a solemn jazz funeral second line to commemorate the great and nearly late daily *Times-Picayune*. "We are one staff, we are one newspaper, and we are one city," McCusker said, his voice cracking, in an emotional impromptu speech to the roughly 150 who attended the party. "So, no matter what fates have dictated where we're being shuttled off to, I just wanted y'all to know that one of the proudest things I could ever say in my life is that I worked for the *New Orleans Times-Picayune*. . . . If we want to pay it forward, let's just treat each other right. We know all about deadlines, and September 30 is our final deadline."

It didn't take long, however, for the staff to fracture. Fissures often played out at the newspaper's cafeteria, a cavernous hub on the second floor of the newspaper's main facility at 3800 Howard Avenue. (Although closed since January 31, 2013, the giant, light-blue neon *Times-Picayune* masthead above the now-empty serving line remains visible to motorists on the adjacent Pontchartrain Expressway, who can spot it through the room's expansive plate-glass windows.) In the cafeteria, "The Table of the Fireds" — where veterans such as Kovacs, Nolan, Parker, suburban editors Kim Chatelain and Dennis Persica and others sat — "migrated toward each other, we all had lunch every day," Parker recalled.

One of the complications of the news leaking early and the minimum sixty-day notice the company was required to provide employees under the federal Worker Adjustment and Retraining Notification Act (better known as "WARN") was that those who were leaving were expected to work professionally and amicably alongside those who were staying for another three-and-one-half months. Countless laid-off employees shared anecdotes of being awkwardly and painfully left behind in the newsroom or bureaus while colleagues who had been asked to remain at the company attended meetings closed to the laid-off workers. The resulting discomfort in the St. Tammany Bureau prompted Thibodeaux, the thirty-one-year veteran and bureau chief who was being laid off, to privately call aside longtime colleagues Robert Rhoden and

Bob Warren, who were staying with the company, to assuage their survivors' guilt and offer them the use of his office for sensitive or confidential conference calls or meetings.

This painful exercise was repeated a couple of months later in New York and Pennsylvania, when Advance announced similarly deep cuts at its *Post-Standard* in Syracuse, and *Patriot-News* in Harrisburg. A total of 180 ultimately lost their jobs at those publications. "Hundreds of years of reporting experience and knowledge of Syracuse history were wiped out in a day," the alternative weekly *Syracuse New Times* reported about the cuts there. "Dick Case, who has worked for a Syracuse newspaper since the year Fidel Castro marched into Havana, is gone, fired at age 77. Award-winning education and community reporter Maureen Nolan, music editor Mark Bialczak, police reporter Robert Baker and other fixtures are all gone. Court reporter Jim O'Hara, with his unequaled grasp of the justice system, is gone. Most of the copy editors, long considered the quality control department of any newspaper, were sent packing."[15]

Like the *Times-Picayune*, the *Patriot-News* is now printed only three days a week, but Advance made concessions in Syracuse: although home delivery was cut to three times weekly, effective February 1, 2013, residents could still get a daily print newspaper — if they were willing to leave their homes four days a week to buy one. Print newspaper die-hards could go in search of 12,000 copies of a sixteen-page version distributed to newsstands in Syracuse's Onondaga County on the days the newspaper was not delivered.[16]

After seeing what had happened in New Orleans and the seeming advantage the element of surprise there had given Advance, newsroom employees of the *Cleveland Plain Dealer* launched their own pre-emptive move in anticipation of being the next Advance newspaper in line for the "digital-first" experience. (Like the *Times-Picayune*, Advance officials acknowledged that the *Plain Dealer* was still profitable, at least as of the end of 2012.) The "Save *The Plain Dealer*" campaign borrowed some of New Orleans's tactics, although it was able to launch a true advertising campaign thanks to the financial support of Newspaper Guild Local One, one of only four unions left at Advance newspaper nationwide, and the guild's parent organization, the Communications Workers of America. (The other three unions at Advance newspapers are at the company's largest, the *Newark (N.J.) Star-Ledger*, where employees responsible for printing and production of the newspaper are represented by the Graphic Communications Conference Local 8-N, Teamsters Graphic Communications Conference Local 1L, and Teamsters New Jersey Mailers Local 1100.[17])

The *Plain Dealer's* campaign included half-page ads in the newspaper, bus placards, and YouTube video spots featuring union members and Cleveland celebrities alike (actress Valerie Bertinelli from the TV show *Hot in Cleveland* was one), emphasizing the importance of a daily newspaper and lobbying for its preservation. "We're trying to get out ahead of this thing and give people a stake and a say in what happens," John Mangels, the leader of the guild committee that created the marketing campaign, told the *Plain Dealer* in early November 2012. "It really ought to be the community's fight as well as ours."[18]

Advance's target in Cleveland, however, appeared to be less the daily print newspaper, and more the newsroom's union. In a deal reached in late 2012 between the guild and Advance, the union accepted a workforce reduction of fifty-eight employees in exchange for a guarantee of no further large-scale layoffs through 2019. Without the agreement, Advance warned it would purge eighty to eighty-five *Plain Dealer* employees when the current contract expired in a few months, and also would likely begin docking employees' wages for a portion of health insurance premiums now covered by the company. The new contract instead protects most existing guild members, restores the 8 percent wage cut they had taken to avoid layoffs in 2009, and provides for Advance to shore up their underfunded pension and health care funds.

Although potentially devastating for the roughly sixty employees who have or will ultimately lose their jobs, the union contract looked surprisingly generous on the part of Advance — until one looked at the fine print. Previously, work by non-union Cleveland.com journalists was prohibited from appearing in the pages of the *Plain Dealer*, while *Plain Dealer* reporters' work appeared both in the newspaper and on Cleveland.com, an arrangement that assured the union local would be supplied with new members as long as a print newspaper existed. That, however, changed under the new contract, with online reporters' work now also being allowed into the pages of the newspaper. "It's a major concession by the newspaper guild, and it'll weaken the union over time, since new hires will likely be on the online side," *Cleveland Magazine* senior editor Erick Trickey wrote on the publication's blog. The change will result in a "shrinking unionized newsroom and a new, non-union digital news staff."[19] The union acknowledged as such. "A big part of that is we've given them some language that could, over the years, really diminish our numbers," guild chairman Harlan Spector told Poynter.org.[20] "That was probably the biggest and hardest thing we gave up, and it was a very contentious point," the guild's administrative officer, Rollie Dreussi, recalled in a May 2013 interview with me. "We understand what it could mean in the long run, but no one knows for sure how it will work out. Sometimes you have to do what you can to stay in the battle just to keep fighting the war."[21] The symbolism of Advance's checkmate also probably resonated with its historically anti-union owners. The "1" in "Local 1," after all, represents the first. The *Plain Dealer* was "the birthplace of the [country's Newspaper] Guild," on March 20, 1934.[22]

After the fifty-odd layoffs that occurred the final day of July 2013, the newsroom stood at 110 employees, down from 350 a decade ago. In earlier negotiations for the union contract now in force, the newspaper guaranteed that only five more employees would lose their jobs in the subsequent six years. Union members have suggested that their campaign may have saved its daily newspaper status. It, like the *Post-Standard* and the *Oregonian*, will be printed daily, but home-delivered only four days a week, beginning August 5, 2013.

When the layoffs finally occurred, management apparently was keen on avoiding the unemployment "death march" scene that had unfolded in New Orleans and Alabama. It directed newsroom employees to stay home but be by their phones between 8 and 10 a.m. for calls telling them whether they'd be "separated from employment," according to the internal memo circulated the day before.[23] Those receiving the "bad call," as staffers referred to it, were then directed to pick up their severance materials the next day, not at the newspaper, but at its distribution facility ten miles away. (The story on the website of *Bloomberg Businessweek* detailing the indignities included a photo from the 1996 slasher movie "Scream," in which actress Drew Barrymore is screaming into a phone moments before encountering a grisly death.[24]) One-third of the newsroom ultimately was slashed, and the resulting flood of tweets told the story in a way neither the company nor the union could. "I just got the call from [assistant entertainment editor] John Kappes," columnist and former longtime *Friday!* magazine editor Chuck Yarborough tweeted. "I still have a job, but I want to throw up . . . if I can just stop crying long enough." Among those not so fortunate: business editor Randy Roguski, photo technician Cynthia Baecker and graphics artist James Owens.[25] "Newspaper bosses keep opening veins on the sick patient, thinking if they can drain the body of blood, they can make it better," author and *Edmonton, Canada Journal* columnist Terry McConnell tweeted in response to the news. (The next day, layoffs began at newspapers across the country owned by the Gannett Company, Inc., the nation's largest newspaper chain.)

If contentions by the *Plain Dealer* union were true, the day's events did seem to further demonstrate that the guild itself was a target as much as any employee. By the time the specific cuts were announced, about two dozen newsroom employees already had voluntarily left the newspaper, Cleveland.com reported, which the union assumed meant that fewer than the previously agreed-to fifty-eight would face the chopping block. Guild President Spector and "Save the Plain Dealer" Leader Mangels both volunteered for layoffs, in an attempt to spare others,[26] and at least a half-dozen other employees also voluntarily left the newspaper (in addition to the earlier departures that occurred in the months since the news of the coming cutbacks first broke). However, the guild cried foul, saying the company reneged on the original agreement to first extend offers to any employees it wanted to hire at Cleveland.com and count those "transfers" against the original number of mutually agreed upon layoffs. The company instead distributed its telephonic pink slips and plans to extend employment offers at Cleveland.com later, meaning that any departures of survivors who choose to leave the *Plain Dealer* in favor of Cleveland.com will further reduce the ranks of unionized employees at the company. For its part, the company insisted that it had bargained with the guild in good faith. "This has been our practice in the past and we will continue to do the same in the future," publisher and president Terrance Eggers said in a statement reported on Cleveland.com.[27]

Another twenty employees lost their jobs at the Sun News, a chain of eleven Advance-owned weekly newspapers circulating in the Cleveland suburbs. "Will the last journalist out of the newspaper business please turn off the lights?" one tweet asked.

By the middle of September 2013, "digital first" would claim about 1,600 jobs at Advance newspapers from Portland, Oregon, to Mobile, Alabama. "We knew the pain was coming. We knew the layoffs would be huge," Alabama-based blogger, sports broadcaster, and communications researcher Dylan McLemore wrote shortly after the cuts were announced in Alabama. "The cuts hit newsrooms surprisingly hard, especially in the wake of Advance's earlier commitment to 'significantly increase online news-gathering efforts' and offer 'richer,' 'deeper,' 'robust,' 'enhanced printed newspapers,'"[28] albeit on the reduced printing schedule. More than six hundred employees at the *Times-Picayune* and Advance's Alabama papers were told in a single day that they would lose their jobs. A legion of newspaper carriers waited weeks longer to learn whether they still had their paper routes.

Many bemoaned the wholesale loss of institutional memory, in the form of the numerous experienced, older, and often more expensive employees that all six newspapers discarded, or failed to retain. Although it wasn't explained to a half-dozen laid-off employees I talked to about it, in compliance with the federal Older Worker Benefit Protection Act of 1990, the *Times-Picayune* included a copy of a spreadsheet in each soon-to-be-laid-off employee's severance packet. It detailed the more than six hundred positions at the company, by department, title, and age, and whether the employee holding each post would be retained or terminated. "I've seen these types of layoffs, where everyone gets a list," said New Orleans labor discrimination attorney James L. Arruebarrena. Although likely not the federal age discrimination law's intended objective, "the purpose of it [from the company's perspective] is probably to discourage laid-off employees from pursuing age discrimination lawsuits by showing that the layoff was relatively fair, at least when it comes to age," he added. "It's fairly typical and was probably done on the advice of their lawyers."[29] The spreadsheet also led to a perverse consequence. Because it was so detailed, employees who had their meeting early in the day were able to deduce who would be laid off later in the day, before those employees were officially notified.

An analysis of that spreadsheet shows that the average age of laid-off *Times-Picayune* employees was 49.2 — an age at which roots in a community are often deep and careers are winding down, not a point in life at which people are generally poised for relocation to another market or reinvention in another industry. Employees sixty years old and older were hit more disproportionally by the layoffs than other age groups. While employees in that age group made up 10 percent of the newspaper's total employment, they constituted 16 percent of those who lost their jobs. Although their rate of layoffs was roughly proportional with their overall representation within the *Times-Picayune*'s total workforce, employees age fifty to fifty-nine bore the brunt of firings: 38 percent of those who lost their jobs fell into this age category.[30] Those older individuals also face tougher employment prospects than their younger counterparts: too young to retire and more likely to face age discrimination as they seek new employment, the fifty-somethings also typically expected to rely on pensions that had been frozen in 2009. "Decent, hardworking people, who got the paper through Katrina and who were never told to do anything different in their work, were gotten rid of and replaced by people not who were better, but who were cheaper," Shea said in March 2013. Their discarding, of course, had its roots in the rescinding of the Pledge. Employees "in their 40s, 50s and 60s, would be most affected by the Newhouses' revocation of the Pledge. The Newhouses would be taking away these employees' ability to plan for their golden years, or forcing them to dramatically alter their life plans," Bronson's lawsuit read.[31]

Amoss took a far more indifferent position on the matter during a May 2013 appearance on the *The 504* talk show, jointly broadcast by WWL-TV and WUPL-TV. "We wanted to create a new company with journalists who not only had great depths of talents, and who knew this community inside and out, but who also understand, or were willing to grasp, what it meant to move into the digital world," Amoss said. "And there are lots of journalists in our industry who are fantastic journalists who don't necessarily embrace that future, and that was our guiding principle.

That comment drew quick and sharp rebukes on the Friends *Times-Picayune* Facebook page, with several people angrily countering that the group of editors who made the decisions about whom to lay off and whom to keep, had little knowledge of the relative digital and social media skills of the employees they evaluated. In response to a later question during his *The 504* interview, this one about the resignations and defections to other news media outlets that had occurred within the *Times-Picayune's* ranks since the changes, Amoss said:

> I hate to lose great talent. In this case, I hated to lose the talent we have lost. I've seen lots of great talent walk out our door and I've seen lots of great talent walk into our door. That is going to continue, that is part of the business. . . . On a professional level, the talent is still in my newsroom and there's new talent that's added to it, so I feel very very good about what we have.[32]

"Talent comes, and talent goes. That's disgusting," a longtime and deeply respected former member of Amoss's editorial staff practically spat out when talking about the remark. "On one hand, he's right: talent does come and talent does go, but usually one at a time, and usually separated by six months, or a year. Not more than eighty people who get laid off, followed by ten more who turn down offers to continue working there, followed by ten more who bide their time until they can get a job somewhere else, followed by ten more who defect to the competition. All in less than a year."

Amoss earlier tried to squelch a tidbit reported in Carr's original story that *Times-Picayune* staffers who kept their jobs, like Advance employees in Michigan, would be forced to accept steep pay cuts. "Concerning pay in the new companies, I want to dispel some rumors: There could be some salary adjustments, depending on changes in job descriptions," Amoss wrote in the May 31, 2012, memo that was published on *Gambit's* website almost as quickly as it was distributed to the staff. "But most people will make what they make today, if not more." Rick Edmonds, an analyst with the Poynter Institute, penned an analysis in June 2012 that combined what little hard data was known about the *Times-Picayune* situation and industry figures available from publicly traded newspaper companies to show that the *T-P's* "digital-first" strategy made financial sense only if the newspaper purged more-experienced, presumably more-highly compensated veterans and replaced them with less-experienced, less-costly new employees. "The disgruntled staff and readers of *The Times-Picayune* are getting it right," Edmonds concluded. "The move only makes financial sense as the occasion for dumping many well-paid veterans and drastically slashing news investment."[33] Some current and former employees thought drastic pay cuts originally had been in the cards for the retained staff, but that the outcry—both locally and in the national journalism community—had caused Advance to think better of slashing pay as it had done in Michigan. Although a handful of retained *Times-Picayune* employees told me privately that their wages remained roughly equal, and had even increased in a couple of instances, rising health insurance premiums likely translated into an overall reduction in net pay for many employees.

Whether executives actually backed down from wholesale pay reductions or simply focused on hiring less-experienced—and thereby less-expensive—new employees to fill the jobs being created or vacated by soon-to-be-laid-off veterans, some older, and presumably better-compensated, employees who hoped to secure jobs with the new company quickly found themselves passed over. Hughes, the fifty-three-year-old senior copy editor who lost her job because of the changes, applied in December 2012 for a newly posted job for a "quality assurance producer," whose job description was basically identical to her previous job. The application included a question about her salary history and expectations, which Hughes detailed. A response from Kelly Nelson, a "recruitment partner" with Decision Toolbox, the company to which NOLA Media Group outsourced its post-layoff recruitment, thanked Hughes for her application, but added, "Before we chat about it, let me determine the salary range. . . . I will keep you closely posted."[34] It was the only communication Hughes received about the job.

Lori Lyons, a veteran high school sports reporter in the newspaper's River Parishes Bureau who most recently had been covering breaking crime while also working as the bureau's clerk, found herself in a similar situation after being laid off and reapplying for a general assignment sports reporting position posted by the new company. An automated email acknowledgement to her online application was quickly followed by a rejection email. "I think I made too much money," Lyons flatly responded in April 2013, when asked why she thought she didn't get the job. "I'm fifty-one. I was at the top of the reporting scale. They weren't going to keep me." Kelly Morris, a thirty-something sports writer recruited from the *Shreveport Times*, instead was hired. Lyons, who is now covering prep sports on a freelance basis for other outlets, has regularly crossed professional paths with Morris, and said she has routinely assisted Morris with information and insight gleaned from her decade on the beat. "She's live blogging, she's live tweeting," Lyons said of Morris. "She's working hard, but they've got her doing so much, there's no wonder she's missing half of the games she's supposed to be covering."[35]

Other new hires proved even trickier. Megan Braden-Capone was a twenty-seven-year-old freelancer primarily for *Gambit* and member of a prominent New Orleans family when NOLA Media Group recruited her in late October 2012, after they had pursued her for several months she said. Almost from the beginning of her employment, she was prone to surprisingly frank Facebook posts about her frustrations working for NOLA Media Group. She voluntarily resigned in March 2013, four-and-one-half months after joining the company. "I left because I didn't believe in the things they were doing and because it seemed like no one could agree on anything," Braden-Capone said in May 2013. "I also spent a lot of my time daydreaming about tripping [her last supervisor, newly promoted NOLA Media Group managing producer] Paula Devlin or dropping a banana peel in her path. I also had four different editors in four-and-a-half months. That's insane. I felt like no matter how hard I tried, it wouldn't work."[36]

Presumably because the sheer logistics and organization of a transition of this magnitude required more institutional memory than Advance or *Times-Picayune* executives had anticipated, other employees were asked to extend their employment with the company for weeks or months. Many held the impression that a strong performance during the interim would put them in good stead for a job with the new entity, although none of those interviewed was ultimately re-hired. Part-time photographer Matthew Hinton, whose employment was extended through December 23, 2012—"I was laid off in time for Christmas," he recalled sardonically in April 2013—was then asked to continue working as a freelancer, at a rate roughly one-third of his hourly wage as a part-timer, and with the added financial burdens of providing his own equipment, being responsible for repairs to it, and paying his share of Federal Insurance Contributions Act taxes previously covered by the company. He declined. "I told them it wasn't a mutually beneficially relationship, [that] the only people who benefited was them," Hinton said.[37]

Special sections manager Victor Andrews, who had been at the paper nearly twenty-five years, had perhaps the dubious distinction of having his employment extended the longest—six months, or through the end of March 2013—at which time he also was offered freelance work that would have paid one-third of his previous salary, and with no fringe benefits. He, like Hinton, declined the offer, but when management had difficulty recruiting a replacement at the new rate of pay, Andrews said he was asked to stay for two more weeks, again at a reduced rate of pay, which he again turned down.[38]

Other veteran employees whose very identities were perhaps inextricably linked to their *Times-Picayune* personas agreed to remain with the organization, as lower-paid contractors without continued access to the company's relatively rich fringe benefits.

"Social Scene" columnist Nell Nolan, who since 1979 has spun alliterative prose detailing the composition of New Orleans Carnival courts and dissecting the region's debutante season, agreed to continue to report and write her column as a freelancer, along with eighty-four-year-old local sports icon Pete Finney. However, the end of an era passed less than a year later, when Nolan—the impeccably coiffed and appointed Uptown doyenne who inhabited the same social circles as longtime publisher Ashton Phelps, Jr. and had long been regarded as protected by him—terminated her relationship with NOLA Media Group at the end of July 2013. Her decision to leave the newspaper came after a series of perceived indignities, including being laid off, then brought back as a contractor; being forbidden to continue to work out of the *Times-Picayune* offices on Howard Avenue; and having her freelance budget reduced for the stable of photographers who captured the smiling faces at the multiple events she covered on any given evening. Three days after NOLA.com | *Times-Picayune* published a report about Nolan's "retirement," the *Advocate* published its own article announcing that she would be joining "the city's daily newspaper."[39]

With few other employment options readily available, other former veteran employees, including thirty-two-year veteran illustrator Kenny Harrison and sports writer Jim Derry—the latter who began work with the company twenty-one years to the day he was told he no longer would have a job with the newspaper—continued freelancing on a limited basis for NOLA Media Group, generally at rates presumed or known to be far below their previous wages. So, whether they were retained as contractors or dismissed, veteran staffers absorbed the harshest of the career-and-earnings body blows inflicted by the changes.

However, it looked as though the kids, perhaps not surprisingly, might be all right. Of the *Times-Picayune* journalists who voluntarily left for new jobs before the changes took effect, most were in their thirties or early forties. The organization has since hired a number of fresh-faced, eager and generally more-digitally savvy employees to post continuously on NOLA.com, and to fill the newspaper's thrice-weekly traditional and new thrice-weekly *TP Street* tabloid editions that launched in late June 2013. ("Not to be braggin', but the entertainment team of 7 plus 2 freelancers kicked out 112 reviews during Jazz Fest. Boom," thirty-one-year-old community engagement specialist Grace Wilson posted on her Facebook page[40] following the conclusion of the 2013 New Orleans Jazz and Heritage Festival. In keeping with NOLA.com's new sports and entertainment focus, it covered the event exhaustively.) Later in the summer, the *Oregonian* began advertising for new employees only a few days after cleaving close to 30 percent of its newsroom. "Experience as a journalist is strongly preferred, but if you can show us some writing samples that have the 'wow' factor, we want to hear from you!" a sentence in an advertisement for a new general assignment reporter read, a statement that previously would have been unthinkable in a solicitation for a journalist at a major metropolitan daily newspaper. Northeast Ohio Media Group (Cleveland.com | *Plain Dealer's* new corporate entity) was sharply criticized on social media for having jobs posted on its own website and industry websites (including Poynter.org, which included the advertisements side-by-side with a report about the layoffs) on the same day it notified the fifty-odd newsroom employees they were losing their jobs. (The company had waited three days after its layoffs in Portland a month earlier before posting "help wanted" ads for jobs there.) As defections from the *Times-Picayune* continued through late spring 2013, a number of younger staffers benefited via promotions precipitated by the resulting musical chairs.

Elsewhere, *Patriot-News* reporter Sara Ganim, who in August 2012 became one of the youngest Pulitzer Prize winners in history for her reports uncovering the Jerry Sandusky child-abuse scandal at Penn State University (she was twenty-four), tore up the Twitterverse in the days after the layoffs were announced, with unequivocal support for Advance's new strategy—before jumping ship to CNN three months before the changes took effect in Harrisburg.

New Orleans, however, wasn't going down without a fight. Beginning almost immediately and extending through the summer, angry New Orleanians organized rallies, signed petitions, sent letters, and created social media accounts to protest the perceived decimation of their beloved *Times-Picayune*. "Citizens . . . are rallying, demanding that Advance save that city's daily newspaper," the alternative weekly *Weld for Birmingham*'s Kyle Whitmire editorialized. "The community rallying behind that paper is as diverse as they come. Grassroots community organizers, musicians, celebrities, and business heavies have voiced their support." A few months later, the newspaper guild-funded public awareness campaign began in Cleveland, marking only the second organized protest in any Advance market undergoing "digital first."

In sharp contrast, the landscape remained quiet in Alabama. "Something is happening in New Orleans, but it's not happening here," added Whitmire, who later joined AL.com | *Birmingham News* and did not respond to a request for an interview.[41] Protests in Birmingham were non-existent, freelance writer and former reporter with the now-defunct *Birmingham Post-Herald* Wade Kwon told *Gambit*.[42]

John Archibald, a metro columnist at the *Birmingham News*, wrote a column questioning why there were protests in New Orleans, but none in Birmingham, and chalked it up to New Orleans's "identity and pride" and Birmingham's "division and hostility."[43] Whitmire said that while New Orleanians were disappointed in the loss of a daily newspaper, Birminghamians were simply disappointed in the *Birmingham News* as the community's newspaper. Rob Holbert, managing editor and co-publisher of Mobile's alternative biweekly *Lagniappe*, had accurately predicted in a January 2012 column that the city's Advance-owned *Press-*

Register would no longer be a daily newspaper by year's end.[44] "We didn't have the same level of outrage here," he recalled in May 2013. "There was unhappiness, but [then-*Press-Register* and now *Times-Picayune* publisher] Ricky Mathews had already been here for a while, the cutbacks already were occurring, so we were somewhat anesthetized. We didn't have the same shock to the system that New Orleans did."[45]

In reality, the difference was likely attributable to what had transpired in New Orleans seven years earlier, in the days and weeks after Hurricane Katrina made landfall, when tragedy and heroism bonded a community and its newspaper in the most extraordinary of ways.

CHAPTER IV

"We Publish Come Hell and High Water"

Although the *Times-Picayune* had published in print form every day for 168 years before Hurricane Katrina's aftermath devastated New Orleans, in many ways the newspaper didn't begin truly connecting with its readers until the hours after the storm struck. As most of the city and region was inundated after the monumental failure of the elaborate levee system designed to keep metropolitan New Orleans's low-lying terrain from flooding, the *Times-Picayune* played a critical and often heroic role—informing, educating, warning, consoling, rallying, enraging, and empowering the region's residents, leaders, and institutions.

About 250 employees and family members, including some eighty newsroom staffers, arrived at the *Times-Picayune*'s headquarters Sunday afternoon, August 28, 2005, in preparation for landfall of the already ominous storm. Journalists in hurricane-prone communities are accustomed to the storm-preparation ritual, which often involves packing sleeping bags, clothing, food, water, family members, and even pets, then heading to a newsroom contained in an appropriately fortified building to ride out the worst and be ready to be deployed as soon as it is safe to venture out to report on the aftermath.

Environmental reporter Mark Schleifstein, whose 2002 five-day series "Washing Away," accurately predicted what would happen to New Orleans when it was hit by the inevitable Big One, has frequently recounted the now-famous telephone conversation he had that afternoon with Max Mayfield, then-director of the National Hurricane Center. During it, Mayfield sharply quizzed

Schleifstein about the elevation of the newspaper's headquarters and its structural ability to sustain hurricane-force winds. "By Sunday night, the outer bands of the 450-mile-wide storm were upon us, growing in intensity until 4 A.M., when one of the Lexan [bullet-proof] windows in the publisher's suite blew in," Schleifstein later recalled in a story he wrote for the magazine of his alma mater, George Washington University.[1] Within a few hours, however, the staff, along with much of New Orleans, thought the city had dodged another barometric bullet as Katrina passed over New Orleans as a Category 3—albeit, a strong Category 3—storm. But as morning broke and photographers and reporters ventured out into the still-howling winds, they discovered what would lead to the real horror of Katrina's aftermath: the region's devastatingly failing levees.

Reporters Bruce Nolan, Gordon Russell (later promoted to city editor), Mike Perlstein, Jim Varney, Brian Thevenot, and Doug MacCash; photographers Ted Jackson, John McCusker, David Grunfeld, and Kathy Anderson; and editor James O'Byrne chronicled much of the early devastation. Jackson discovered a Lower Ninth Ward "inundated by seawall breaches and storm surge," O'Byrne and art critic MacCash reported. Jackson and Thevenot then took a boat to find neighboring St. Bernard Parish also under water. Later in the day, O'Byrne and MacCash bicycled toward the city's lakefront, about five miles west of the newspaper's headquarters. "The [levee] breach sent a churning sea of water from Lake Pontchartrain coursing across Lakeview and into Mid-City, Carrollton, Gentilly, City Park, and neighborhoods farther south and east," the duo wrote in a report posted that evening. "As night fell on the devastated region, the water was still rising in the city, and nobody was willing to predict when it would stop."[2] On that trip, O'Byrne surveyed his and Schleifstein's completely flooded homes.

By midmorning Tuesday, "you couldn't walk out the building without walking in water up to your waist," managing editor

Peter Kovacs told the *New York Times*.[3] As flood waters continued to rise around the newspaper's three-story headquarters, Phelps and Amoss ordered employees to evacuate via a fleet of waiting newspaper delivery trucks. "We ran through the building of our newspaper—people were still asleep in their sleeping bags, people were having breakfast in our cafeteria, people were already beginning to work—and we just ran through the building, shouting, 'Get out, get out, go to the loading dock!'" Amoss recalled in a January 2006 interview on National Public Radio's *Fresh Air* program. "At the loading dock, where normally newspapers are shipped out for delivery, we started shipping out people for delivery to we-did-not-know-where, in the backs of our delivery trucks. We just pulled up a dozen or so delivery trucks and started loading people into the back of them."[4] At 9:40 A.M., an obviously hastily written and typo-strewn brief was posted to the newspaper's website: "*The Times-Picayune* is evacuating it's New Orleans building. Water continues to rise around our building, as it is throughout the region. We want to evacuate our employees and families while we are still able to safely leave our building."[5]

After regrouping at the newspaper's still-dry West Bank bureau on the opposite side of the Mississippi River, an initial plan to travel to Baton Rouge or the Cajun burg of Houma and send reporters back in with the National Guard drew immediate protests from journalists unwilling to "*just leave* the world's biggest story in our own hometown," Thevenot remembered in his *American Journalism Review* article. Then-sports editor David Meeks—who would later write about taking a kayak to his inundated Old Lakeview home and literally swimming through the structure to rescue the family dog[6]—asked Amoss for a delivery truck and permission to remain with a small group of reporters to chronicle the devastation. The eclectic team included Russell, Thevenot, editorial page editor Terri Troncale, assistant editorial page editor Dante Ramos, Perlstein, music critic Keith Spera, MacCash, and McCusker. (Nolan, who had struck out on his own to check on his elderly parents, whom he had arranged to evacuate to a downtown hotel, later rejoined the group.) They departed "with a few days' supply of water, hardly any food or clothes, very few notebooks and one laptop," Thevenot recalled. Russell's, Troncale's, and columnist Stephanie Grace's dry Uptown homes became ad-hoc bases of operation.

Other reporters and photographers already were spread across the city. Varney and Grunfeld documented destruction in New Orleans and nearby parishes, while photographer Alex Brandon rode with a local SWAT team, and crime reporter Trymaine Lee was embedded at the city's emergency command center in the downtown Hyatt Hotel,[7] which became a symbol of Katrina's fury because most of the windows in the thirty-one-story hotel blew out during the storm. Photographer Rusty Costanza, who was embedded with city officials in suburban Kenner, learned that the levees had failed when he saw the news on a nurse's computer at St. Jude Hospital. He also then discovered that the *Times-Picayune* had evacuated its headquarters. He remained with Kenner officials for much of the next several weeks. When Costanza made an appearance at the newspaper's temporary Baton Rouge headquarters a couple of weeks later, Amoss's face flashed with shock and concern. He asked me, "'Are you OK?'" Costanza recalled. "I didn't realize how much weight I had lost. I couldn't find a belt, so I had a rope tied around me, holding up my pants."[8]

Manuel Torres had just been named bureau chief of St. Bernard Parish, which was essentially destroyed by the storm. He teamed with reporter Paul Rioux and the duo initially planned to embed in the St. Bernard Parish Government Center. However, after surveying where officials planned to station them — near windows on the first floor — and learning that Katrina had been upgraded to a Category 5 storm as it churned toward the Gulf Coast, the duo opted instead to work out of the newspaper's downtown offices. The government center subsequently was completely flooded and its inhabitants had to be rescued from the building's roof. Torres and Rioux instead ended up in Baton Rouge, and made daily, before-dawn pilgrimages to New Orleans, reporting all day and then traveling to wherever they could get a cell phone signal to transmit their reports.

For three days after the city flooded, the *Times-Picayune*'s reports appeared only online, in the form of constantly updated blog posts and a portable document format, or PDF, version of the newspaper available for download on NOLA.com. Shea, joined by a dozen employees including reporters and editors Schleifstein, Bob Warren, and Kim Chatelain, set up shop in the offices of the *Courier*, a newspaper sixty miles from New Orleans in Houma. Without access to any of the *Times-Picayune*'s production software, templates, or fonts, copy editor Mary Chauvin—on her first day as a full-time employee—"was able to replicate the look of the newspaper on the fly by cobbling together graphic elements from earlier online editions," the *New York Times* reported.[9] As Chatelain and Warren made intermittent contact with reporters who had stayed behind in the city, they began blogging again on NOLA.com. Metro zone layout editor Jennifer Brown organized her copy desk colleagues to put out a thirteen-page paper—"an oddity because we knew we weren't printing" a physical newspaper, Shea recalled in May 2013.[10] That Houma crew posted to NOLA.com and produced the PDF newspaper during those three days, while a larger news operation numbering about sixty (which Nolan joined) assembled in Baton Rouge, initially at the Manship School of Mass Communication at Louisiana State University. The first edition that appeared the morning after the evacuation as a PDF contained seventeen articles and an editorial, all written by staff members, and twelve photographs, only one of which was not a staff-generated image, the *New York Times* reported.

When a print edition returned September 2, 2005, it was an abbreviated sixteen-page version, initially with no advertising or syndicated features, with 50,000 copies printed on contract by *The Courier*. (In contrast to that limited print run, the *Times-Picayune*'s daily average circulation before the storm was about 260,000.) Despite its lack of physical heft, the condensed edition was greeted like beads on Mardi Gras by residents desperate for news and normalcy, as columnist Chris Rose recalled in his *Oxford American* essay. Rose, who worked at the newspaper from 1984 until 2009, remembered spotting a stack of the scarce post-Katrina print newspapers in a French Quarter hotel, grabbing it, and heading into the streets:

> When I arrived at the first responders' emergency post outside of Harrah's Casino, I was mobbed by local cops, firemen, and EMTs, who reached for copies like sub-Saharan refugees grabbing for water or baby formula. . . . I walked into several French Quarter bars with copies and was greeted with joyous calls of "*The Times-Picayune!*"
>
> Driving towards Uptown, I spied two women who appeared to be in their sixties sitting on their front porch fanning themselves in the crushing afternoon heat. . . . They eyed me suspiciously until I held up the newspaper and identified myself. "Oh my God!" they said in unison and rushed down the steps to embrace me. Then they stepped back and I handed them each a copy of the paper. Tears rolled down both of their faces. One said very softly to herself, "*The Times-Picayune,*" and clutched it to her breast. They thanked me and returned to their porch, holding each other's arms and their papers, lost in the reverie of a familiar feeling in their hands, the return of a cherished ritual, a fabled institution, their daily bread.[11]

The *Times-Picayune* and its website became a linchpin to residents who stayed and those who evacuated. The newspaper's reporters and photographers emerged as larger-than-life characters, including Rose, quickly anointed as the city's heart, soul, and sage as he detailed the unraveling of his own post-Katrina life in his thrice-weekly column, and McCusker, who pushed himself so far beyond the brink in visually capturing the trauma that he delusionally attempted "suicide by cop" a year after the storm. Rose's *1 Dead in Attic*, a compilation of his post-Katrina columns — titled for the message spray-painted on the exterior of an Eighth Ward house noting "the untimely passing of a citizen, a resident, a New Orleanian" — became the seminal emotional account of the catastrophe.[12]

Only a fraction of *Times-Picayune* subscribers were physically in the region to receive copies courtesy of the reduced print run on the *Courier*'s presses, and essentially no delivery infrastructure was available to distribute them to the few areas of the city that were habitable. However, it quickly became apparent that evacuees and millions of people around the world were eager to devour every word and image the *Picayune* could report about Katrina's aftermath — regardless of the medium of distribution. For months after the storm, many of the newspaper's regular readers remained exiled by either flood waters or destroyed homes, meaning they read the newspaper's reports exclusively online. NOLA.com's reportage became the definitive accounting of the worst natural and engineering disaster in the country's history and made the website the pre-eminent source nationally and internationally for news about the aftermath.

NOLA.com established a missing person's forum on the Wednesday after the storm that allowed readers to post queries about friends or family whose whereabouts were unknown. By late Thursday, it had 7,400 posts,[13] a number that grew to nearly 23,000 a few days later.[14] NOLA.com also created forums for people wanting to volunteer in rescue and rebuilding efforts, and to open their homes to people left homeless by the levees' failure. Rescuers — ranging from public-spirited individuals piloting single motorboats to the US Coast Guard — monitored NOLA.com for locations of people in need of rescue. "Through its stories, blogs, and forums, thousands of disjointed families and friends found one another," Rose recounted in his *Oxford American* essay. "It provided stability amid the chaos. Some folks claimed it saved lives."

Other evacuees quickly came to regard the site as simply the most reliable source of information about their ravaged city. "We've been checking the NOLA.com blog religiously," resident James Lien, who had evacuated to Tennessee, told the *Online Journalism Review (OJR)*. "We were checking it literally almost every hour. They had so many small details, and covered nooks and crannies of New Orleans that an Associated Press or major network person would *never* have known, or gotten right. . . . This was the first storm I've ever weathered where New Orleans people were obsessed with looking at satellite photos online. Looking for a tiny speck of your house to find out if that tree in the yard fell down, or counting the number of front steps you could see on the church down the block to guess how high the water got over the curb. New Orleans people who evacuated were absolutely feverish about it."

NOLA.com's page views soared from a typical 800,000 to 900,000 per day to 30 million on the Friday after Katrina's landfall. *OJR*, a joint project of the University of Southern California's Annenberg School for Communication and Journalism and the Knight Foundation, called the website's ability to quickly post information and photos from individuals and its role as an emergency response-and-rescue tool a "watershed moment in journalism."[15] Coincidentally, the 2006 Pulitzer Prize competition (for work published in 2005, the year Katrina hit) for the first time opened all of its award categories to digital content.[16]

Although the public service they provided was clearly invaluable, *Times-Picayune* reporters paid a steep emotional price for the horrors they chronicled, as DigitalJournalist.org recounted in a harrowing story about the morning after the storm passed:

> When day broke, [photographer Ted Jackson] went out in his truck to photograph the customary aftermath of what he thought was just another normal hurricane. Arriving on the bridge above St. Claude Avenue and discovering the road below flooding from the storm, Jackson found himself powerless to rescue several women

and their children, trapped and clinging to the rails on their front porch. Partially submerged by the rushing, rising waters, they desperately beseeched him for help. There was no possible way to get to them across the road just 50 feet away without being swept away himself. Amid much anguish, he did shoot a few frames, but the images left in his mind were perhaps more haunting than the photographs he did take. Realizing he could not deliver them from their peril, and understanding the power of hope, he called out to them to stay where they were, reassuring them that help would come.

It would be several months before Jackson would learn that the women and children he felt powerless to aid had been rescued and safely evacuated to Houston.

As part of a photographic gallery he compiled for DigitalJournalist.org, Jackson wrote about being on a boat with rescue workers and spotting a hole hacked through the roof of a home in the city's Lakefront neighborhood. "We jumped . . . onto the rooftop and scampered to the opening and peered in. The old man had laid down on the rafters in the attic, crossed his hands across his chest and died in the intense heat. His crippled sister had drowned in her wheelchair below. It was my first dead body of the flood. It certainly wouldn't be my last."[17]

Two days after the storm's landfall, "the haunting fear of flooding was replaced by a raw fear for life and public safety," NOLA.com reported in a post headlined "City not safe for anyone." The account described "a landscape of lawlessness where [reporter Russell] feared for his life and felt his safety was threatened at nearly every turn." Hordes of hungry and desperate people at the Superdome and Ernest N. Morial Convention Center overwhelmed a handful of first responders "in a near riot situation."[18] The stench of excrement nearly caused Russell to vomit at the Superdome, where 30,000 had gathered, Thevenot recalled in his *AJR* account. Six days later, Russell reached his breaking point. Thevenot was ordered by metro editor Jed Horne to high-tail it to Russell's house "and get him the f— out of there. He's in a bad way. He said he's got heat exhaustion or something and he's been throwing up. He keeps calling here, which makes me think he's in deep, deep trouble." Thevenot was able to help transport Russell to Russell's mother-in-law's house outside of the metropolitan area, where he quickly recovered before returning to the city to continue his reporting.[19]

Nearly a year after the storm, the accumulated stress and sadness of documenting so much destruction and misery, of losing his family's home, and of battling insurance companies for the money to rebuild it, caused McCusker to snap. In an incident that started as a traffic stop, he pinned a police officer between cars, then fled and crashed before being stopped again, when he was finally subdued with a Taser gun. He then begged officers to shoot him. "He kept saying, 'Just kill me, just kill me,'" James Arey, commander of the New Orleans Police Department's SWAT Crisis Negotiation Team, told the *New York Times*. "Our officers are well trained to recognize crises and attempts at 'suicide by cop,' and that's what this was."[20]

McCusker recovered with the help of thrice-weekly therapy sessions and anti-depressants. He was ultimately allowed to plead to misdemeanor charges, which were later expunged from his record. His wife, Johanna Schindler, an assistant community news editor at the newspaper who became director of communications at the University of New Orleans after the storm, however, fared far worse. Several former employees shared disturbing stories of Schindler's psychological meltdown that began essentially as soon as they fled the *Times-Picayune*'s headquarters in the delivery trucks. "Johanna lost her mind, and she never recovered," McCusker, who had three children with Schindler during their twenty-two-year marriage, said in a March 2013 interview. "It completely destroyed her. I never kissed my wife again after Katrina."[21] Schindler died in 2010 of complications from a brain aneurysm[22] about a month after she and McCusker separated.

Rose's struggles—in the damaged city and with the now-damaged souls that occupied it—played out in his columns, which were a finalist for the 2006 Pulitzer Prize, losing to the *New York Times*'s Nicholas Kristof's work chronicling the genocide in Darfur.[23] In one of his early columns after the storm, Rose wrote of a neighborhood couple who returned home and made a drunken suicide pact a few weeks later because they couldn't bear living in "the smoking ruins of Pompeii." The man killed himself, but the woman didn't, prompting Rose to ask, "Where are we now in our descent through Dante's nine circles of hell?" He wrote about "crying jags and fetal positionings," the "thousand-yard stare," "the inability to hold conversations," according to a 2008 *Columbia Journalism Review* profile of him. "I'd . . . reach for my kids, always, trying to hold them, touch them, kiss them. Tell them I was still here. But I was disappearing fast."[24] He slid into substance abuse, and it took an intervention by family and friends, a stint in rehab, and anti-depressants to ultimately pull him from his "rabbit hole." In the end, his marriage failed and after accepting a buyout from the *Times-Picayune* in 2009, he accepted a position with FOX New Orleans, which he left in April 2013. As this book goes to press, he's working on a follow-up to *1 Dead in Attic*, titled *As Not Seen on Oprah: A story of struggle, fame, fatherhood, madness, addiction, rehabilitation and redemption in post-apocalyptic New Orleans*.[25]

The journalists' inability to escape the pervasiveness of the destruction and despair was particularly overwhelming. "I watched a colleague crack one night; she was sent away to stay with relatives," veteran *Times-Picayune* reporter John Pope wrote in an essay for the fall 2007 edition of *Nieman Reports*, a publication of the Nieman Foundation, sponsor of the prestigious journalism fellowships at Harvard University by the same name. "One of my roommates had aging relatives and in-laws who had lost their home on the Mississippi Gulf Coast. His wife, who had taken their children to stay with friends several hours away, was wondering whether to enroll them in school there because there was no way to know when anyone would be able to return. At four o'clock in the morning, he awoke with stabbing chest pains and had to be rushed to the hospital. It wasn't a heart attack, but it served as a warning of the toll stress could take."[26]

Although several *Times-Picayune* journalists talked of being almost on automatic pilot and of knowing what needed to be done and instinctively doing it, the sheer ineptitude of the government's response to the crisis came to fuel their work. "For the rest of the world, we felt an obligation to show that New Orleans was in dire crisis, that the slow government response cost lives, and that our longstanding neglect of the poor had created Third World conditions in a First World country," Perlstein, who left the newspaper in 2006, first for academia and then for his current position with WWL-TV's investigative team, wrote in an essay published in the winter of 2006. "We were re-energized by the desperation of mostly poor, mostly African-American citizens begging us to tell the outside world of their plight. Police officers begged us to tell the same story. So did firefighters and doctors and elected officials."[27]

Those frustrations led much of the newspaper's editorial staff to toil that much harder. After months of overwork, Schleifstein blew out a disc in his back in February 2006. "The doctor told me I needed emergency surgery, but this was not a time during which you wanted to have health problems in New Orleans," he recalled in 2013, referring to the region's post-storm shortage of medical professionals and overburdened healthcare system. He was discharged the morning after surgery to minimize the risk of contracting an infection in the overrun hospital. "And I started writing again the day after I got home," he remembered.

Although Nolan's home in Algiers, the only Orleans Parish community on the west bank of the Mississippi River, survived relatively unscathed, he talked about how others close to him didn't fare nearly as well. "I have so many friends who lost literally everything," he told American Public Media's the *Story* radio show in 2012. "The way they kept their sanity was by working, by plunging into work, working furiously, and working collaboratively, and touching base with family to make sure that they were OK, and by just sort of focusing on the next fifteen minutes, or the next half-hour, or the end of this day, until things slowed down a little bit and some clarity began to emerge."[28]

Not only did the paper powerfully document the death and destruction in its news pages, but it also forcefully advocated for its residents and city on its editorial pages. "On the elevated portion of Interstate 10 near Orleans Avenue, a group of displaced people pushed a wheelchair carrying a dead woman. She wore pink pajama bottoms—and a white kitchen garbage bag on her head," began one of the first editorials the newspaper published after the storm. "Hurricane Katrina has created a humanitarian crisis of unimaginable proportions. And if the main strategy for addressing that crisis is to evacuate the east bank of New Orleans, then local, state and federal officials need to move much faster to get people out."[29] In "An Open Letter to the President" five days after the storm made landfall, the newspaper called out the "bald-faced lies" of Federal Emergency Management Agency Director Michael "You're doing a heck of a job, Brownie" Brown:

> Despite the city's multiple points of entry, our nation's bureaucrats spent days after last week's hurricane wringing their hands, lamenting the fact that they could neither rescue the city's stranded victims nor bring them food, water and medical supplies. Meanwhile there were journalists, including some who work for the *Times-Picayune*, going in and out of the city via the Crescent City Connection [bridge across to the West Bank of the Mississippi River]. On Thursday morning, that crew saw a caravan of thirteen Wal-Mart tractor trailers headed into town to bring food, water and supplies to a dying city. Television reporters were doing live reports from downtown New Orleans streets. . . .
> Our people deserved to be rescued. No expense should have been spared. No excuses should have been voiced. Especially not

one as preposterous as the claim that New Orleans couldn't be reached.[30]

A week later, Brown resigned.

The paper understandably reacted particularly vociferously when public officials and other news organizations questioned whether New Orleans should even be rebuilt. After an editorial in Connecticut's *Waterbury Republican-American* questioned the wisdom of rebuilding New Orleans[31] and then-US House Speaker Dennis Hastert was quoted as saying, "It looks like a lot of that place could be bulldozed," the *Times-Picayune* responded with a forceful editorial headlined, "Yes, we are worth it."[32] "Who'd have thought that we'd ever be talking about threats to the city's existence?" *Times-Picayune* editorial columnist Jarvis DeBerry wrote in the fall 2007 edition of *Nieman Reports*. "Or that there would ever be a debate as to whether this city — this city of all cities — should continue to exist? The *Times-Picayune* can't have but one forceful opinion on that topic, and I've been fortunate enough to be one of the ones who gets to express it."[33] For weeks and months, and then years after the storm, the paper editorialized about the lack of federal, state, and local leadership, about the corruption that pervaded the rebuilding process, and about the need for stronger safeguards protecting all areas of the country vulnerable to natural disasters and dependent on the protective nature of healthy coastlines and marshlands.

"I think the newspaper has been an extraordinary leader in trying to define the agenda and trying to raise the issues that are important to the future of the city," O'Byrne said at a presentation at Harvard University about a year-and-a half after the storm. "Your hometown is hit by a disaster and the nation wants to talk about, 'Well, should we really have a town there after all?' I mean, it's an extraordinary conversation to have, but as a newspaper in New Orleans, which was a city before the United States was a country, it's strange to have a conversation about whether or not you're going to have a city at the mouth of your major river. . . . 'We'll just let those people rot, essentially, let that city rot. Sorry we didn't build a strong enough flood protection system, but life's tough. Move on,' — is not an acceptable position to have."[34]

Heroic work, sacrifice, and crusading by the *Times-Picayune* didn't go unheralded by the New Orleans citizenry. The newspaper's reporters and photographers were practically sainted as the city began to recover. "The people gave the paper love," Rose recalled in his *Oxford American* essay. "Reporters were treated like heroes by returning residents and businesses. In the year after the flood, *Times-Picayune* staffers couldn't pay for their own drinks." Immediately after McCusker's arrest, the Friends of the *Times-Picayune* Katrina Relief Fund, which had been established by four newspaper alumnae to raise money for employees harmed by the storm, made a special appeal on his behalf. Within two days, more than $10,000 poured in. The fund ultimately raised more than $300,000 to aid some 200 employees and their families.[35]

In a second commentary for the *American Journalism Review* published a year after Katrina, Thevenot talked about what the city's affection and admiration meant to the staff:

> More gratifying than anything has been the close, almost intimate connection the newspaper has forged with its readers through our shared struggle. Like most reporters, I've grown used to dealing with the kind of people who love to hate the media, including their hometown paper. But those people have all but vanished in the post-Katrina media landscape. No one here complains about the paper anymore, and I can't count the number of regular readers I've met recently who have gushed with gratitude when they learned I work for the *Picayune*. As I took a long walk down St. Charles Avenue recently, I ran across a newspaper box with a heart spray-painted on it. Another recent day, I sat in a bar watching a young woman read the paper, then heard her remark to a friend, "This paper has just been fantastic lately."[36]

The work of the *Times-Picayune*'s news staff was highlighted in a yearlong exhibit, "Covering Katrina," at the Newseum in Washington, DC, which coincided with the fifth anniversary of the storm in 2010. *Photograph courtesy of the Newseum/Sarah Mercier.*

The adoration and esteem extended well beyond New Orleans. The *Times-Picayune's* two Pulitzers for its Katrina coverage were for breaking news, and the even-more-coveted Gold Medal for "meritorious public service." In addition to numerous other national awards detailed earlier, the staff also won the Medill Medal for Courage in Journalism awarded by the Medill School at Northwestern University, widely regarded as one of the country's leading journalism schools.

Recognition kept coming. In 2010, the newspaper's Katrina coverage was named one of the country's top ten works of journalism during the decade by New York University's Arthur

L. Carter Journalism Institute, topping even the *New York Times*'s reporting on the September 11, 2001, terrorist attacks. "The *Times-Picayune*'s coverage was heroic in every sense," Dan Fagin, director of NYU's Science, Health, and Environmental Reporting Program, told the *Columbia Journalism Review*. "The content was fearless, and the fact that there was any coverage at all in those initial days borders on the miraculous."[37]

During this time, Advance remained extraordinarily committed to the *Times-Picayune* and its employees. "Everyone [in our family] has their own personal feelings about the paper," Steven Newhouse told the *New York Observer* in a rare interview given in September 2005 to debunk an Internet rumor that the Newhouses planned to stop publishing the newspaper in the wake of Katrina's devastation. "I certainly have close relationships with everyone down there. For me, at a time when it's fashionable to badmouth journalists, [the coverage] shows the amazing dedication and craft of the people at *The Times-Picayune* and many other newspapers."

During a visit to the newspaper's temporary offices in Baton Rouge about a week after the storm, Steven Newhouse's father, Donald, acknowledged that the accolades for the *Times-Picayune* were also reverberating in the Big Apple. He "expressed immense pride . . . He said he was surrounded by praise in New York, and it was tremendously gratifying," Amoss told the *Observer*. On the visit, Donald Newhouse affirmed his company's intention to continue to employ all employees, and to pay their full wages through mid-October, even if they did not return to work during that time.[38] Advance also continued to provide company-paid health insurance, and employees who were working received an immediate $300 cash payment, a $75 *per diem* if they were working away from their homes, and an up-to-$3,000 no-interest loan. "The biggest thing was the sense of security that I didn't have to worry about my job," Shea said. "They were so incredibly generous. It was Ashton, but it was also Donald."

But most important, the newspaper continued to publish, even as the region's population listlessly rebounded. "The reality was that we lost major advertisers," Schleifstein, dubbed the "Prophet of Katrina" for his years of prescient reporting about the inevitable Big One, said in March 2013. "The department stores disappeared and the grocery stores were a mess, but [the Newhouses] made a conscious decision that this newspaper was not going to die. What I saw was a newspaper that was hurt dramatically, that was being underwritten by the parent company for several years until it got back on its feet. [Donald Newhouse] walks on water, as far as I'm concerned."

Two employees with knowledge of the newspaper's financial performance who spoke on the condition of anonymity reported that it enjoyed relatively strong advertising revenues—especially in light of the scale of the devastation and population loss—in 2006 and 2007. "Everyone needed an apartment, a [new] mattress, a refrigerator, a job," one commented. The newspaper's finances also were aided by some thirty-five newsroom employees who either never returned or quit relatively quickly after the storm, which reduced the organization's payroll expenses. "The newspaper, oddly enough, is stabilizing, albeit at a reduced level from before the storm," Amoss told the *New York Times* in April 2007. "It has not come roaring back—it is a smaller business, but it is healthy business, and that can't be said of many American newspapers."[39]

As the city's population fell by nearly two-thirds, the Sunday *Times-Picayune* circulation declined nearly 30 percent, to just fewer than 200,000 in 2007, the first time after the storm the newspaper was required to report figures to the industry group, now known as the Alliance of Audited Media, or AAM.[40] By July 2011, the Census Bureau estimated New Orleans's population had rebounded to 360,740 or 74 percent of its 2000 level.[41] The newspaper's circulation, however, continued to plummet, registering at almost 146,000 on Sundays and about 128,000 Mondays-Fridays, as of September 30, 2012, the last AAM report issued before the latest changes at the newspaper went into effect.[42] Two former senior-level managers said the *Times-Picayune* remained profitable in 2008 and was marginally so in 2009, helped in part by the buyouts that began that year and the unpaid furloughs that started in 2010.

While the *Times-Picayune* may have been in the black, it clearly was not enjoying anything close to the hefty margins it had achieved consistently for much of Advance's ownership. Seemingly unfazed by this reality, the newspaper produced a memento of its hard-fought Katrina battle, a T-shirt that would become very popular, and then particularly pointed after the 2012 changes were announced. It was emblazoned with the newspaper's Olde English font-influenced masthead, and what had become the *Times-Picayune*'s post-Katrina battle cry: "We Publish Come Hell and High Water." It was donned often at gatherings and farewell parties in the weeks and months after Advance announced the coming changes.

CHAPTER V

"Katrina Without the Water"

Rather than diminishing over time, outrage both inside and outside of the *Times-Picayune* only seemed to grow, especially after the humiliating way in which the June 2012 layoff notices was handled. Angry and frustrated that editor Jim Amoss and online editor Lynn Cunningham never responded to the initial list of questions they submitted, a group of seventeen primarily senior reporters signed a new, more detailed list of concerns and questions posed to Amoss, Cunningham, and features editor Mark Lorando.[1] "We thought it would make a bigger impression if we could get as many people as possible in hard news" who had been asked to stay to sign the letter, one former employee who signed the letter recalled. "We hoped it would signal to them that we weren't going to automatically say 'yes' because we were scared, and that they needed to explain to us why it was worth it to go along with them."

The only response offered was a meeting between a handful of the signatories, and Amoss, Cunningham, and Lorando. The reporters in attendance, however, felt they received few definitive answers. "Several days later, many of us who were in the meeting turned in forms declining the job offers," one attendee recalled. "Jim seemed stunned." All told, close to a dozen of the nearly ninety editorial employees the newspaper sought to retain instead tendered their resignations within a few weeks. Investigative reporter David Hammer and criminal justice reporter Brendan McCarthy jumped ship for WWL, the region's leading TV station and CBS affiliate. "He asked why I would want to do that, that 'we're newspaper guys,'" Hammer recalled in April 2013, about the conversation he had with Amoss when he tendered his resignation. "And I said, 'But you're taking away the newspaper.'"[2] (Less than a year later, McCarthy departed WWL to head the newly established Kentucky Center for Investigative Reporting, a project of Louisville Public Media.)

Special projects reporter Cindy Chang, who led an eight-part exposé into the state's prison system that received a prestigious national award the week the layoffs occurred, decamped for the *Los Angeles Times*. Married couple Bill Barrow, who covered statewide education issues, and Michelle Krupa, who covered City Hall, departed with their toddler son for the Associated Press's Atlanta bureau and CNN, respectively. Pulitzer Prize-winning outdoors editor Bob Marshall, who had been with the company for about four decades, declined an offer to stay, and then went to work for New Orleans's investigative and public policy website the Lens.

Longtime City Hall reporter Frank Donze, a beloved thirty-five-year veteran who was far-and-away dean of the City Hall press corps, earlier had directed city editor Gordon Russell "not to fight for me" during meetings in which individual layoffs were decided. Donze soon accepted a position as director of communications for the Audubon Nature Institute, which operates the city's renowned zoo and aquarium. Business writer Jaquetta White, a New Orleans native who delicately navigated the politically unenviable task of reporting for the newspaper and NOLA.com the stories about the layoffs, quietly accepted a position covering the music industry at the *Tennessean* in Nashville. Stephanie Grace, a sixteen-year veteran who worked her way up from the City Hall beat to statewide political columnist, turned down an offer to return to reporting.

"This has been an amazing disaster," New Orleans-based author and freelance writer Jason Berry said in late June 2012 on the news media public affairs show *Informed Sources* that airs on New Orleans's public television affiliate WYES. "Here you have a newspaper that won four Pulitzer Prizes in twenty years, and they've wiped out their institutional memory, they're losing many of their best reporters, and they're making money in the process."

New Orleans Magazine associate publisher and editor in chief Errol Laborde considered it almost his duty to spotlight the situation via the pages of his magazine. "To me, this is an issue

New Orleans Magazine commissioned former *Times-Picayune* editorial cartoonist Mike Luckovich to draw three cartoons satirizing the newspaper's changes. *Image courtesy of Mike Luckovich.*

about New Orleans and the dignity of New Orleans," said the native and Mardi Gras expert. Although the magazine's "Speaking Out" feature previously had never been done on the same issue more than once, it was devoted to the changes coming to the *Times-Picayune* for four consecutive issues over the summer, and Laborde has continued to regularly devote his column on the magazine's website to developments related to it. He also commissioned three original cartoons by the *Times-Picayune's* former editorial cartoonist Mike Luckovich, now the Pulitzer Prize-winning editorial cartoonist at the *Atlanta Journal-Constitution*.[3]

An anonymous newsroom source told *Gambit*'s Kevin Allman that executives were "sh—ting bricks" because of how many and how quickly employees the organization wanted to retain were instead finding new jobs, an assessment a second unnamed source confirmed to Allman. In their apparent panic, managers rescinded layoffs of at least ten employees, including business writer Thompson and photographer Scott Threlkeld. Thompson chose to return, while Threlkeld declined.

Both graphic artist Emmett Mayer III and metro zone layout editor Jennifer Brown were "unfired," or asked to stay after first being told to go, but then moved on as quickly as possible. Mayer, who created highly detailed, yet accessible infographics explaining everything from the region's elaborate levee system (for the 2002 "Washing Away" series) to how 2010's BP's Deepwater Horizon oil spill disaster occurred, was offered a position in the print operation shortly after first being laid off. Hopeful that other employment opportunities he was pursuing would pan out, he declined the offer, but when nothing else had materialized by September, he asked about staying on, and was hired. Three weeks later, he jumped ship for New Orleans-based professional services firm GCR, Inc., where he is creative graphic design manager. Unsure of the future of NOLA Media Group, "I didn't really want to go through all of that again and when a good opportunity presented itself to me, I took it," Mayer recalled in April 2013.[4]

Brown, a twelve-year veteran, went into her June 12, 2012, meeting with sports editor Doug Tatum relatively confident that she would survive. She had, after all, crossed the picket line at Advance Publications' behest, when union employees at the *Vindicator* in Youngstown, Ohio, went on strike in late 2004, and Advance came to the aid of a fellow Buckeye state newspaper publisher with replacement workers.[5] "'Do the Newhouses know what I've done for them?'" Brown recalled asking Tatum. A few days later "someone friendly with management" told Brown that "I shouldn't be too worried, 'I think things are going to work out for you,'" she said, but no management entreaty immediately followed. While she was on vacation more than three weeks later, then-page one editor Terry Baquet called Brown and offered her a position at "essentially the same salary, but he couldn't tell me what I would be doing, what my job title would be, or who I would be reporting to—and I had two days to decide," she recalled. After assessing the other job opportunities she was pursuing, and reflecting upon the way she had been treated, Brown turned down the position. "A few days later, Terry came back to me and said, 'We can't do this without you. What can we do to make you stay?'" She again declined to stay.

"I was just really, really hurt" by being targeted in the layoffs and that "no one in management came to me afterward to officially say, 'Don't worry, we're looking out for you, things will be OK,'" she remembered. Still not taking "no" for an answer, dayside copy desk chief Kathy Roa Luther then approached Brown, who again declined the request to stay past the across-the-board September 30, 2012, severance date. She was appointed night metro editor at the *Daily Advertiser* in Lafayette, Louisiana, in February 2013. "I wish [editor] Jim [Amoss] had reached out me and said, 'I'm sorry, you fell between the cracks, please stay, I'll make it right,'" Brown recalled in May 2013. "If he had done that, I would have stayed."[6]

Brown in mid-July 2013 became the latest of close to three dozen former *Times-Picayune* editorial employees who would ultimately land either full- or part-time positions at the *Advocate*, joining the newspaper as executive news editor. Despite Brown's short tenure at the *Daily Advertiser*, management there was gracious when she broke the news. "I got a high-five from the executive editor," she said. "I was amazed. I work five months for a company, get a cake, and a promise of a nice farewell. Twelve years at the *Picayune*, and not one acknowledgment from any direct supervisor or editor for my work." Intent on seizing her silver lining, Brown said, "I was sad and hurt by the events of last summer. But since the beginning of this year, it's all been positive changes for me. I never would have grown without leaving the *Picayune* and my past there will remain fond, [except] for the last few months."[7]

Although he failed to make an overture to Brown, Amoss did make such an appeal in September to another longtime employee, but without success. Shortly after yet another editorial employee the company had sought to keep tendered her resignation—longtime business reporter Becky Mowbray, who left in September 2012 for a position with the Office of the New Orleans Inspector General—Amoss asked Bruce Nolan to stay. Over lunch, Nolan said, Amoss told him, "'I had to make a lot of decisions on short notice, and I made some bad ones. Laying you off was a bad decision. I'd like you to come back.'" Nolan briefly considered the offer before declining to stay. "I didn't need the job financially, the place I had known was about to change utterly, and was in new hands that didn't seem very hospitable," he recalled seven months later. "It was an easy decision."

Perhaps the most sensational and well-publicized employment dance at the newspaper involved "occasional" reporter Kari Dequine Harden. The now-eliminated "occasional" classification is one that most *Times-Picayune* employees assigned to it came to despise. It was, essentially, a freelancer with a recurring, if not regular, schedule at the newspaper. Occasionals worked throughout the news operations, including in the downtown newsroom, photography, and the bureaus. They were generally paid a flat hourly rate but were prohibited from freelancing for other news outlets in the region. They also were ineligible for overtime, vacations, sick leave, holiday pay, or mileage reimbursements when driving to assignments, and they weren't allowed the use of company equipment, such as cameras or cars. Over the years, the newspaper — probably fearing a crackdown after high-profile companies such as Microsoft came under federal scrutiny over their questionable, yet widespread use of contractors — eventually began paying occasional employees' FICA contributions and allowed them to vest into the company's pension plan before it was frozen in 2009. Dequine Harden was an occasional who was paid $18 an hour (compared to the roughly $33 an hour a senior staff writer earned) to work Saturdays and Sundays at the newspaper, and regularly filled in for vacationing or absent reporters on other shifts. As a newsroom personality, she was even more ingenuous and self-absorbed than many early-thirty-somethings. (She's thirty-two.) She brandished her reporter's idealism like a badge of honor and talked incessantly about how much she loved her job, while also offering sometimes-uninformed criticism of the newspaper. (For example, in an email to newsroom brass, she criticized the decision to prominently feature a story "about a flight that happened a long time ago," instead of three overnight murders she would be following up on her upcoming shift. That flight, Pan Am 759, crashed in 1982 at take-off from New Orleans International Airport into a suburban Kenner neighborhood, killing all 145 on board and eight on the ground, and remains the fifth-deadliest crash in US aviation history. The story was about a documentary commemorating the thirtieth anniversary of the disaster.) The rest of that email, however, is what Dequine Harden soon came to be known for.

"Sometimes I just want to scream about what is happening around me," she wrote to noted news media blogger Jim Romenesko, who promptly posted her missive to his well-read blog. "Those of us laid off still have jobs to do until the thirtieth of September, but it's going from bad to worse. . . . I desperately want my job until October because I love it. But I also can't just keep my mouth shut and pretend everything is okay, or that it doesn't matter." She went on to supply Romenesko with the letter she sent to Mathews, Amoss, Cunningham, and another online editor: "I take a lot of pride in my work, even after I've been fired and told my experience, skills, and talents are of no use after September 30. I know that I am good at what I do. But compared to other news outlets, our website is a joke. We break news — but no one would know because of the worst news website known to man and the priority setting — whoever is doing it, is totally f — ed. . . . And yet we are focused on digital now? . . . Who is buying this crap?"

Her email went viral on social media and was reported by such respected media outlets as the *Washington Post*, Politico.com, and Atlantic.com. It led to a subsequent calm "and without expletives" meeting with Amoss and Cunningham, she said, during which they re-affirmed that she was welcome to continue with the newspaper until September 30. She instead bailed three weeks later by sending an even more audacious email to Steven Newhouse. (An excerpt: "I thought I'd be able to go down with it, but I don't even recognize the ship anymore. . . . You have betrayed my most esteemed colleagues, my city, my belief in journalism, and my belief in people.") At least one veteran newsroom alumna flatly predicted that Dequine Harden would leverage her new notoriety into a new journalism job, and in early September, she did just that, landing one of the three coveted news reporting positions with the new daily New Orleans edition of the Baton Rouge-based *Advocate* newspaper. The photogenic blonde was even introduced to *Advocate* readers in a full-color house ad. Nine months after she accepted the job and a month after the newspaper was acquired by New Orleans businessman John Georges and beats were reassigned as additional employees were hired, she resigned.

"I'm tired of getting jerked around," she said in late May 2013, the day before she tendered her resignation. "After seeing how people are treated in the industry, I don't want to work for a daily newspaper. There's absolutely no job security, and things change overnight. I want to own my name, I want to own my stories."[8]

CHAPTER VI

Ricky Go Home

As the weeks passed, pressure on the *Times-Picayune* not only escalated within its own ranks, but also in a community intent on saving its daily newspaper. Philanthropist Anne Milling's *Times-Picayune* Citizens' Group sent a second, and far blunter, letter in early July 2012, this time directly to twenty-two members of the extended Newhouse family, urging them to sell the paper:

> Unfortunately and sadly, the considerable goodwill your family enterprise has created in New Orleans in the last fifty years has dissipated in just a few short months because of the decision that took our entire community by surprise. . . . It is painful to report that right now it is nearly impossible to find a kind word in these parts about your family or your plan to take away our daily newspaper. . . . If your family does not believe in the future of this great city and its capacity to support a daily newspaper, it is only fair to allow us to find someone who does. If you have ever valued the friendship you have shared with our city and your loyal readers, we ask that you sell the *Times-Picayune*. Our city wants a daily printed paper, needs a daily printed paper and deserves a daily printed paper.[1]

Donald Newhouse's response was swift and equally uncompromising: "We have read the letter with great respect and concern," he said in a statement issued the day after the letter was received. "Advance Publications has no intention of selling the *Times-Picayune*."[2]

National interest in the saga also continued to grow. Coverage expanded to appear in the *Los Angeles Times*, the *Nation*, and the

CBS Evening News. CBS News's *60 Minutes* arrived in town to conduct interviews with editor Jim Amoss, Mayor Mitch Landrieu, Milling, and others, for a segment about the daily newspaper's demise. Staffers speculated that newsroom managers simply stopped providing written updates because anything issued in writing was funneled to *Gambit*'s Kevin Allman essentially as soon as it was distributed, who in turn devastatingly dissected the organization's arguments and assertions. Erik Wemple, who reports a blog about the media for the *Washington Post*, also took the newspaper's management to task for its convoluted and deceptive declarations. In a post headlined *"Times-Picayune*

The satirical newspaper and website, the *Levee*, wrote an obituary for the 175-year-old newspaper, noting that it's "survived by two children, a three-day-a-week version and by Nola.com." *Image courtesy of the* New Orleans Levee.

publisher spews standard workforce-reduction garbage," Wemple called out language in Phelps's memo sent in response to the initial *New York Times* story: "Strikes me that if you **reallocate** to **accelerate**, you **necessitate** more people, not fewer people," Wemple wrote about a passage in the memo that promised a stronger news product with a smaller staff. "The memo rhetoric is just another variation on the we're-going-to-do-more-with-less cant that fools no one and insults everyone, every time."[3]

A master in the art of devastatingly cutting satire, the city's sardonic newspaper and website, the *New Orleans Levee*, featured a front-page obituary accompanied by an image of the *T-P*'s faux crypt. "She was 175 years old, so maybe poor circulation isn't all that surprising, but her time had come," the obituary quoted Steven Newhouse as saying, adding that "the company provided hospice service to her until her death Oct. 1. When she could not support 20 percent to 30 percent profit margins anymore as a seven-day-a-week daily, we knew it was time to pull the plug."[4]

NOLA Anarcha, "a collective of anarchists running a website to spread the resistance to all forms of oppression," was blunter and darker in its assessment: "The *Times-Picayune* was murdered, and it was murdered for money. Specific men with names and addresses murdered the *Times-Pic* for money. It's a long and sordid story, and it's one I'm not sure we can rely on corporate-owned media to accurately report."[5] In a six-part diatribe posted over three weeks, NOLA Anarcha also reminded the community that the daily *Times-Picayune* remained profitable. "Was it as profitable as selling cocaine? No. Was it as profitable as Wal-Mart? No. But it was profitable, even notably so among U.S. dailies."[6]

Around the same date as the Rock 'n' Bowl rally, Rolfes launched RickyGoHome.com, a website that offered protesters two easily downloadable fliers designed to let incoming new *Times-Picayune* publisher Ricky Mathews and everyone else know what they thought of his arrival in the city and his plans

Anne Rolfes, founding director of the environmental health and justice organization Louisiana Bucket Brigade, created fliers and a website to let new *Times-Picayune* publisher Ricky Mathews know he was not welcomed in New Orleans. *Image courtesy of Anne Rolfes.*

to decimate their beloved newspaper. The western outlaw-themed leaflets featured Mathews' smiling photo under a bold headline "WANTED: Ricky Mathews for attempted ruination of the *Times-Picayune*" and "WANTED: Ricky Mathews for unnecessary slaying of the *Times-Picayune* Staff." The website, which was still live as this book went to press, also groups Mathews in a "Rogues Gallery" including former disgraced FEMA Director Michael Brown, universally despised in the region for his abysmal management of Katrina rescue efforts; NFL Commissioner Roger Goodell, almost as loathed for his seemingly punitive suspensions of New Orleans Saints coaches and players following the team's 2009-11 "Bountygate" scandal; the Atlanta Falcons, whose rivalry with the Saints is regarded as one of the most-heated in pro sports; a mosquito, one of the semi-tropical region's most injurious, annoying, and exterminated pests; and Edward Pakenham, director of British forces during the 1815 Battle of New Orleans.

"The most important thing about Ricky Mathews from a New Orleans perspective is that he has the gall to move to town and dismantle our newspaper," the site declares. "Even Hurricane Katrina couldn't do that. Ricky Mathews doesn't know us. He doesn't know our city. Yet he is attempting to dismantle a lifeline and a common thread. Ricky, please go home. And give us our newspaper on your way out of town." The fliers quickly began appearing in shop windows around town, including in several within easy walking distance of the luxury Windsor Court Hotel, where Mathews was known to stay when in New Orleans. And although it was amusing to perhaps everyone except him, and of some comfort to the scores of employees and residents troubled by what his arrival portended for the newspaper, the "Ricky Go Home" effort failed to acknowledge one critical reality regarding his arrival at the *Times-Picayune*: he was nothing more than a hired gun brought in to do a dirty job ordered by the bosses. "I certainly don't want to defend Ricky, but I was surprised at how

"What the hell is a 'robust' website anyway?"

Television newspaper editor Lou Grant mysteriously appeared around the *Times-Picayune* during the summer of 2012, courtesy of fliers embellished with acerbic captions targeted at Advance Publications and NOLA Media Group.

much the anti-Mathews efforts missed the point," one veteran editor who lost his job because of the changes observed in May 2013. "It's not like he came here and decided to do this. This wasn't his decision. What's that line from [the movie] *Apocalypse Now*? 'You're an errand boy, sent by grocery clerks, to collect a bill.' That's what Ricky Mathews is."

About the same time, the *Times-Picayune* newsroom was mischievously papered with fliers featuring a photo of veteran actor Ed Asner in his well-known television role as no-nonsense newspaper editor and TV news director Lou Grant. The fliers were embellished with acerbic captions including: "What the hell is an 'enhanced' newspaper?" (taking aim at corporate-speak descriptions used in newspaper editorials about the coming *Times-Picayune*); "What the hell is a 'robust' Web site anyway?" (deriding the hackneyed adjective of choice invoked by Mathews and Amoss when they described promised future enhancements to NOLA.com); "How exactly do we do more with less?"; "Fewer ad dollars, huh? What about a paywall?"; and "A 3-day-a-week newspaper in New Orleans? When did Ted Baxter become an executive at Advance Publications?" (the latter drawing analogies between Advance and the witless fictional TV anchor on TV's *The Mary Tyler Moore Show*, on which Lou Grant also was a character).[7]

In another skillful grassroots ploy designed to boost morale among the newspaper's rank-and-file, freelance writer and Rock 'n' Bowl rally co-organizer Michael Tisserand reached out to Asner's Hollywood agent and asked whether the actor would send words of encouragement to the beleaguered staff. A longtime left-leaning political activist and former president of the Screen Actors Guild who played a front-and-center role in the organization's 1980 strike, Asner responded with a note that likely rankled the union-despising Newhouses:

To the employees of the *Times Picayune*:

I've been on strike and I've always identified with the working press, knowing they're not fat cats and knowing job security is zilch. Freedom of the press belongs to the man who owns one. I identify totally with your plight and hope that a decent resolution may be arrived at!

Sincerely,
Ed Asner

In addition to Asner's note of support, actor Alec Baldwin—generally known more for savagely castigating the news media than defending it—tweeted his encouragement around the same time.

Other New Orleans businesses beyond the media also got involved in the battle. Within days, local shops Fleurty Girl, Dirty Coast, and Gerald Haessig Designs created their own T-shirts that

Local shirts and apparel company Dirty Coast created one of many T-shirts that sprung up around New Orleans skewering the *Times-Picayune's* changes. *Photo Courtesy of Zack Smith/Zack Smith Photoraconteur.*

quickly rivaled the "We Publish Come Hell and High Water" design in their popularity and ubiquity. One declared, "Save the Picayune: Don't Let Bylines Be Bygones," while the other two proclaimed "The Some-Times Picayune" and "Throw me ~~Something~~ a daily newspaper, Mister!", the latter a take-off on the common refrain of spectators to New Orleans Carnival krewe float riders.

Mark Schleifstein, the veteran and much-lauded environmental reporter who was asked and agreed to remain with the new company, labeled the aftermath as "Katrina without the water."

The community outcry grew to include protests from elected officials. Amid weighty questions about the federal Patient Protection and Affordable Care Act, NBC's *Meet the Press*

A group of local politicians, New Orleans restaurateur Ralph Brennan, and "Save the Picayune" founder Anne Milling underwrote creation of 1,500 signs imploring Advance Publications to keep the *Times-Picayune* a daily newspaper. They sprung up in yards and storefronts across the metro area. *Photo courtesy of Kim Lieder Abramson.*

moderator David Gregory in July 2012 peppered Louisiana Gov. Bobby Jindal—then rumored to be on Republican presidential candidate Mitt Romney's vice presidential shortlist—with questions about the *Times-Picayune*.[8] Mayor Landrieu and City Council President Jackie Clarkson claimed that a less-than-daily newspaper reflected poorly on New Orleans's status as one of the world's great cities. In an open letter to Steven Newhouse, US Sen. David Vitter roundly panned NOLA.com and the company's digital efforts before demanding, "Do the right thing. Sell."[9]

A group of progressive Louisiana representatives elected since Katrina—Neil Abramson, Wesley Bishop, Jared Brossett, Walt Leger III, and Helena Nancy Moreno—chipped in to produce 500 campaign-style yard signs demanding a daily newspaper.

Four Mardi Gras krewes, including Le Krewe D'Etat, satirized the *Times-Picayune* via their 2013 parade floats.

Restaurateur Brennan and Milling underwrote a tripling of the order, and the signs quickly began to dot yards and shop windows, with Abramson's wife, attorney Kim Lieder Abramson, delivering them to anyone requesting them in every corner of the metropolitan area during the brutally hot summer.

In late July, New Orleans Saints owner Tom Benson publicly emerged as one of the two individuals Milling had said were interested in exploring the purchase of the newspaper. In a letter he sent to Steven Newhouse, Benson referenced an earlier in-person meeting between the two men and Benson's wife, Gayle, in Newhouse's Manhattan office. "I would welcome the opportunity to speak to you about my interest in purchasing the Times-Picayune, with others," Benson wrote. In a handwritten post-script, Benson indirectly reminded Newhouse that he earlier had saved another beloved New Orleans institution from abandoning the city: "In 1985, the Saints were leaving. I would hate for this to happen with our paper."[10] But Donald Newhouse, Steven's father and president of Advance Publications, again immediately declared to WWL-TV that the paper was not for sale.[11]

Through the fall and into the New Year, New Orleans's displeasure with Advance and the newspaper's management did not diminish. Even New Orleans's annual Mardi Gras parades got in on the act. Four krewes known for their clever and cutting satire took direct aim at the Newhouses and the newspaper's top executives. The first parade of the Carnival season, Krewe du Vieux, featured three floats targeting the newspaper's management: "All Out of TP?", "Times Prickayune Fails to Deliver," and "Black and White and Dead All Over." Two of the floats were so ribald that photographs of them were labeled "NSFW" ("not suitable for work" viewing) on social media sites. Krewe d'Etat's "Gone With The Wind" float was preceded by a sign that said, "I Don't Know Nuthin' 'Bout No Internet," and poked fun at Advance.net chairman Steven Newhouse ("Frankly, my dear New Orleans, I don't give a damn") and former *Times-*

Picayune publisher Ashton ("Ashley") Phelps. The Krewe of Muses's float, "Canned Goods," took aim at longtime newspaper editor Jim Amoss, featuring a huge caricature of him on the side of the float under the banner "Famous Amoss" and his "Cold Cuts." (A number of former and current NOLA.com | *Times-Picayune* employees are members of Muses.)[12]

Chapter VII

The Michigan Model

As profit margins at US newspaper companies continued to narrow or altogether disappeared in the early-to-mid 2000s, Advance Publications wasn't alone in its mission to arrive at a way to reinvigorate the once-highly lucrative financial returns generated by its newspapers. Newspaper publishers have adopted different approaches to righting their businesses in recent years, but the precipitous decline of advertising revenue and rising costs of producing and delivering a print newspaper to thousands (if not hundreds of thousands) of doorsteps have put the focus squarely on ways publishers can take advantage of the increasingly popular Internet and digital devices as much more cost-effective distribution platforms. In an August 2012 commentary Steven Newhouse wrote for the website of the media think tank and journalism education center the Poynter Institute, he said Advance had spent the past four years on a "quest to find long-term answers to the profound challenges to local newspapers . . . and to find a business model that makes sense in today's economic environment."[1]

But newspaper companies still had to deal with the pesky problems that emerged from the precedent they set early on when they chose to give away their product on the Internet: the decreased demand for print products and the devalued advertising that supported both their print and digital editions. In an effort to cut print production costs without forsaking the still-far-more-lucrative print advertising rates, Advance in 2009 began experimenting with reducing the number of days some of its newspapers published print editions, while simultaneously focusing on improving those publications' websites. The company would continue to print editions on days of the week important to advertisers—"food Thursdays [although the *Times-Picayune* and a few other Advance newspapers ultimately settled on Wednesdays], entertainment Fridays and the always content-rich Sunday paper," as *T-P* editor Jim Amoss wrote in a June 2012 *Times-Picayune* front-page commentary[2]—while working to lure readers to its websites the remaining days of the week.

Although early online-only success had been perhaps inadvertently achieved by NOLA.com during Katrina's aftermath, Advance chose its eight smaller newspapers in Michigan for its initial "digital-first" experiment, which introduced the reduced print schedule. In early 2009, the company announced that its daily *Ann Arbor News*—founded two years before the *Times-Picayune*, in 1835—would cease to exist. Beginning July 1, 2009. It would be replaced by its companion website and a twice-weekly "print product" (apparently not to be confused with a "newspaper") carrying the "AnnArbor.com" masthead. "We have shared with you before in our pages the extreme challenges that our industry and our newspaper have faced over the last couple years," *Ann Arbor News* publisher Laurel Champion wrote in a March 2009 open letter published on MLive.com, the online home of the other seven Michigan newspapers owned by Advance. "Out of those challenges has come a new opportunity. As we say hello to AnnArbor.com, we will say good-bye to the *Ann Arbor News.*"[3] The company also announced that Advance's *Bay City Times*, *Saginaw News*, and *Flint Journal* would cut back to three editions weekly (although the former two later produced a joint Tuesday edition initially offered only on newsstands, but expanded to home-delivery in late 2011). Advance's Michigan operations also laid off almost half of their 1,200 employees, only to rehire dozens. Some who declined their offers reported that they did so because they had been offered dramatically less pay.

Two-and-a-half-years later, the company announced that it was maintaining daily publication of its remaining four newspapers in the state—including its largest, by far, the *Grand Rapids Press*—but reducing home delivery in those markets to three days a week. "Our new structure will allow us to innovate and compete in an overwhelmingly digital age," Dan Gaydou, president of the MLive Media Group, wrote in a November 2011 open letter published on the site. "We will be better able to serve consumers, who are increasingly going online for their information."[4] Although it had not held much import at the time, many *Times-Picayune* newsroom staffers later recalled that Mark Lorando, the newspaper's longtime features and entertainment editor, disappeared from the newsroom without explanation for two weeks in the spring of 2012, a traditionally very busy time for him and his staff because of the annual New Orleans Jazz & Heritage Festival. Staffers presumed he was in Ann Arbor, studying what came to be known as the "Michigan Model," because a garish and widely panned redesign of NOLA.com clearly modeled after MLive.com launched while he was gone, and the mysterious "Rapture" meetings of a half-dozen senior editors began immediately upon his return. When personnel changes were announced in June 2012, Lorando was named director of metro content, becoming one of the most-powerful editors in the newsroom, behind Amoss, and a peer to James O'Byrne, who was appointed NOLA Media Group's director of state news and sports.

Reviews of Advance's changes to its print product in Ann Arbor generally have not been kind. Charles R. Eisendrath, director of the prestigious Knight-Wallace Fellows in journalism at the University of Michigan, declared, "If this is the model for the future of traditional news organizations, they need to begin calling themselves something else. Not news organizations." The publication had become so irrelevant that Eisendrath—someone with clearly more than a passing interest in the evolution of newspapers—no longer bothered to read his hometown newspaper.[5] Although less harsh, Ann Arbor resident and freelance business writer Micheline Maynard offered this May 2012 assessment on Forbes.com: "The printed edition is newspaper-like, but with a different style and less gravitas than its predecessor."[6]

Advance executives have never publicly pegged the changes in Michigan to the *Times-Picayune*'s and NOLA.com's online success in reporting about Hurricane Katrina. Steven Newhouse declined to be interviewed for this book, but it seems as though the Katrina experience served as strong motivation for the Michigan Model. Amoss acknowledged as much in his June 2012 front-page commentary justifying the newspaper's decision to publish only three days a week. In it, he recounted observing his reporters in the newsroom in the early hours as Katrina bore down on New Orleans and knocked out the region's electricity:

> A dozen editors and reporters were sitting at terminals, powered by a generator . . . . Cell phones to their ears, they were typing furiously, hammering out dispatches from our reporters throughout the New Orleans metro area. None of these reports would ever see a printing press. They would never be part of a bundle of paper landing on someone's doorstep. No reader would physically turn a page and stumble upon them. They were vital pieces of digital journalism, written by a news staff driven to get word out, posted on our website, NOLA.com, as they happened . . . I didn't realize at that moment that I was witnessing the beginning of our part of the revolution that is [now] transforming our business.[7]

Not everyone with a vested interest in the newspaper industry agrees with the move to less-than-daily print frequency. Billionaire US investor and philanthropist Warren Buffett began acquiring small- and medium-sized US newspapers in late 2011[8] and dedicated a significant portion of his Berkshire Hathaway Inc.'s widely read annual shareholders' letter in 2012 to the company's burgeoning newspaper investments. "I believe that papers delivering comprehensive and reliable information to tightly-bound communities and having a sensible Internet strategy will remain viable for a long time," Buffett wrote in the letter, released in March 2013. "We do not believe that success will come from cutting either the news content or frequency of publication. Indeed, skimpy news coverage will almost certainly lead to skimpy readership. And the less-than-daily publication that is now being tried in some large towns or cities—while it may improve profits in the short term—seems certain to diminish the papers' relevance over time. Our goal is to keep our papers loaded with content of interest to our readers and to be paid appropriately by those who find us useful, whether the product they view is in their hands or on the Internet."

Another high-minded mogul who believes in the power of the printed daily newspaper is Aaron Kushner, CEO of 2100 Trust LLC, a holding company Kushner founded in 2010 specifically to buy and grow major newspapers. (Kushner was nicknamed the "anti-Advance" by leading consumer news analyst Ken Doctor, drawing direct contrast between Kushner's business approach and Advance Publications' "digital first" strategy.) 2100 Trust acquired Freedom Communications, owner of California's *Orange County Register*, the country's fifteenth largest newspaper by circulation, and six other papers in July 2012 and named Kushner publisher. "The 2100 Trust name was derived from Kushner's belief in newspapers' long-term future and their fundamental strength as community institutions," his biography on the *Register* website reads. Since acquiring the *Register*, 2100 Trust has increased its staff by 50 percent to 270 (roughly what the *Times-Picayune*'s was pre-Katrina). It also redesigned many of its twenty-four neighborhood weeklies, and throughout the summer of 2013, announced increased days of publication for several of them. In addition, Kushner's company has dramatically boosted the *Register's* overall page count and amount of color printed on its pages and added a substantial daily business section, along with additional global, national news, prep sports, food, and sports coverage.[9]

During a spring 2013 Newspaper Association of America conference discussion with Berkshire Hathaway Media president, Terry Kroeger, Kushner contended that print reinforces the relevance of a newspaper and offers unique opportunities to bond with readers that simply don't exist in a digital format. "Will you ever tape your iPad to your refrigerator?" he asked. Kushner also underscored 2100 Trust's commitment to investment, as opposed to cost-cutting. "If you focus your time on reducing costs, you get good at it," he said. "But you lose sight of how to grow revenue. The first and most important thing we do as a management team is focus on how we grow our business, not on how we cut our business."[10] And Kushner upped the ante in August 2013 by launching his own newspaper war, *a la* the *Times-Picayune* and the *Advocate*, in southern California. Kushner's *Long Beach Register* will go head-to-head five days a week with that city's *Press-Telegram*, a MediaNews Group newspaper that has been so reduced in recent years that "you could say it was a shadow of itself if you could find the shadow," Doctor jokingly told *USA Today's* media editor and columnist Rem Rieder. The *Long Beach Register* will offer sixteen pages of news specific to the second-largest city in Los Angeles County, wrapped around issues of the *Orange County Register*, the latter which will provide readers with state, national, and international news coverage. Mirroring the *Advocate's* moves into New Orleans, Freedom Communications initially will have twenty reporters and photographers covering Long Beach, a number Kushner told Rieder he intends to increase.[11]

However, the Nieman Journalism Lab at Harvard University less than five months earlier had predicted that fewer than half of the country's daily newspapers would be printed daily by the end of 2015, primarily because the soaring popularity of electronic tablets, such as iPads, would continue to erode print newspapers' profitability. Former newspaper executive Martin Langeveld wrote: "That's why the Newhouse family is systematically converting their Advance Publications newspapers into two- and three-day print operations. And that's why the rest of the industry is trying to figure out when, not if, they should follow suit."[12] In addition, a March 2012 study by the Pew Research Center's Project for Excellence in Journalism involving thirteen companies that own a total of 330 daily US papers, or almost one-quarter of the country's English-language daily newspapers, found that the most-common industry prediction for the next five years was that newspapers would be published and delivered only two or three times a week, or maybe even only on Sundays,[13] the day on which some newspapers generate as much as one-half of their advertising revenues.

Greg Hywood, chief executive officer of Fairfax Media, one of Australia's largest diversified media companies, gave some additional credence—but not an unqualified endorsement—to Advance's approach in an April 2013 presentation to the International News Media Association World Congress in New York. Fairfax is "absolutely on the journey from print to digital," Hywood declared, adding that print newspapers of the future will be "expensive, bespoke (and) narrowly distributed. We know that at some time in the future, we will be predominantly digital or digital-only in our metropolitan markets. We can't say whether it's three, five or ten years. That depends upon print revenue trajectories, but it will happen. Media consumption continues to shift and fragment and the advertisers follow." Although his company also initiated a dramatic restructuring in June 2012 that eliminated 20 percent of its workforce, Hywood wasn't ready just yet to jettison days of print publication of the company's newspapers, which include national titles the *Age*, the *Sydney Morning Herald*, and the *Australian Financial Review*, along with five regional newspapers and thirty-five community newspapers. Profitability shouldn't be judged on the basis of performance of individual daily editions, he said, and the benefits that inure from the printed newspaper to the digital business— including branding—should be carefully evaluated before print is jettisoned."A commitment to profitable newspapers doesn't mean every edition, every day has to be profitable, but it does mean we need to fully understand the full economic effects that shutting down a paper, either collectively or on a selective basis, delivers," he said. "Simply shutting down one day [a week] won't inherently or immediately lead to a reduction in fixed costs."[14]

The high-tech city of Portland, Oregon, home of Advance's 163-year-old *Oregonian*, seemed to be a natural for the company's digital-first approach to newspaper publishing. The publication, however, also has a revered standing, in both its fiercely independent Pacific Northwest home and among US newspapers overall: tied with *USA Today* as the twelfth-best US newspaper and the only Advance/Newhouse newspaper in a late 1999 *Columbia Journalism Review* ranking of the nation's top twenty-one newspapers,[15] the *Oregonian*'s Pulitzer Prize record is even more impressive than the *Times-Picayune*'s. It has won seven in total, five since 1999, and produced another nine Pulitzer finalists since 1993.[16] It, too, had managed to remain profitable, its publisher N. Christian Anderson III, acknowledged to the *Portland Business Journal* in late June 2013.[17] Anderson had, as recently as August 2012, denied that the newspaper planned to change its publishing schedule,[18] but ten months later, it announced plans it would adopt another variation on the emerging, popular hybrid of "digital-first": beginning in October 2013, the *Oregonian* will continue to be published daily but will be home-delivered only four days a week.

Anderson refused to disclose how many of the *Oregonian*'s 650 employees would lose their jobs in the resulting workforce reduction, which was announced in late June 2013, with laid-off employees shown the door August 30. (Their notice equated roughly with the sixty-day notice employers are required, under WARN—the federal Worker Adjustment and Retraining Notification Act—to give employees who lose their jobs in mass layoffs. The assumption had been that the *Times-Picayune* had probably planned a similar notice period but was forced to reveal its plans earlier than desired by the May 2012 *New York Times* report). Editor and Vice President Peter Bhatia told newsroom employees that the reductions would be "significant," the newspaper reported. But as was the case in New Orleans, he said the new Oregon Media Group would also be hiring, and the staff and industry watchers presumed new hires would be younger, more digitally savvy, but also less-expensive. *Willamette Week* reported that one hundred employees in total lost their jobs, including up to forty-nine in the newsroom.[19] A staffer who was retained and spoke on condition of anonymity because of the staffer's fears of retribution, pegged newsroom layoffs closer to fifty-five, which would be more than 31 percent of the newsroom.

During an interview with Oregon Public Radio's *Think Out Loud* show the day after the layoffs were announced, Anderson appeared to follow the Advance playbook that had been so carefully adopted by Amoss, as he first announced the cutbacks in New Orleans and later continued to justify them. "We're not firing a third to a half of our newsroom," Anderson said. "We have ninety reporters on our staff today. We will have ninety reporters on our staff at the start of the new company, with plans to grow, not contract, from there." He allowed that there would be an overall reduction in newsroom personnel, just not in the reporting ranks. "Some of those [laid-off] people will be in the newsroom because we won't be producing as many pages on non-home-delivery days . . . There will be some turnover in the reporting staff, and some of that will be involuntarily, and that's a very sad part of this process, but some of it will be voluntary as well."[20] Laid-off staffers were further humiliated when Bhatia and Anderson made good on their statements regarding hiring: Oregon Media Group (the acronym "OMG" was quickly seized upon by skeptical employees and critics, along with the tentative new name of the website: "MyDigitalO") began advertising for new reporters three days after delivering the pink slips. "While we value experience, talent is the pivotal factor, and we are proactive about professional development, whether you are a ten-year veteran or just starting your journalistic career," the advertisement read.[21] ("What about if you're a fifteen- or twenty-year veteran?" a long-time laid-off *Times-Picayune* editorial staffer asked pointedly on the private Facebook page, in response to the solicitation.) Although later removed from the website launched by the newspaper's recruitment contractor, Decision Toolbox (the same company used by the *Times-Picayune*), the *Oregonian* initially solicited for a replacement for its quite digitally savvy laid-off music critic Ryan White, prompting a tweet from White: "HEY GUYS, we're hiring a music critic," with a link to the now-deleted online job posting.

The *Oregonian* by-and-large used the same marketing-speak that other Advance newspapers had employed. "Today we are unveiling exciting plans for the future of our company," Anderson wrote in his June 20, 2013, staff memo that did not discuss the layoffs and what those losing their jobs could expect in the way of notice, severance, and benefits until the end of the memo.[22] "While we believe these changes will create growth opportunities for our employees, the reality is that some employees will lose their jobs," Anderson acknowledged at the very end of a report posted to the OregonLive website.[23] Others were willing to call it as it was. "Another city. Another mélange of limited information, confused storytelling, and an unsuccessful attempt to put on a happy face to mask a huge change in newspapering and civic life," Doctor wrote less than a week after the layoffs were announced.[24] Bhatia said he made all of the decisions personally, and personally delivered the news to each newsroom employee losing his or her job, including his wife, commentary editor Liz Dahl, Mesh reported. Some of the cuts were particularly heartless. The married couple and veteran editors Randy Cox and Joany Carlin both lost their jobs, despite the fact that Cox was fighting advanced kidney cancer.[25]

As had been the case in New Orleans, *Oregonian* employees

took to social media and the web to share the news of their fates. "Laid off and leaving Omaha," sports reporter John Hunt tweeted from Nebraska, where he was covering the Oregon State Beavers baseball team in the College World Series when he received a phone call that he was being terminated.[26] Music critic White shared his sad news on his blog, and he reminisced about a fifteen-year career that began with a call to his parent's Ann Arbor, Michigan, home from a former college classmate who was working at the *Oregonian* and alerting him to the job opening he'd ultimately fill:

> I was twenty-three and my life fit in my car. I'm thirty-eight now, with a wife and a kid and a mortgage. I grew up in that newsroom (though I'm sure a few colleagues will read that and say, "grown up?") . . . August 30 will be my last day, and I don't know what comes next . . . This town needs the *Oregonian* — in whatever form its packaged — and it needs the talented people who remain in that building.[27]

"This is the graceful, evocative, wonderful writing the *Oregonian* is losing. Screw you Little Stevie Newhouse," the newspaper's former US Capitol correspondent Charles Pope tweeted with a link to White's blog post.[28]

One aspect that initially is very different in Portland than in New Orleans is the areas of focus the newspaper spared and gutted. According to a veteran *Oregonian* staffer who will remain with the newspaper, consistent with what occurred in New Orleans, the *Oregonian*'s copy desk, photo department, and community news (called the "hyperlocal" team in Portland) were eviscerated. However, in sharp contrast to the *T-P*, the *Oregonian*'s features department and health/environmental team also were slashed, while the bureaus were essentially spared, as were the business, politics, and breaking news teams. (In New Orleans, the bureaus and business desk were gutted, while star environmental reporter Mark Schleifstein was retained.) "Clearly, [Bhatia] wants a much harder edged product going forward," the *Oregonian* staffer said of the newspaper's editor.

Despite the sometimes-public lament for the daily newspapers in the towns where "digital-first" has been implemented, their websites remain a linchpin in Advance's business strategy. And critics pull no punches when detailing their weaknesses. "Their sites are among the worst in newspaper journalism," Joshua Benton, director of the Nieman Journalism Lab, declared in an August 2012 interview about the topic. "They're clunky. They all look like they were built in 1998."[29] In an oft-cited comment, freelance writer and author Maynard opined in her Forbes.com report, "AnnArbor.com . . . is a constantly updated blog, which gives equal play to impaled cyclists and rabid skunks as it does to politics and crime." John McQuaid, a former *Times-Picayune* reporter who contributed work to two of the newspaper's Pulitzer Prizes and spent years in the Washington, DC, Newhouse News Bureau before embarking on a career as an author and freelance writer, made the following observations on Atlantic.com about Advance websites in June 2012:

> They are generic, ugly and notoriously hard to navigate. They share DNA with Parade.com (the website of *Parade Magazine*, the newspaper insert also owned by Advance). They present news in a rolling blog format . . . In this framework, news is primarily a click-generating engine, featuring movie listings, weather forecasts, or the doings of the Kardashians.[30]

In its defense, NOLA.com has made changes since McQuaid's assessment designed to make the site friendlier to use, including a less-jarring color palette and increased reader control over the "river" of content (as it is called internally) displayed on the home page. While acknowledging that Advance's newspaper sites generate traffic and foster active forums (the latter of which the company does not universally moderate and can be littered with crude and sometimes racist comments left by anonymous readers), the *New York Times*'s Carr in July 2012 labeled them "a miserable place to consume news. Balky and ugly, with a digital revenue base below much of the rest of the industry, they seem like a shaky platform on which to build a business."[31] Nearly a year later, little had changed in Carr's assessment. "I spent a fairly significant amount of time with [NOLA.com] a couple of weeks ago, and I didn't notice any great improvement," he said during an interview in mid-May 2013. "I don't think the site has gotten that much more reader-friendly, and a lot of alternatives have sprung up."[32] In a piece written by Carr in May 2013, retired *T-P* metro editor Jed Horne remarked that, in NOLA.com, the company "promised a Tesla and it performs more like an Edsel."[33]

Jason Fry, then a member of the adjunct faculty with Poynter (and a former *Times-Picayune* intern), said he initially thought the closure of the *Ann Arbor News* and creation of AnnArbor.com was a sad but necessary decision. "I had to revise that once I saw how thin and generic AnnArbor.com felt — it's journalism on the cheap, with crummy materials making blueprint irrelevant. NOLA.com . . . has always looked and felt cookie-cutter despite repeated redesigns — a crying shame given it represents America's liveliest city,"[34] he wrote in May 2012, and reaffirmed in an email exchange with me a year later.

McQuaid, the former *Times-Picayune* reporter, agreed. "There are many promising experiments underway, whether with aggressive community engagement and social media, or paywalls and premium content," he wrote in his Atlantic.com piece. "But with NOLA.com, the owners have so far promised to deliver only the barest bones of what an online news operation does: 24-hour coverage. In a click-centric website, this can mean a hamster-wheel ethic, with staffers churning out blog posts, tweets, and video snippets 24/7, with little time to go deeper."

That "click-centric" mentality, coupled with smaller staffs, concerns many. "There are three levels of the problem," Alan Mutter, media consultant and publisher of the "Reflections of a

Newsosaur" industry blog, told the *American Journalism Review* in the summer of 2012. "The first is that there are fewer reporters, the second is that the people left can't look at stories as intensely or thoroughly as they had in the past, and the third is that stories become less ambitious. It's not what's there in front of me that I worry about. It's the stuff that's not there because they weren't able to get it."[35]

But veteran *T-P* environmental reporter Mark Schleifstein believes NOLA.com critics are holding fast to an outdated view of the site. "I think they look at the site and see what they want to see," he said in a March 2013 interview. "And I look at the site and see what I want to see, and I understand that the truth is likely somewhere in between." Both Schleifstein and colleagues who spoke on the condition of anonymity because they fear retribution for talking to me said too many critics are harking back to the pre-Katrina *Times-Picayune*, when readership and, as a direct result, profits were larger, so economic pressures were lower. "This is not the *Times-Picayune* that it used to be, but it's not a house of horrors, either," said one veteran staffer who spoke on the condition of anonymity. "I'm reporting the same types of stories I reported before. The difference is I tweet them, I blog them, I video them. It's a different kind of job, but if you look at the work we're doing, we're reporting hard news. Is there more news reporting, or less? I'm not sure, but I know I'm personally reporting more."

Schleifstein said the site strives to balance the content readers want with the news they need. "NOLA.com is a news site that clearly recognizes that the Saints are a key part of the news in New Orleans," he said. "But at the same time, so is hurricane protection and BP. Yes, we're struggling. We're re-creating ourselves in a new image with limitations placed on us by our management and our industry. At the same time, we're also covering the major issues that are important to New Orleans." I remain convinced that this news outlet will remain a quality product, it still is a quality product, but there's no doubt that it's a different product.

It's small-townish, while also being national in scope."

However, another NOLA Media Group reporter said the constant pressure to produce for the site is at the expense of enterprise and investigative work. "They want NOLA.com to be the one-stop shop for everyone to get everything they want," said the reporter. "That comes at a price—the reduction in enterprise and investigative stories. I think a lot of us are working on our enterprise and investigative stuff on our days off, which isn't ideal and isn't right. I think they underestimate how much time it takes to chase minor stuff down and do a post on it, add links and a picture." Another longtime editorial employee who spoke on the condition of anonymity because of the employee's fears of retribution for questioning NOLA Media Group's business strategy, acknowledged the loss. "I like what I'm doing, but I don't like that we're not a daily, I don't like that we gave up our pre-eminent position," the staffer said. "The two unanswered questions are, A, if their model—if they have one—is right, and B, if our audience will accept it."

A veteran *Ann Arbor News* editor, writer, and columnist who lost his job there gives AnnArbor.com and the changes Advance has made "passing" marks. "They have a good staff, albeit a far smaller staff, of young, hard-working journalists that don't cost as much as the old staff did," said Geoff Larcom, who spent twenty-five years with the newspaper before being laid off in 2009, and now regularly interacts with the company's reporters in his job as executive director of media relations for Eastern Michigan University in Ypsilanti. "They're making headway," including more in-depth reporting and interactive features and polls. The staff does a "terrific job on weather and disasters," he added. "On a personal level, I had planned to work for the *News* until I retired, and wish it had been able to sustain itself at a reasonable size, but it went through a long, protracted decline as it struggled to sell advertising in an extremely competitive ad market. And that will be the key question going forward: Can they attract enough advertising to keep it economically sustainable?"[36]

At least publicly, the Newhouses insist they are pleased with the performance of the company's Michigan newspapers since their dramatic transformation, as evidenced by the commentary Steven Newhouse wrote for Poynter.org in August 2012:

> AnnArbor.com . . . exceeded our expectations for audience growth and performed well by increasing our digital revenue . . . The changes we have made in Michigan have strengthened our confidence that we can secure a vital future for our local journalism elsewhere. While we believe that our print revenue will decline further, we are hopeful that our increased focus on digital will allow digital revenue to become an even greater revenue growth engine.[37]

That satisfaction has continued more broadly with MLive.com's performance, according to Dan Gaydou, president of MLive Media Group."We're better at delivering significant and meaty journalism, reaching a broader audience and doing it in a most timely and interactive way," he wrote in an open letter to readers that somewhat curiously noted the sixteen-month anniversary of the launch of MLive, in late June 2013. "Journalism has never been healthier in our company." Although AnnArbor.com | MLive did not report optional web usage figures in its 2012 or March 2013 semi-annual reports member newspapers file with industry group the Alliance for Audited Media, Gaydou wrote that the company's "digital core business, both on the desktop and on mobile platforms," grew 27 percent year over year in 2012, which "is being surpassed by a 43 percent growth pace in 2013."[38] Randy Siegel, president of Advance's local digital efforts, also called out the performance of the company's Michigan newspapers as proof of the fledgling success of the company's digital strategy. "We're nearly two years into this [digital] transformation—and we've made our share of mistakes—but I am pleased to report that our new companies are performing well," Siegel wrote in late July 2013 in an internal memo published the same day by media blogger Jim Romenesko. "In Michigan, for example, digital ad revenue from January through June was 42 percent higher than the first half of 2012 and 74 percent higher than the first half of 2011."[39]

Others concur that the Michigan Model has been successful — at least from a market penetration perspective, and probably from a profit standpoint as well. "We can document that we have a larger audience reading our content today than when we just had the print product," an individual with knowledge of Advance's Michigan operations said on the condition of anonymity. "The fact that Newhouse continues to do this — the logical assumption is that they wouldn't be doing it if it weren't profitable, or showing strong signs of becoming profitable soon." Doctor, consumer news industry analyst for global research and advisory firm Outsell, and author of *Newsonomics: Twelve New Trends That Will Shape the News You Get*, has estimated that Advance has slashed 25 percent of its expenses and retained 90 percent of its advertising revenue, "which means that strategy is working pretty well" from a financial perspective, he said in a May 2013 interview.[40]

If the ultimate goal is to do away with the print products — as some suggest, and Steven Newhouse seemed to insinuate with his predictions about the continued decline of print revenue — the new, less-than-daily publication schedule appears to be advancing that goal. Average Sunday circulation of the print AnnArbor.com fell almost 38 percent, between September 2009 (the closest circulation report corresponding with the July 2009 switch to twice-weekly publication) and March 31, 2013, the most recently available figures when this book went to press, while Thursday circulation dropped about 38 percent. Circulation of the print Sunday *Times-Picayune* fell about 9.4 percent year over year, while combined average Sunday circulation at Advance's three Alabama newspapers declined about 8 percent.[41] Amoss, in a May 2013 appearance on New Orleans TV talk show *The 504*, and Siegel, in his July 2013 memo, expressed satisfaction with the pace of decline in print circulation, with Siegel reporting that in the first half of 2013, "average circulation declines in [Advance's] relaunched markets were in line with newspaper industry averages." Doctor said those declines are exactly what Advance has bargained for as it strives to improve profitability. "Falling print circulation is an acceptable tradeoff for the cost savings they're realizing," he said. "You're accepting fewer readers, you're accepting lower advertising revenues, you're accepting less civic impact, but you're driving short-term profits."[24]

At the same time, the *Times-Picayune* and Advance's other newspapers need to hang on to print readers, at least for the foreseeable future, because they continue to be coveted by many print advertisers who, at least at this juncture, pay far more of the freight than digital advertisers. Doing so, however, has proved to be a challenge, both in the wake of the overall downward trend in print newspaper circulation and the poorly executed and ill-received changes at several of the company's newspapers. For example, anecdotal reports began to surface almost immediately that people across New Orleans were canceling their subscriptions, either immediately, or effective on the scheduled last day of daily publication of the *T-P*, September 30, 2012. Reports continued to erupt from those who canceled subscriptions and complained that the newspaper kept appearing on their doorsteps, even after they repeatedly called, demanding that it be stopped. "How do I put a vacation stop on the delivery of the *T-P* if I don't have a subscription and they deliver it anyway?!?" a frustrated Kim Lieder Abramson asked on the "Friends" Facebook page in January 2013. "Do I call and say: 'Hi, can you stop bringing the paper while I'm out of town that I already cancelled three-and-a-half months ago?'" (Although she and her husband, State Rep. Neil Abramson, had canceled their subscription at the time, they subsequently re-subscribed when the 2013 Louisiana Legislature convened so that they could more comprehensively monitor media coverage of the session.) Soon-to-be-laid-off employees who cancelled their subscriptions the day they learned they were being terminated reported still receiving the newspaper weeks, and even months later. In reporting his March 1, 2013 update on the *Times-Picayune* and NOLA Media Group, *Columbia Journalism Review*'s Chittum also talked to former subscribers who confirmed that the newspaper has continued to throw papers, even after they had canceled their subscriptions.

The semi-annual statements member newspapers are required to file with the AAM reflect that a number of Advance newspapers that have reduced the number of print editions of their newspapers have simultaneously increased — oftentimes dramatically — the number of complimentary editions they distribute in their communities, along with significantly increasing the number of subscriptions they extend on credit. For example, the *Times-Picayune* increased by more than twenty-fold the number of Sunday newspapers it throws to past-due accounts year over year, according to its March 2013 AAM report, while its Sunday "average unpaid distribution" — newspapers it provided for free, to advertisers or agencies, or to customers who had stopped paying for their subscriptions — grew 83 percent. While newspapers thrown on credit in Birmingham decreased about 5 percent, the *News*'s overall unpaid distribution grew nearly 80 percent.[42]

While declining to comment specifically on the *Times-Picayune*'s figures, Ken Shultz, senior vice president of Audit Services for the AAM, said a significant increase in "arrears and credit allowances" is not uncommon in these types of situations. "The *Times-Picayune* has obviously undergone a significant transformation and it wouldn't be a surprise to most people [in the circulation profession] to hear that they have increased their arrears allowance after such a significant change, to give their subscribers an opportunity to experience the new product," Schultz said.[43] (The AAM allows member newspapers to continue to throw newspapers essentially on credit to past-due subscribers for up to ninety days after they stop paying for their subscriptions — and to count up to 4 percent of those issues as part of their official circulation figures. "Average unpaid circulation" distribution, however, may not be counted toward a newspaper's official "total average circulation," the number upon which advertising rates are generally set.)

The increases were equally stark in Mobile, where Sunday "average unpaid distribution" of the *Press-Register* increased almost ten-fold year over year—and was equal to almost 9 percent of the newspaper's total print circulation. The *Press-Register*'s "credit and arrears allowances" grew 28 percent during the same time period.

Those same tactics have not been applied at all Advance newspapers that implemented "digital first" either much earlier or later than New Orleans and Alabama. For example, AnnArbor.com initially increased its "average unpaid circulation" in the nine months after it implemented digital first, but that rate has since fallen dramatically. Harrisburg's *Patriot-News*'s average unpaid circulation actually declined almost 41 percent between March 2012 and March 2013. Although the total newspapers thrown were fewer than 1,800, the *Syracuse Post-Standard*'s overall rate increased nearly 18 percent over the same period.[44]

AAM regulations require that member newspapers be paid for at least 70 percent of the issues they circulate, but the organization offers methods that allow publishers to continue to distribute newspapers to readers whom advertisers want to reach—regardless of whether those readers pay for the publication. One method is a category called "Targeted Verified" circulation, which allows publishers to throw newspapers for up to twelve weeks to readers who do not pay for the publication, or may have not even requested free editions. It can be "sponsored" by another entity, such as an advertiser that wants to reach a certain demographic or neighborhood, and can be extended indefinitely.

The *Times-Picayune* also began or increased a variety of marketing tactics to entice subscribers to re-up, offering them everything from comic-embossed umbrellas to gift cards from local grocery stores and Walmart in exchange for renewing their subscriptions. Deep discounting also is part of at least the short-term strategy to hang on to the print subscribers that advertisers still covet. Subscribers who stopped paying for their subscriptions after unsuccessfully trying to cancel them complained that they then often began receiving solicitations from out-of-town telemarketing firms offering cut-rate renewal offers. As recently as May 2013, one former employee received a mail promotion offering three months of the three-day-a-week newspaper for $29.85 — a 41 percent savings off of the customary $16.95 a month rate, the solicitation touted — or three months of Sunday delivery for $18, or $6 a month. Interestingly, the mailing made no mention of NOLA.com or any of its offerings. Another tactic also surfaced in the spring of 2013. Former longtime subscriber Tisserand gave a telemarketer who was again trying to persuade him to re-subscribe to the newspaper his standard response: he would re-subscribe when the newspaper began printing daily again. The agent offered a new rejoinder to Tisserand's riposte: "The more people who subscribe, the better the newspaper will do, and the more likely it will be that it will start printing daily papers again."[45] A *Press-Register* subscriber told Rob Holbert, co-publisher and managing editor of *Lagniappe*, Mobile's bi-weekly alternative newspaper, that after her family purchased a Sunday-only yearlong subscription for $52 in the winter of 2013, a *Press-Register* circulation representative called to say they also would be getting Wednesday and Friday newspapers for no additional charge. "They told me they're calling everyone," the subscriber told Holbert, who calculated that those discounts brought the price of the home-delivered, per-newspaper issue down to 33 cents.[46]

As they strive to hang on to print subscribers still necessary to appeal to the more-lucrative print advertisers, many newspaper owners are maintaining a firm gaze on their perhaps now-longer-term hopes that successful digital distribution is the elusive prize that could restore their profit margins. To that end, the AAM also collects and compiles numbers that take into account digital editions of newspapers that readers are viewing. Although the *Times-Picayune* did not report a circulation figure for its digital editions in its March 2012 AAM report, when its total average print circulation figure from that report is compared to its March 2013 print and digital circulation, the newspaper's Sunday circulation grew about 13 percent year-over-year, to slightly more than 175,000. Nascent "digital replica" editions—essentially a PDF of the newspaper that subscribers may download to their computers—at Advance Alabama newspapers meant their inclusion had little effect on total circulation there.

MLive Media Group—which has had the longest experience with "digital first"—posted a nearly 20 percent year-over-year decline in "total Sunday circulation" for its eight Michigan newspapers combined, according to numbers Advance supplied to the AAM for the same period. However, bolstering Advance's contentions of its digital success in the Great Lakes state, several of its eight newspapers there have seen dramatic circulation increases of their "digital replica" editions. Led by the *Grand Rapids Press,* which is by far the largest of Advance's Michigan newspapers, MLive's digital replica Sunday circulation more than doubled year over year and was equal to more than 7 percent of the group's total paid Sunday print circulation.

The Internet has introduced new levels of complexity to the newspaper business, not the least of which is measuring—and valuing—website traffic. A number of businesses compile and help newspaper companies analyze their website and mobile data. They parse Internet traffic any number of ways, including page views (how many pages on a website readers visit), visits (how many individual visits to a site, including multiple visits by the same person over a specific time period), and unique visitors (how many different people access a website over a specific period of time, with no additional credit given for multiple visits during that designated window).

NOLA Media Group executives—notably president Ricky

Mathews, Amoss, and O'Byrne—have regularly referred to NOLA.com's skyrocketing growth. The Media Audit, a company that compiles syndicated, local-market audience survey data for companies and to which Advance Digital executives frequently refer, did not respond to a request for access to its data. I instead reviewed figures compiled by Quantcast "one of the most recognized names in measuring web traffic," according to technology website and magazine *Wired*[47] (which incidentally is owned by Advance Publications' Condé Nast magazine subsidiary). Millions of websites, including all Advance and numerous other US newspapers, allow Quantcast to access and aggregate detailed website traffic information, which Quantcast in turn makes available for free on its website.

Quantcast's publicly available data does not go back far enough for each Advance site to make year-over-year comparisons possible, and the company declined to make historical data available. However, the site's figures show that, with the exception of MLive.com and al.com, the websites of Advance newspapers that have adopted "digital first" have seen their early rates of growth tumble.[48] For example, NOLA.com's unique visitors grew steadily between August 2011 and January 2012, when they exceeded 3 million in a single month for the first (and only) time to-date, but they then began to list downward for the remainder of the year. They recovered somewhat in early 2013, but did not again approach 3 million, even during February 2013, when the Super Bowl was in New Orleans. (To appeal to the thousands of visitors the game brought to the city, NOLA.com produced more than 2,000 stories, photos, and videos specifically about the game or related activities, Mathews boasted to an industry conference later that month. The site, in turn, attracted 2.7 million unique visitors that month.[49])

The trend line for page views, another popular barometer, is roughly consistent with that for unique visitors. NOLA.com delivered almost 25.7 million page views in February 2012, but that number again gradually drifted downward until a year later, the month of the Super Bowl, when the site's content efforts did pay off in the page view category: NOLA.com delivered more than 26.2 million page views during the month, a record for the site. Page views on mobile devices slowly increased through 2012, and then significantly climbed in the first three months of 2013, before listing downward again through May 2013 and rebounding in June. Mobile growth, however, appeared to be cannibalizing website growth: although mobile usage grew, combined web and mobile page view numbers continued to decline through spring and early summer of 2013. "I would have thought, given the amount of time and energy they've invested, it would have improved," the *New York Times*'s Carr, said in a May 2013 interview. "I think they were hoping for more [traffic], but I'm not surprised they haven't gotten more."

However, different web traffic numbers that several Advance properties reported to the AAM paint a far rosier picture. Most show double-digit, year-over-year growth in both unique visitors and page views. For example, according to NOLA.com's self-reported AAM figures, total 2012 unique visitors grew 25 percent year over year, to slightly more than 29 million, while its page views grew 13 percent, to 428.6 million.[50] In his July 2013 internal memo posted publicly by media blogger Jim Romenesko, Siegel, Advance Publications' president of local digital strategy, said that the company's websites averaged 29 percent year-over-year growth in unique visitors in the first half of 2013. He also reported that the latest Media Audit research ranked six Advance sites in the top ten US newspaper-affiliated websites for local market penetration.[51] Numbers like these, however, get little attention "because it contradicts the attacks on us that our websites suck," Steven Newhouse told Poynter.org in August 2012.[52]

Acknowledged or not, those figures aren't as impressive as they may sound, Doctor said. "We'd expect huge increases in digital reading if the *T-P* was really reaching readers that could no longer read print, so even 15 percent-to-35 percent isn't a great achievement." Doctor estimates that to grow digital revenue substantially, NOLA.com needs to be experiencing a 35 percent to 50 percent increase in page views "to show it is engaging at the same level now with forced print/digital access compared to the seven-day print model." He projects that the site is increasing digital ad revenue at a rate of about 10 percent, "which is good, but not world-beating. Remember, the basic model is a cost-cutting strategy, rather than a big revenue growth model." Amoss boasted to Doctor in late June 2013 that internal NOLA Media Group numbers showed that overall page views on NOLA.com were up 15 percent, and "eyes on content" — or views of articles, videos, and photos across the site — had increased 35 percent, with views of photos skyrocketing 150 percent year over year, and now representing 16 percent of the site's traffic." In a subsequent interview for this book, Doctor said that while NOLA.com's "photo galleries are spinning lots of traffic, it's traffic that's not particularly valuable for advertising."[53]

A fundamental question for Advance — and for all newspaper publishers — is whether they can generate sufficient revenue from web traffic to offset the decline in revenue that undoubtedly will accompany falling print circulation and advertising. NOLA.com's online revenues grew 20 percent year over year, Mathews told the *Wall Street Journal* in September 2012, but he wouldn't say from what base, only that the company's percentage of online ad revenue compared with print ad revenue was larger than the then-industry average of 13.5 percent. (That number has grown to 15 percent, according to the latest annual Pew Research Center's "State of the News Media" report, released in March 2013.) NOLA Media Group's goal is to have a "50/50 split between print and digital revenues within five years,"[54] Mathews told the *Journal*.

One strategy to generate more online revenue that Advance seems to have rejected — at least for the time being — is erecting what is known as a digital "paywall" and ending its long-standing practice of providing its content to consumers free online. In the past several years, more newspapers have moved to a paywall business model, in which some or all of their content is inaccessible to anyone who hasn't paid for a subscription or limited-time access to it. The movement accelerated dramatically in the final months of 2012 and into 2013. About 450 of the country's almost 1,400 daily newspapers have or will soon have paywalls,[55] including nine of the nation's twenty largest newspapers, meaning about one-third of all daily newspaper readers now or will soon access content behind a paywall.[56] Among the notable newspapers now relying on or soon to be instituting paywalls are the *Wall Street Journal*, which was the first major daily to adopt the model; the *Financial Times*; the *Washington Post*; *Dallas Morning News*; *Boston Globe*; *Baltimore Sun*; *San Francisco Chronicle*; and the *New York Times* and its *International Herald Tribune*. Large US newspaper chains that have recently jumped on the paywall bandwagon include the Gannett Company (all of its more than eighty newspapers except for the flagship *USA Today* are erecting paywalls), and the E.W. Scripps Company. Many grant access to a limited number of free articles each month before a "metered paywall" kicks in and requires readers to subscribe before accessing more content.

Metered paywalls—some more bluntly refer to them as "leaky paywalls" because they offer some free access and are not difficult to circumvent if readers are intent on defeating them—provide newspapers with dual benefits. First, search engines and social media links can still direct casual readers to a site's content, which helps to ensure larger audiences upon which higher advertising rates can be based. Second, they also ostensibly capture, "higher access" online readers by enjoining them to pay up once they exceed access to a basic threshold of content. "Every other American newspaper company is putting paywalls in place and saying to readers, 'You're no longer just a print customer, you're an all-access customer—tablet and phone apps, and website,'" analyst Doctor said. "That's the sole growth driver of American newspapers. By producing less content and not having a reader revenue strategy, [Advance] essentially has a no-growth strategy, which stands in distinction to what other US newspaper companies are trying to do."

Among the leaders who have a record with a paywall strategy is the *Wall Street Journal*, which restricted access to some online content beginning in the mid-1990s, and had close to 900,000 digital subscribers as of May 1, 2013.[57] Thanks largely to its paywall and the 738,000 readers who, as of June 30, 2013, subscribed to the digital version of the *New York Times* and the *International Herald Tribune*, the New York Times Company in 2012 saw circulation revenue surpass advertising revenue for the first time in its storied history.[58] But it's unclear whether these publications are models for the future or exceptions to the rule. As the *Economist* pointed out in December 2012, the *Wall Street Journal* and the *Financial Times* offer specialized business content directed at a more sophisticated and affluent readership from which newspapers historically have been able to command a subscription premium.[59] And in the case of the *New York Times*, its status "as a national newspaper with international resources" gives it "a pool of many million potential readers, so the fact that over a half million of that audience has opted in is a good sign for the organization, but not necessarily for the industry," the newspaper's media reporter Carr noted in a December 2012 article.[60]

Former Wall Street analyst Henry Blodget, co-founder, CEO, and editor-in-chief of BusinessInsider.com — one of the world's fastest-growing business and tech news websites — makes an argument that no website can make a go of it based solely on digital revenue — unless it wants to significantly reduce its heretofore print-supported expenses accordingly. Blodget did an analysis of the print and digital circulation and advertising revenue of the New York Times Media Group and concluded that average print subscribers of the company's products consume about $450 in advertising per year, and are willing to pay about $650 annually to get both the print and digital versions of the paper. Conversely, the average paying digital subscriber consumes only about $100 of digital advertising a year, and digital subscribers are willing to pay only about $150 annually for their subscriptions—at least so far, Blodget's analysis shows. "When you put those numbers together, what you find is that the *New York Times*'s digital business cannot replace the revenue being lost in the print business, even with the paywall," he concluded. "So, as the print business continues to shrink, the newsroom has to shrink."[61]

Some regional newspapers, however, report success with paywalls while keeping their daily print editions firmly intact. *Dallas Morning News*'s publisher Jim Moroney made a persuasive case for this approach during a February 2013 presentation at the same industry conference where Mathews and Amoss also presented. He noted that the *Morning News* had created a combined digital-and-print subscription and increased rates by 40 percent and was in the process of raising them again. Although total subscriptions had fallen 12 percent, the increased revenue per subscription meant that about one-third of the newspaper's total revenue was now coming from subscribers. "Hardcore news subscribers don't see digital as a substitute for print," Moroney told the gathering. "They won't trade down. We say in Texas, 'You are going to have to take this paper out of my cold, dead hand.' I don't think we should apologize for that. We should celebrate that."[62]

The *Orange County Register* plans to underwrite its significant recent investments in the print newspaper by also increasing subscription prices and launching a metered paywall. With those changes, Doctor concluded that the company could make enough on additional print and digital subscriptions to offset the increased payroll, redesign, and production costs. "Once that [paywall] goes up, the *Register*'s subscribers will no longer have the choice of dropping their [print] subscriptions in favor of free digital," he opined in January 2013. "That loophole will be closed—and that supports the higher prices."[63]

Advance, however, appears poised to stand by the free, advertising-supported, increasingly digital model. "We've looked at paywalls, and we believe there's revenue in it, but there's not nearly enough revenue to really support the kind of journalism that we aspire to continue," Steven Newhouse told Poynter in August 2012. "The real revenue growth is this tremendous increase in digital spending." He added that with the "superior local product" Advance provides in each market, the company is confident "we can capture our fair share" of that growth.[64] However, the topic was apparently at least being deliberated within Advance. "From a company standpoint, there's a robust discussion going on about that at this moment," *Oregonian* publisher Anderson said during his Oregon Public Radio interview in June 2013, but quickly added that there are no imminent plans for a paywall, metered or otherwise, for Advance newspaper websites.[65]

The lack of all-access subscribers paying more of the freight amid falling advertising revenue is Advance's Achilles heel, Doctor wrote in late June 2013. "Why? Advance depends on and will depend much more on ad revenue than its peers. Many of those peers believe that reader revenue may reach 50 percent of total revenue within two to five years," he wrote. If that is true, a paywall-less Advance going forward "will have two major choices: find currently unknown large sources of revenue—or keep cutting expenses, including newsroom staff."[66]

Plenty of people are watching to see if Advance's Michigan Model will work.

"We're definitely on the front end of something," NOLA Media Group's O'Byrne said during a December 2012 interview on *Out to Lunch,* a weekly business and public affairs show produced by New Orleans's public radio station, WWNO. "What we hear from other publishers and editors around the country, privately, is 'good luck, we hope you make it. We want someone to show us a way out of this constant mode of decline. And if your business model is the one that shows us the way, we're all going to follow.'"[67]

Others in the industry are reserving judgment. "They are betting their franchise" on eschewing paywalls and reducing print editions, Poynter analyst Rick Edmonds wrote. "Either Advance is bolder and smarter than everyone else or they are wrong. Time will tell."[68]

CHAPTER VIII

"Noise Out There"

The day the details of the changes and the resulting layoffs were spelled out for Advance employees in New Orleans and Alabama, Steven Newhouse, chairman of Advance.net and presumed arbiter, if not mastermind, behind the company's digital-first strategy, gave a rare interview to a publication not owned by Advance. Most of his reported conversation with Campbell Robertson, the *New York Times*'s New Orleans-based Southern correspondent, was unremarkable, but one thing Newhouse said about the *Times-Picayune* raised the ire of just about every New Orleanian who read or heard it: "We have no intention of selling, no matter how much noise there is out there."[1]

Although stunning in its insensitivity, Steven Newhouse's pronouncement confirmed the type of relationship the secretive and tight-knit Newhouse family was seen to have with its nearly three dozen newspapers spanning both coasts: a seemingly contradictory combination of laissez faire management that generally deferred to the sensibilities and predilections of local publishers and their perceptions of the community, but a stance that also could enforce a corporate overlord mentality on major, and usually controversial, issues — or as a 1992 *New York Times* headline described it, "Newhouse Maintains Loose Reins with a Tight Grip."[2] It also perhaps revealed a shift in how the third, and latest generation, of the Newhouse family viewed and expected to conduct business with the *Times-Picayune*, and by extension, its other newspapers.

Advance had owned the *Times-Picayune* just a few months short of fifty years at the time of Steven Newhouse's proclamation, and the utterance was a slap in the face to New Orleanians who cared deeply about their daily newspaper. "Hello? Steve Newhouse? It's WTF calling" was the headline on a column appearing on NolaVie, the nonprofit lifestyle and culture website that shares select content for posting on NOLA.com. "That was the eulogy Steven Newhouse read at Tuesday's funeral for our beloved *Times-Picayune*," columnist Brett Will Taylor wrote. "Only he didn't deliver it in person. He read it over the phone. To the *New York Times*. Which leads me to ask all of us mourners, we family members of the dearly departed, the following question: What. The. F%*#?"[3]

Others also weighed in, including an editorial in the region's alternative weekly *Gambit*, published two days after Taylor's column:

> "*Noise*?" Is that what he thinks New Orleanians have been pouring out from their hearts? What Mr. Newhouse calls "noise," we recognize as the voices of our friends and neighbors. When a billionaire absentee owner refers to the heartfelt pleas of his customers as "noise," it tells us that all the pretty puffery about a more "robust" news product is pure bunk. Local business owners, many of whom for years have faithfully advertised in Mr. Newhouse's paper, know all too well that ignoring the voices of customers — particularly in New Orleans — is a recipe for failure. Oddly enough, we suspect that's the Newhouse plan: sooner rather than later, there will be no printed edition of the *Times-Picayune*.[4]

Steven Newhouse later in the summer backpedaled from the harshness of his remark and some of the tactics that had been employed by Advance newspapers as they implemented "digital-first."

"Some of the criticism was well founded," he wrote in the August 2012 commentary on Poynter.org, about outrage and negative media coverage that greeted the company's "forced march to digital," as newspaper analyst Ken Doctor labeled it. "We could have communicated our decisions more openly and sensitively to our employees, our readers and our communities."[5] It nonetheless is almost impossible to imagine Steven Newhouse's father, Donald, the family member who has overseen Advance's three-dozen-odd daily and weekly newspapers for roughly six decades, making such a tone-deaf public comment about any of the company's properties. Although he had infrequent direct contact with the rank-and-file, *Times-Picayune* employees had for years spotted the elder Newhouse at the newspaper's downtown headquarters during his regular business updates with Ashton Phelps, Sr. and Jr. Many Newhouse relatives and Advance executives had trained or worked at the newspaper over the years, including the younger Newhouse brother, the late Norman Newhouse, and the family's support of the newspaper following Katrina had strengthened employees' gratitude to the family.

Advance, however, had been operating for close to a decade in a very different era than it did in the heyday of the media empire amassed by Steven's grandfather and Donald's father, S.I. "Sam" Newhouse, Sr. During the newspaper industry's financial zenith that began in the late 1970s and extended through the middle of the first decade of the new millennium, publishers almost printed money along with their newspapers, and few were better at it than Sam Newhouse. "It used to be that running a newspaper was slam-dunk easy. It was a beautiful business to be in," said Alan Mutter, a former newspaper reporter, editor, and columnist turned industry analyst and consultant who bills himself as "perhaps the only CEO in Silicon Valley who knows how to set type one letter at a time." "You were the only one in town, you could raise rates at will any time you needed to, and back in the day, people didn't have a choice. You needed to hire a secretary? You took out a [help wanted] ad in the [local] newspaper for $600 because there wasn't another option. Monster.com or Craigslist didn't exist. Now, the newspaper business is anything but easy.

It's incredibly complicated. It has gone from being stupid easy to being almost unbearably difficult."[6]

Newhouse newspapers, before the full-bore arrival of the Internet as an information and entertainment medium, routinely enjoyed profit margins among the best in the industry—between 20 percent and 30 percent, leading newspaper analysts John Morton[7] and Ken Doctor[8] estimated. Morton projected that Advance's profit margin is now probably half of what it was at its apex, while Doctor said the company's newspapers probably would fetch 10 percent of what they would have a decade ago.

Because Advance is a privately held company—and a secretive one at that—it is essentially impossible to obtain financial information that provides meaningful insight into its performance. While the company and the *Times-Picayune* released limited financial data after public sentiment developed so forcefully against them, it has by-and-large been cherry-picked information that supports their narrative or a particular position they are trying to advance. For example, NOLA Media Group president and publisher Ricky Mathews told the *Wall Street Journal* in the fall of 2012 that NOLA.com's online revenue grew 20 percent year over year, but he wouldn't say from what base, making it impossible to assess the website's relative performance, or evaluate it against industry standards. Even when executives do release figures, they don't always match up. In a January 2013 commentary published on NOLA.com that assessed NOLA Media Group's performance since the change, *Times-Picayune* editor Jim Amoss wrote that, "In 2012, 41 million viewers came to NOLA.com, 7 million more viewers than in 2011."[9] "Viewers" is not a recognized industry metric, so in writing about the commentary for *CJR*, the magazine's the "Audit" editor Ryan Chittum presumed Amoss was referring to unique visitors.[10] Amoss's numbers averaged 3.4 million unique visitors a month in 2012, and 2.83 million in 2011. However, Mathews and Amoss presented numbers to an industry conference in New Orleans some six weeks later that were significantly larger than the figures Amoss cited in his commentary.[11] Although independently compiled figures often vary widely, numbers generated by nationally recognized web analytics company Quantcast indicate that both men overshot the runway, and that the website actually received hundreds of thousands of fewer unique visitors a month, on average, in 2012. (Full 2011 figures aren't available on the Quantcast site for a 2011 comparison.)[12]

In a comprehensive story published by *Columbia Journalism Review* in March 2013 about the *Times-Picayune* since it became a less-than-daily publication, the magazine estimated that the newspaper and NOLA.com annually generate roughly $90 million in revenue and $9 million in operating profit, "which come overwhelmingly from the print side." In a report he wrote for the *Nation* that cited both publicly available and proprietary figures shared by employees, New Orleans author and freelance investigative journalist Jason Berry concluded that the newspaper probably made about $8 million in 2011.[13] *CJR* estimated the *Times-Picayune's* circulation revenue at roughly $25 million to $30 million annually, which, if true, meant the print newspaper generated more than 90 percent of the company's revenue before the changes "and still likely brings in five of every six dollars in revenue," *CJR* concluded. "If NOLA Media Group were a standalone business with no newspaper to support it, its costs would exceed its revenue by many times."[14] As mentioned earlier, global market research company Kantar Media projected that the *Times-Picayune* brought in $64.7 million in print advertising revenue in 2011, while NOLA.com earned less than one-tenth of that, or $5.7 million.

Given that the *Times-Picayune* has publicly acknowledged that it was still profitable before the changes were implemented, the situation is likely no better, and potentially far worse, at other Advance newspapers. For example, *New York Magazine* in 2009 reported that the company's largest newspaper, New Jersey's

Newark Star-Ledger, may have lost as much as $40 million in 2008. The newspaper will lose a projected $51.6 million in 2011-13, publisher Richard Vezza disclosed in June 2013, a figure the newspaper's three labor unions flatly reject.[15] Mobile, Alabama's *Press-Register*—earlier nicknamed the "Cash Register" in journalism and Mobile business circles because of its reported historically high levels of profitability—saw its profits sink from $7.3 million in 2006, to about $4 million in 2007, and $313,000 in 2008,[16] before its 2009 budget projected a loss of $200,000,[17] according to information presented in the lawsuit former *Press-Register* publisher Howard Bronson brought against the newspaper and Advance in 2009. "No one in the [Newhouse] family believes the newspaper business is coming back," *New York Magazine* reported in 2009.[18]

Aside from the obvious fiscal pain, another problem with the sinking fortunes of Advance's newspapers is the widely held industry assumption that the company historically has met the financial obligations of its other print media properties largely on the backs of its newspapers. Those benefiting from the newspapers' historic largesse included the magazines of Advance's Condé Nast, which include some of the world's most recognized titles, such as *Vanity Fair*, *Glamour*, *The New Yorker*, *Vogue*, and close to two dozen others. The historically notorious extravagance of the magazine side of the house, run by Donald's brother, Si, was a primary reason the magazines were often beholden to their less glamorous—but far more profitable—corporate siblings, the newspapers. "Donald makes the money and Si spends it," was an often-heard comment about the Newhouse media empire. In an October 1979 report published two months after patriarch Sam Newhouse's death, *Forbes* noted that "75 percent of Newhouse [Advance] is still the Newhouse newspapers, and in unguarded moments, Si Newhouse is apt to call everything else 'peripheral.'"[19] As author Carol Felsenthal noted in her 1998 book, *Citizen Newhouse* "that, over the years, has largely remained true."

Sam Newhouse's unauthorized biographer, Richard Meeker, told Felsenthal in an interview that the Advance newspapers "fund everything else"[20] in the company, an assumption widely accepted in industry circles.

As the Great Recession further eroded the magazines' performance, and took a harsh toll on the newspapers' once-lofty profits, Advance in recent years was forced to shutter several of its better-known magazines, including *Portfolio*, the much-ballyhooed business publication (said to be a personal favorite of Si Newhouse's), after it burned through a considerable chunk of its $100 million in start-up money in its short two-year life.[21] "We will not be in that position after today—we won't have businesses that don't make a contribution," Condé Nast CEO Richard H. Townsend told the *New York Times* in 2009 after announcing the closure of four magazines, including well-known titles *Gourmet* and *Modern Bride*.[22] "Resources are now spread thinner," *New York Magazine*'s Steve Fishman reported. "The company no longer has the luxury of pumping cash into a struggling title."[23] (At least one Advance business is assumed to be performing much better. The Advance/Newhouse Partnership owns Bright House Networks, a digital cable, phone, and broadband Internet company with about 2.2 million residential and business customers in Alabama, California, Florida, Indiana, and Michigan. The division also owns a significant interest in cable TV's Discovery Communications, Inc.[24])

Fishman's 2009 article, which quoted insiders and dished on the Newhouse family and their empire in more detail than many reports have done in recent years, detailed how Si and Donald Newhouse continued the ritualistic family meetings begun by their father, which typically included about twenty extended family members. "The family works hard for unity. At meetings, family members voice opinions, but respectfully. Nothing is voted on. 'At the end of the day, Si and Donald lead the decisions,'" an executive who had attended meetings told Fishman.[25] The *New*

York Post's Keith Kelly, however, reported in early July 2013 that Si Newhouse "was gently bumped aside for health reasons" in 2012 and that an informal group of top executives—including Townsend, Condé Nast President Bob Sauerberg, Donald Newhouse, Steven Newhouse, and Jonathan Newhouse, a cousin of Si and Donald's who runs Condé Nast International—now oversees the magazine division.[26]

But the still-sputtering economy and consumers' defection from print media to the Internet has ramifications not only for the company. "Without profit, there's no 'distributable cash' for the family," Fishman reported, and conventional wisdom in the industry suggests that the dramatic restructuring of the company is likely driven at least as much by shoring up the family's massive wealth as by a desire to reshape US newspaper journalism. "The privately held Newhouse empire provides a comfortable living for dozens of family member owners, and tight times in the newspaper industry apparently have cut their payouts and perhaps their lifestyles," author and Central Michigan University journalism professor John K. Hartman wrote in *Editor & Publisher* in late June, following the beginning of the "digital first"-driven layoffs at the *Cleveland Plain Dealer*. "The only way to push the stipends back in the direction of comfortable is to dramatically cut expenses while maintaining advertising revenue."[27]

Regardless of the continued day-to-day involvement of octogenarians Si and Donald Newhouse, it's clear they have begun to pass the mantle to younger Newhouse family members. The third generation not only must manage the radical shift in the very underpinnings of the family business, but they also are likely intent on defying that traditional "third-generation jinx" that fells so many previously successful family-owned enterprises. Front and center is Steven Newhouse, labeled in 2012 by the *New York Observer* as "the third-gen Newhouse to watch," who, with the changes at the *Times-Picayune* and other Advance newspapers "has proven himself a savvy businessman who little relishes underwriting a failing business model."[28]

An unlikely defender of Steven Newhouse is Dan Shea, one of the *Times-Picayune*'s two former co-managing editors who was unceremoniously forced out by the 2012 layoffs, and has since been hired as chief operating officer and general manager of the *Advocate* by its new owner, New Orleans businessman John Georges. "When I see people condemning [the Newhouses] and saying that they're doing this just because they're greedy, I don't think that's the case," Shea said in March 2013, six weeks before landing the job with the *Advocate*. "Steve Newhouse doesn't want to be the generation that runs this off the rails. I don't ascribe evil motives to it. People don't understand business and the serious role Steven Newhouse has in preserving his family's fortune."[29]

But Steven, his two siblings, and their cousins have limited options, given the company's overwhelmingly "legacy media" assets in today's increasingly digital media world. "They're saddled with the legacy, and they're a prisoner of that legacy," Mutter observed. "They got caught when the music stopped. The value of their newspaper assets is shrinking, and they long ago missed the opportunity to get out while the getting was good."

Although Donald and Steven Newhouse have been adamant that their company will not sell the *Times-Picayune*, Mutter's observation points to the reality that the Newhouses' intransigence may very well represent less of an unwillingness to sell, and more of an unwillingness to sell at the price their newspapers would fetch in today's market.

Morton estimates that a metropolitan daily today generally commands between $300 and $400 per average subscriber, down from $1,000 to $1,200 a decade ago. Based on the most recent— and most generous—reading of circulation figure the *Times-Picayune* supplied to the voluntary industry auditing group the Alliance for Audited Media, for the period October 2012-March 2013, the newspaper's total Sunday print and digital circulation of about 175,000 means it would go for between $53 million and $70 million today under Morton's formula, down from $258 million to $310 million ten years ago, when the newspaper's average daily circulation was about 258,000. And that 2013 estimated value is likely high, Morton added, given Georges's April 2013 acquisition of the competing *Advocate,* his seeming willingness to pump money into it to compete effectively with the *Times-Picayune,* and the community's still-raw hostility over the boorish manner in which the *Times-Picayune* handled its cutbacks.[30]

Based on a different formula that takes into account a newspaper's profits, Doctor pegs the *Times-Picayune*'s value at a broader, yet consistent range: between $50 million and $100 million. *CJR* in March 2013 calculated the newspaper's value at only $40 million.[31] (Writing about what the *Times-Picayune* and other newspapers are facing amid today's seemingly irreversible decline, Reuters's media columnist Jack Shafer in June 2012 noted that the *Philadelphia Inquirer* and *Daily News* sold for $515 million in 2006, for $139 million in 2010, and $44 million in April 2012.[32])

The declines in valuations are linked to newspapers' falling profit margins, freelance journalist Dan Mitchell wrote on Fortune.com in June 2012, just as the *Times-Picayune* debacle was unfolding. Mitchell noted those margins often exceeded 40 percent two decades ago, "but those days are gone, and publishers have known it for years. Estimates vary widely, but margins now tend to average somewhere between 8 percent and 15 percent,"[33] a still-respectable return in many industries, and one that may be the new reality for newspaper publishers. (Doctor estimates today's profitability at closer to 5 percent to 10 percent and asserts that even that level is only maintained through continual cost-cutting.) Legendary billionaire investor Warren Buffett appeared to acknowledge as much in writing about his company's newspaper-buying spree. "At appropriate prices — and that means at a very low multiple of current earnings — we will purchase more papers of the type we like," he noted in Berkshire Hathaway's most-recent shareholders' letter.[34]

The third generation of Newhouses are "pissed because they didn't sell when they should have, they're pissed because they couldn't do anything about New Orleans after Katrina, and they're pissed now that they've got this rich guy [Georges] who's suddenly confronting them with a form of potentially asymmetrical warfare, a competitor who appears to have the assets and desire to do what it takes to be the dominant publisher in southern Louisiana," analyst Alan Mutter observed. "They're between a rock and hard place. They don't want to be the ones to turn off the lights at the newspapers. They don't want to be the ones who fail."

The buyouts, furloughs, and pension plan suspensions were the Newhouses' initial responses to the encroaching red ink. As mentioned earlier, Advance executives evidently began contemplating a less-than-daily-publication scenario for at least some of their newspapers before mid-2008, at which time the company revised the Pledge to narrowly cover only employees of newspapers published daily in a newsprint form. And the February 2010 outright revocation of the Pledge opened the door to large-scale layoffs the company would undertake about two-and-a-half years later, long after other large newspaper companies.

In the case of the *Times-Picayune*, Amoss has consistently denied that the newsroom has been greatly reduced, and as late as mid-May 2013, was touting a workforce of 156.[35] However, a careful review of NOLA.com's own publicly posted staff list and its internal employee phone directory show the number was closer to 130 full-time employees — down from NOLA.com's self-reported 175 before the layoffs[36], but still almost forty more than survived the fall 2012 staff massacre. Amoss would achieve his higher number and then some by including fourteen high school sports stringers and fourteen entertainment freelancers listed on NOLA.com's public staff list in May 2013.

That level of staff reduction has been or will be instituted at all sixteen Advance newspapers that have undergone or are facing "digital-first." In addition to the fifty-eight newsroom layoffs previously agreed to by the editorial employees' union at the *Cleveland Plain Dealer,* the newspaper in late June 2013 began cutting an undisclosed number of additional non-unionized positions in its marketing, finance, information technology, pre-press, and building service departments. And an estimated 100-105 employees were laid off from the *Oregonian* in June 2013, including forty-nine-to-fifty-five from the newsroom, following buyouts, pay cuts, and more than three dozen layoffs since 2010, mostly in the newsroom, according to *Willamette Week.* Across Advance's three Alabama newspapers, 400 employees lost jobs, while 550 positions were eliminated in Michigan, 70 in Harrisburg, and 112 in Syracuse. Another thirty-some-odd full-time and twenty-six part-time jobs were eliminated in two rounds of layoffs in the winter and spring of 2013 at Advance's *Easton (Penn.) Express-Times,* which had employeed 230 before the cuts.[37] And eleven more people lost their jobs in January 2013 at Advance's *South Jersey Times,* which employed about 150 at the time.

In what it termed its "first-ever large-scale layoff," the *Newark Star-Ledger,* Advance's largest newspaper, eliminated thirty-four jobs, or about 10 percent of its workforce, in January 2013, blaming the continuing decline of the newspaper industry and the lingering effects of Hurricane Sandy, which had hit the region only three months earlier. At the time, publisher Richard Vezza indicated that the newspaper would seek significant contract concessions from its three printing and production unions when their contracts expired in the summer of 2013.[38]

He also told his newspaper that, "This is not a foreshadowing of the demise of the paper. We have no plans for further layoffs." That quotation, however, disappeared from the online version of the report sometime between the story being published in mid-January 2013 and late June 2013,[39] perhaps because the layoffs actually were a forewarning of the possible shuttering of the newspaper. Vezza in late June dropped one of the biggest bombshells in the Newhouses' reengineering of Advance: If the *Star-Ledger's* unions don't agree to what the unions' leader characterizes as brutal concessions that would approximate the estimated $9 million in annual savings the company calculated it could realize by outsourcing production and packaging, Advance will close the newspaper. Citing a projected three-year loss of $51.6 million through the end of 2013, Vezza told *Star-Ledger* reporter Ted Sherman, "This is not a ploy. This is reality. We cannot afford to keep operating the paper like this."[40] Less than two weeks later, the newspaper also announced that it is putting its headquarters of fifty years at 1 Star-Ledger Plaza in downtown Newark up for sale and will move to smaller leased offices.[41]

The company's three unions aren't buying reports of the newspaper's potential demise. Saying the *Star-Ledger's* demands equate to a 55 percent reduction in union members' entire compensation package, Ed Shown, president of the Council of *Star-Ledger* Unions, and of Teamsters-Graphic Communications Conference Local 8N (the latter of which represents roughly 250 of the newspaper's 771 employees), contends that the newspaper remains profitable. "We did exhaustive studies. We presented what we thought they were making, as opposed to what they're saying they're losing," Shown said in an interview two days after Vezza sent a letter to employees and the unions outlining the newspaper's demands. "They're telling us they're losing money, but we don't believe them. They're making $30 million a year just in obituaries. They're making tens of millions on legal advertisers. They're running as many as twenty full pages of color ads on Saturdays, the slow day of the week for newspapers. It'll never be like its heyday, but we believe the *Star-Ledger* is holding its own." Shown also predicted that a new contract will be ratified by September 2013,[42] after this book goes to press.

When the Pledge was still in force, Advance had first threatened to sell the *Star-Ledger* in 2008 if it did not win substantial union concessions and acceptance of voluntary buyouts from a significant portion of the newspaper's non-union, full-time workforce. Ultimately, 304 employees took buyouts, including 151 in the newsroom. Even with those and the 2013 layoffs, the *Star-Ledger*'s newsroom headcount stood at 175.[43]

One thing the newspaper is unlikely to do (presuming it continues to publish) is cut the number of days it publishes, Vezza said in January 2013[44] and reaffirmed in June, citing the intensely competitive New York metropolitan media market as the primary deterrent. "There are no plans for that. This is strictly a labor issue at the *Star-Ledger*," Vezza told the *New York Post*'s Kelly the same day he issued the staff memo threatening the closure.[45]

With the exception of the *Star-Ledger* and *Express-Times*, Advance's layoffs have been followed by varying levels of cutbacks in print publication and/or home delivery of its newspapers. All of those reductions—in personnel, press runs, and/or home delivery— produced significant reductions in expenses that have no doubt dramatically improved those newspapers' bottom lines. In an October 2012 analysis he did for the Nieman Journalism Lab, Doctor projected that the changes had cost the *Times-Picayune* 21 percent of its circulation revenue and nearly 14 percent of its advertising revenue, but that its sharply lower payroll and newspaper production and delivery costs produce "11 percent more cost savings than revenue losses. It could be high or low, but at 11 percent, it would double or triple the profit margins of many metro papers."[46] He later readjusted his estimate of advertising revenue lost to a mere 10 percent, which would mean even higher profit margins. Poynter's Rick Edmonds, on the other hand, projected that the cutback would yield only a 3 percentage-point savings, assuming the news staff costs were reduced by 50 percent. Any gain beyond that is "a big bet" on growing digital readership, but more importantly on "a sharp pickup in [online newspaper] ad growth . . . [and the belief that the] *Times-Picayune* and other Advance titles will be well-positioned to capitalize on the surge when it happens," Edmonds concluded.[47]

But improved profitability via cost reduction is the real short-term goal, Doctor, Edmonds, Morton, Mutter, and others conclude. "All of this suggests that [Advance is] trying to maximize near-term profitability against the day when [daily newspapers are] no longer a viable business," Mutter said. "What can you do this month, and next month, and for the foreseeable future? You can control your expenses to maximize short-term profitability. The plan is to keep figuring out ways to make money, and the day they figure out that they can't make money anymore, they'll close it."

On his "Reflections of a Newsosaur" blog, Mutter borrowed the term popularized in 2004's *The Vanishing Newspaper: Saving Journalism in the Information Age* by former newspaper editor and University of North Carolina at Chapel Hill professor emeritus Philip Meyer—the "Milk It" strategy:

> Accept the inevitable decline and fall of the traditional newspaper model and then whack costs to extract the most profits from the decaying business for as long as possible. As unfortunate as it may be that Ann Arbor, New Orleans or Mobile are deprived of the power of a vigorous press, the strategy evidently selected by Advance makes sense if you believe that the best days of newspapering are behind us. By cutting staff to a bare minimum and printing only on the days it is profitable to do so, publishers can milk considerable sums from their franchises until the day these once-indomitable cash cows go dry.[48]

Doctor predicts Advance will be more profitable in 2013 than it was in 2012, "but their print advertising is declining with everyone else's. The only way they maintain the newer, higher profit is to continue to cut expenses because they don't have increasing reader revenue. If they want 12 percent, or 15 percent profit, the only way to achieve that is to continue to cut. They will have to continue to cut content, and that's simply not a strategy."

Mutter, Shafer, and *CJR's* Chittum all contend that Advance's end game is liquidation, a perceived assumption by Advance executives that they can get more for the company's newspapers by slowly bleeding them dry and trading on their publications' goodwill, than by selling them in today's languishing newspaper marketplace. "Buffett probably would have paid $60 million [for the *Times-Picayune*], but they'll make that in two or three years" with the new business model, said Shea, the former *Times-Picayune* co-managing editor now with the *Advocate*. "By cutting costs well ahead of perpetually declining revenues from the 'Inkosaurus,' as [state editor] James O'Byrne calls the print edition, the Newhouses can ride the *Times-Picayune* down profitably while minimizing the loss of money," *CJR*'s Chittum concluded in his March 2013 report.

Doctor and Morton, on the other hand, shy away from applying the l-word. "Liquidation? That's too strong," Doctor said. "But a wind-it-down strategy? It definitely could be. It's not a 2025 strategy, but it could work for 10 years."

For their part, Advance's lieutenants contend that the strategy is about growth, a position Steven Newhouse took in his August 2012 Poynter.org commentary:

> For quite a while now, and especially in the past four years, it's been more and more apparent that the economic model that supported our journalism for so many decades was no longer sustainable, and that, as a result, the role we played in civic life was in jeopardy . . . we are hopeful . . . digital revenue [will] become an even greater revenue growth engine, and, eventually turn our local companies into growth businesses once more . . . By taking transformational actions now, as painful as some of them are, we have a chance to continue doing what we do best, as publishers, journalists, business partners and community leaders, for decades to come.

The Newhouses "began in the newspaper business, they began in journalism," *Plain Dealer* Publisher Terrance Egger said in a December 2012 appearance on a local public affairs TV show. "They've taken less profit out of these markets they're in than most newspaper people. Here's the thing: Because they want to try to get it right and they're making a big bet, it's easy for people to vilify them. Their sole intent is to try to get this right, so that it lasts."[49]

The "noise" in New Orleans may very well have prompted Advance to temper the aggressiveness of those attempts in other markets. First up after New Orleans and Alabama was Syracuse's *Post-Standard*, which continues to be printed daily, although like the four Advance newspapers in Michigan that also continue to print daily, it is only home-delivered in print form three days a week.[50] Beginning August 5, 2013, *Plain Dealer* subscribers saw their home delivery reduced to the same schedule as the *Oregonian*'s — Sundays, Wednesdays, and Fridays, with a smaller "bonus edition" on Saturdays — but like in Syracuse and Portland, editions will be available at Cleveland newsstands the remaining four days a week.[51] Egger said he and other *Plain Dealer* executives recruited to craft the newspaper's future business plan recommended to Advance that it continue to publish a newspaper daily in Cleveland. "We think that's a must in this marketplace, and we were listened to on this point," he told the newsroom the same morning the changes were publicly announced in early April 2013.[52] Egger also postponed his previously announced retirement to stay on through the end of 2013 to oversee the transition.

New Orleans began its three-day-a-week *Times-Picayune* on October 1, 2012, but the calculus in that market — easily the most outraged and vociferous of the Advance markets that have gone "digital first" — quickly became much more complicated. Even before the cutbacks were instituted, the company bowed to fanatical New Orleans Saints fans and announced the *Black and Gold Report*,[53] a new tabloid to be produced on Mondays after Sunday Saints football games, and thrown to newspaper subscribers and available on newsstands and in newspaper boxes for everyone else.[54] Then in early October of that year, the *Times-Picayune* began producing an early Sunday edition available on newsstands and newspaper racks on Saturdays. It includes some breaking news

In the days preceding and immediately following *TPStreet's* launch, billboards and bus wraps popped up in and around New Orleans, like this billboard at a well-trafficked intersection in suburban Metairie. *Photo courtesy of Barry Garner.*

and, depending on the season, various high school prep coverage, and Louisiana State University and Saints football reports.[55]

The morning of April 30, 2013, a NOLA.com story carrying editor Amoss's byline announced yet another print product: *TPStreet*, a tabloid that launched in late June 2013 on the weekdays that editions of the *Times-Picayune* are no longer produced (Mondays, Tuesdays, and Thursdays). *TPStreet* is sold at newsstands and newspaper boxes in the New Orleans region, but newspaper subscribers also can access "an exact electronic version" downloadable on NOLA.com in a PDF file. "'In *TPStreet*, we sought to develop a publication that would address our single-copy readers and also respond to a repeated request from our home-delivery subscribers for a front-to-back newspaper reading experience in the e-edition on days we don't offer home delivery,'" Amoss quoted NOLA Media Group president and publisher Ricky Mathews as saying. "'Our success in delivering more news, sports and entertainment to our readers enables us to create this innovative publication, the latest milestone in our evolution as a multimedia news organization. We promised to invest in our community, and we're fulfilling that promise.'"[56] Incredibly—especially given that he only seven months earlier had led the termination of one-half of the newsroom—Mathews told the *New York Times* that executives had not yet determined how many new employees would be hired to work on *TPStreet*.[57]

More than anything, *TPStreet* is NOLA Media Group's concession to *Times-Picayune* advertisers "who prefer the idea of a daily newspaper," consumer news analyst Doctor said. "It's a tweak of their corporate model, a realization that it's better to do single-copy printing the other days of the week at a relatively low cost. It would have helped them to say 'New Orleans, we listened to you.' But it's instructive to the way things are being done at a corporate level within Advance."[58]

Despite Mathews's lofty marketing-speak pronouncements, if *TPStreet* resembles the newsstand-only editions Advance produces in Syracuse, New Orleanians shouldn't expect much, *Columbia Journalism Review's* Ryan Chittum wrote in late April 2013:

> Take Monday's Syracuse *Post-Standard*. It clocked in at 16 pages and had no original content on page one . . . The entire paper had about 2,300 words of original content, including briefs. It had zero ads—literally none, besides classifieds and a couple of obits. It ran more editorial [page] copy . . . from the *Oklahoman* (320 words), of all papers, than it did from Syracuse (0 words). Even by the immiserated standards of Monday newspapers, that's pathetic.[59]

Chittum pointed out that the *Post-Standard* newsstand edition doesn't have many people to either dazzle or appall: its press run is only 12,000, about one-sixth of its former daily circulation. *TPStreet's* inaugural issue, however, signaled it may very well be a different type of publication, clocking in at "sixty pages and a good run of ads," Doctor noted,[60] although it had dropped to fifty-two pages a couple of weeks later. Amoss told a local television station that the initial print run was 50,000.

Although it initially appeared to be an evolving hybrid of Advance's various approaches in its other markets, in hindsight, the April announcement of *TPStreet* was clearly a preemptive strike against an even bigger announcement that came late that same evening: Georges announced that he had completed his-long-anticipated acquisition of the *Advocate* and had hired Peter Kovacs and Shea, the two former co-managing editors of the *Times-Picayune* who had so humiliatingly been discarded, to lead it. In his first interview after announcing *TPStreet*, Amoss incredulously said the timing of Georges's acquisition of the *Advocate* and the announcement of *TPStreet* was coincidental. "It takes a while to plan to reach the point where you can announce a change like that," Amoss said on WUPL-TV/WWL-TV's *The 504* talk show, in mid-May 2013. "So, if there was a coincidence in timing, it takes a while to get to a point to announce."[61]

Regardless of whether *TPStreet* was a response to Georges's acquisition of the *Advocate* or a recalibration of how aggressively the *Times-Picayune* will go "digital-first," the public derision that met Amoss's announcement was striking. Although reader comments on NOLA.com often are not particularly articulate or insightful, those posted to his story were at times both incisive and hysterical, and soon went viral over social media. "Oh for God's sake," one online reader commented. "Why don't you say you're going back to publishing the newspaper seven days a week instead of trying to make up a new name and size for the T-P? People are not that stupid and your credibility suffers in proportion to management's constant missteps."

Others took full advantage of the Internet's multimedia capabilities and inserted new topic-relevant quips into digital clips from movies such as *Office Space* and *The Godfather*, which made hilarious points about the incongruity of the development.

"Hmmmm . . . John Georges just completed the purchase of the *Advocate* on the same day the *T-P* announces a quasi-daily edition," another reader commented. "My, what a coincidence." Several others questioned whether the *Times-Picayune*'s management was following the playbook of Coca-Cola and its much ballyhooed 1985 launch of "New Coke" and quick return to "Coke Classic," which is widely regarded as one of the great marketing fiascoes of all time. "Can we just go back to a paper seven days a week and call it the *Times-Pic Classic*?" a reader asked. And another tried to make sense of NOLA Media Group's new print publishing schedule:

> So, just to recap:
> Monday: We'll print a paper but won't deliver it.
> Tuesday: We'll print a paper but won't deliver it.
> Wednesday: We'll print a paper and deliver it.
> Thursday: We'll print a paper but won't deliver it.
> Friday: We'll print a paper and deliver it.
> Saturday: Sunday's paper!
> Sunday: Yesterday's paper, delivered!

"You now need a spreadsheet to understand the *Times-Picayune*'s print publishing schedule," former longtime Pulitzer Prize-winning *Times-Picayune* reporter John McQuaid tweeted.[62] The headline on *Gambit* editor Kevin Allman's post to the alt-weekly's "Best of New Orleans" blog ripped Mathews's nonsensical quote that appeared in Amoss's story: "*Times-Picayune* to begin printing on days it doesn't print in order to provide 'front-to-back newspaper reading experience.'" Allman then went on to preface his report by reassuring readers that Amoss's story "was not from the *Onion*," the popular national satirical newspaper and website.[63] Northshore resident Bill McHugh, who created the blog DumpThePicayune.com initially "as a tongue-in-cheek response to the blue bloods' attempt to turn the situation around by their 'Save The Picayune' efforts on Facebook,"[64] did the math for New Orleanians insistent on continuing to get a print newspaper daily. "We used to be able to get home delivery of the *Times-Picayune* seven days a week for $18.95 per month," he wrote. But now subscribers pay $16.95 a month for the three-day-a-week newspaper. If they choose to begin buying *TPStreet* three days a week and the $2 for the early Sunday edition that's sold on Saturdays, the new "subscription" cost "is $35.37 per month, and you'll have to drive to the grocery to get it four days a week."[65]

Even the *New York Times*'s Carr joined the fray:

> It's been a jaw-dropping blunder to watch. Advance misjudged the marketplace . . . Now it is in full retreat with new competition.
>
> The company endlessly complicated what had been a simple proposition that has worked since the newspaper's founding in 1837: deliver a printed bundle of its best efforts every day for a fixed price. The new distribution plan is hard to explain, but I will do my best: On Wednesdays, Fridays and Sundays, a broadsheet called the *Times-Picayune* will be available for home delivery and on the newsstands for 75 cents. On Mondays, Tuesdays and Thursdays, a tabloid called *TPStreet* will be available only on newsstands for 75 cents. In addition, a special electronic edition of *TPStreet* will be available to the three-day subscribers of the home-delivered newspaper. On Saturdays, there will be early print editions of the Sunday *Times-Picayune* with some breaking news and some Sunday content.
>
> There's more, but you get the idea—or not. It's an array of products, frequencies and approaches that is difficult to explain, much less market.[66]

Both Amoss and Mathews acknowledged—at least partially—that *TPStreet* was a reaction to the reality that the company had likely moved too forcefully in its zeal to scale back on print. "We're constantly second-guessing ourselves, we're constantly listening to our readers," Amoss said in his appearance on *The 504*, the local television talk show. "We frankly heard from our readers that this was a big void and that they wanted us to fill it."[67]

Regardless of whether Advance actually believes it is pursuing a viable growth strategy and despite its presumed about-face regarding daily print newspapers in many of its markets, the way it has restructured seems to point to the day when it will pull the plug on print altogether. In all of its markets that have adopted the digital-first strategy, Advance's operations have been split into two companies: one handling advertising and news for all of the entity's newspapers and digital products, and the other overseeing human resources and printing, production, and distribution of the physical newspaper. In the case of New Orleans, for example, the *Times-Picayune* Publishing Corp. was disbanded in favor of NOLA Media Group and Advance Central Services Louisiana. "Once the paper reaches terminal velocity, they can shut down Advance Central Services, the print wing, tie up any potential liabilities from the paper, and pitch them into the Mississippi," *CJR's* Chittum wrote about the presumed coming day when a print *Times-Picayune* will no longer be profitable. "If NOLA Media Group is able to turn a profit on its own by then, probably with a dramatically lower headcount than its newsroom has even now, so be it." DumpThePicayune.com's McHugh agreed with Chittum's prediction, suggesting that actions as seemingly minor as eliminating the "timespicayune.com" email domain in favor of "nola.com" "may be part of a strategic move to separate the digital and print organizations, so the latter can be jettisoned when the former reaches a sufficient level of profitability."[68]

In addition, all of the Advance newspapers that have gone "digital-first," have ditched perfectly serviceable facilities in favor of high-profile new digs, ostensibly to accelerate the cultural change the newspapers are seeking and to help establish the "Google-Nike kind-of-vibe work environment" he wants for NOLA Media Group, Mathews told the June 2012 New Orleans tech gathering.[69] In a prominent business story published early in August 2012, the company announced that it had leased 27,000-square feet of new penthouse offices in One Canal Place, a prominent high-rise at the foot of Canal Street at the Mississippi River, and adjacent to the French Quarter.[70] "We felt like the physical move was extremely important," Mathews told a February 2013 industry conference. "We wanted to change a culture and move away from the print-centric culture."[71] The thirty-two-story building is also home to Westin New Orleans Canal Place, the Shops at Canal Place, a food court, health club, scores of offices, and a parking garage. "Take an elevator down [from the parking garage], walk past J. Crew and Anthropologie, dodge the shoppers, and hop on another elevator that goes up, past the floor with the Panda Garden knock-off, to the offices of NOLA Media Group," Chittum wrote in his March 2013 *CJR* article. The lease on the property probably runs between $16- and $19-a-square-foot, according to two knowledgeable New Orleans real estate agents, and mandatory parking rental probably tacks on another $100,000 annually, meaning NOLA Media Group is shelling out an estimated $532,000 to $613,000 annually for its new digs.

"It's absolutely stunning," said New Orleans communications consultant Cheron Brylski, who viewed the new offices during the April 2013, open house NOLA Media Group hosted for select members of the community. "The views are amazing, it's so new and clean, and it's really set up for collaboration and meetings, with Wi-Fi available throughout both floors."[72] About six months after most employees made the move, Amoss told Doctor that it has, indeed, helped reporters make the mental shift of producing news round-the-clock rather than for a daily print publication. Some employees haven't been so impressed. "'I work at the mall for a website,'" one NOLA.com reporter told Chittum. When Mathews referred to the office's view of the crescent-shaped bend in the Mississippi River that gave New Orleans its "Crescent City" nickname as the "money shot,"[73] more than a few current and former employees instead invoked the term's other porn-industry-related subtext.

"OCP," as employees call One Canal Place, also gave me my closest near-miss to buttonholing Amoss or Mathews with questions for this book—but at least one of them had other plans. While scheduling my interview with environmental reporter Mark Schleifstein, he also said he would give me a tour of NOLA Media Group's new offices. But when he and I met a week or so later for the interview and I asked about the tour, he responded, "I've been told you're not welcome on the thirty-first or thirty-second floors." "Really? By whom?" I asked. "I really can't say," he replied. At the conclusion of our interview, I again asked him who had rolled up my welcome mat. "Let's just say 'management,'" he responded, with his characteristic Schleffy smirk. "I'm fairly sure all of management feels that way."[74]

I was surprised, not necessarily by the sentiment, but by the execution. But given NOLA Media Group's seemingly compulsive PR blunders over the course of this saga, I shouldn't have been. A perfunctory five-minute tour would have provided me nothing I didn't already know, but this deliberate snub underscored the organization's bunker mentality, and only strengthened my resolve to tell the story as comprehensively and forthrightly as I could.

Most editorial employees had moved into OCP in January 2013 from the newspaper's longtime Howard Avenue headquarters. Even with a smaller editorial staff, there aren't enough seats for everyone who now works out of Canal Place—by design. The newsrooms features "hotel seating," which means most reporters don't have assigned desks, ostensibly because they're expected to be out in the field with their company-issued iPhones and MacBooks, and to sit at any open desk when they're in the office. Most reporters are forbidden to leave personal effects on company desks and are limited to one file cabinet drawer, which was made available first-come, first-served, for reference materials or other resources needed to do their jobs. "It helps control clutter," Mathews told BusinessJournalism. org in February 2013. "We worked hard to make it feel clean and be as paperless as possible." Like Howard Avenue did, the new newsroom also features a video studio, replete with a green screen and anchor desk.

But NOLA Media Group's location on the top floors of the 440-foot-tall skyscraper belies the "easy for the public to access" mantra other Advance newspapers are touting about their new locations. The streets near One Canal Place are difficult to navigate and frequently congested. Upon learning in late August 2012 of NOLA Media Group's plans to relocate much of its staff to the high-rise, some employees immediately raised concerns about their ability to quickly get to breaking news from the location, especially during Carnival and high-traffic events at the Mercedes-Benz Superdome. One of the staff letters sent to Amoss, Cunningham and Lorando in the summer of 2012 also raised the concern and suggested that the company instead pursue presumably more reasonably priced space in the more centrally located neighborhoods of Mid-City or Bywater.

The newspaper's classified advertising department also moved into the offices in late May 2013. The lack of easy access to OCP may discourage customers who want to personally place ads or obituaries, but that is fine with NOLA Media Group's new director of classified advertising verticals, Tricia L. Etienne, according to a former veteran employee of the department. "Trish does not believe that employees should be wasting their time with customers that come in," the former employee said on the condition of anonymity. "She wants them on the phone cold-calling accounts. She thinks that it's ridiculous that people come into the office [to place ads]. She has told us that customers without Internet [access at home] can go to the New Orleans Public Library [to access the Internet], or they can text their obits in. These people have hard-earned cash in their hands, and come to the paper to place ads, and we're not taking ads from walk-ins anymore." Etienne did not respond to an email request for an interview made before this book went to press.

Production and some editing functions remain on Howard

Avenue, along with the printing presses, and circulation and delivery functions and their employees, the latter of whom now technically work for Advance Central Services Louisiana. Although not in the best part of town, the newspaper's longtime home offered employees easy automobile access to just about any point within New Orleans, as well as to the West Bank and neighboring Jefferson Parish. It also sports one of the city's most recognizable architectural features, the *Times-Picayune* clock tower, which remains easily visible, at least as this book goes to press, from the adjacent Pontchartrain Expressway and Broad Street overpass. (An image of the tower is featured on the dust jacket of this book.) In addition to once housing both the newspaper's presses and its newsroom, Howard Avenue also provided employees partially subsidized meals in the building's cafeteria (which was closed in January 2013) and free lot and garage parking. Some employees who continue to work at Howard Avenue have complained about its ghost-town feel, given that it formerly was home to more than five hundred employees, but now houses somewhere in the neighborhood of three hundred.

Alabama Media Group in January 2013 announced it, too, would move employees of the *Birmingham News* and *Mobile Press-Register* from relatively new downtown offices "to space . . . more suitable for the companies' digitally-focused operations." The nearly 120,000-square-foot home of the *Birmingham News*, which was built in only 2006, and its parking lot across the street, went on the market late that month for $21.4 million, al.com reported, while the company intends to keep the adjacent production facility. In Mobile, al.com is looking to sell its entire 245,000-square-foot building for $21.8 million but wants to lease back the production plant from the new owner.[75] The company also has opened new, modern offices in Montgomery, the state's capital. On Independence Day 2013, the *Star-Ledger* became the latest Advance newspaper to announce that it also would vacate and sell its current home in favor of leased office space.

Earlier in the year, al.com said it would move the *Huntsville*

Times – the newspaper I grew up reading, and "the birth city of al.com 15 years ago," then-Alabama Media Group President Cindy Martin told the local WHNT-TV – from its longtime home on the city's Memorial Parkway main drag, to downtown. In what is no doubt another cost-saving move, the newspaper's presses were shut down in July 2012, and the newspaper is now printed on the *Birmingham News*'s presses[76] and trucked the roughly 100 miles north to Huntsville on the three days a week the newspaper is published. Continuing with that line of consolidation, most of the layoffs at Advance's *Express-Times* were driven by the newspaper stilling its presses for the first time since the Civil War era, in favor of printing the publication on the presses of New York's *Staten Island Advance*, the namesake of the Newhouse company,[77] and trucking it the roughly sixty miles to the *Express-Times*'s home of Easton, Pennsylvania.

Rumors have circulated around New Orleans that Advance has similar plans there: to shutter the *Times-Picayune*'s presses, and print the newspaper on the *Press-Register*'s presses, then truck the finished product back to New Orleans, about 150 miles away. The speculation, however, appears to be just that, especially in light of the launch of *TPStreet*, with one insider familiar with both the *Times-Picayune*'s and *Press-Register*'s operations saying it's unlikely that presses at the latter have the additional capacity needed to also accommodate the *Times-Picayune* press runs.

Also in January, Advance's Syracuse Media Group held a news conference to unveil plans for its new downtown headquarters in "street-level offices in Merchants Commons," a renovated downtown office-and-apartment complex. It will be governed by the same "clutter-free" and no assigned seating policies as OCP.[78] Initially set for an April 2013 move-in, the date was delayed, based on photos of the construction posted in May 2013 on Syracuse.com.[79] As is the case in New Orleans (at least for now), and Mobile, the *Post-Standard*'s sister company, Advance Central Services Syracuse, will remain at the newspaper's existing facility to oversee printing, production, and other functions, such as accounting and human resources. Not so in the Keystone State, where both the PA Media Group and Advance Central Services Pennsylvania will move into new, but separate facilities.[80] All of the moves to new offices continued a precedent that began when Advance closed the *Ann Arbor News*, and AnnArbor.com abandoned the newspaper's downtown headquarters of seventy-three years in favor of a leased "hub" three blocks away. Other hubs also were opened or planned around Michigan.

The one part of the financial equation that doesn't make readily apparent sense is Advance's willingness to spend considerable amounts of money on high-end, leased real estate, especially in cases where the company already owned relatively new and perfectly functional facilities. It's unclear whether legal considerations led to the moves into the new offices and the jettisoning of original and long-established corporate entities. Does creating new companies and physically leaving behind legacy offices help Advance to further legally distance itself from any residual obligations associated with the Pledge and make it more difficult for laid-off or current employees to win lawsuits like the one brought by former *Press-Register* publisher Howard Bronson? "The ultimate question here is whether Advance thought it had a serious legal liability due to the Pledge," *CJR's* Chittum wrote in late June 2013 about the revoked job security pact and whether Advance's company "name game" changes are designed to eradicate any lingering legal liability under it. "Can you promise employees that 'no full-time, non-represented, regular employee will ever be laid off because of economic conditions or because of the introduction of new technology' and then unilaterally say 'Oopsie! We don't mean that anymore'? I don't think so."[81]

To add to their financial challenges, the current generation of Newhouses apparently also will face an enormous tax bill when Si and Donald Newhouse pass away, the result of what is regarded as one of the wiliest tax dodges in the history of US family estate tax law. In the protracted, but little scrutinized US Tax Court lawsuit between the Internal Revenue Service and the estate of Sam Newhouse, the government charged that the estate so grossly underestimated the estate taxes due after the 1979 death of the elder Newhouse that it levied, in addition to the $609 million principal tax bill, a $304 million civil penalty for deliberately attempting to deceive the government. It was then, and perhaps still is, the largest tax assessment ever filed by the US government in a family estate case. In submitting their initial $48.7 million estate tax payment, Donald and Si Newhouse and their army of attorneys, accountants, and bankers claimed that control of the company was shared among the family, and not predominantly held by Sam Newhouse. Under that structure, the elder Newhouse's stake in the company was about $181.9 million, generating the lower tax payment submitted by Si and Donald Newhouse in their capacity as co-executors of their father's estate. (The trial and its implications were detailed in Thomas Maier's 1994 book (updated in 1997), *Newhouse: All the Glitter, Power, & Glory of America's Richest Media Empire & the Secretive Man Behind It.*)

Had the IRS been victorious, its nearly $1 billion tax bill probably would have forced the Newhouse family to sell some of its assets, Maier and other observers concluded, and even could have forced the notoriously secretive private company to take its company public in order to raise enough money via the capital markets to satisfy an enormous IRS judgment. The glacial progress toward a resolution—Sam Newhouse died in 1979, but a final stipulated decision of the US Tax Court was not rendered until September 1990—allowed the company to grow far more quickly than it ever could have had its coffers been depleted or even emptied entirely by paying the government's original tax bill, Maier observed in *Newhouse*. The family, however, prevailed in the seven-week 1989 trial that the IRS is widely viewed to have bungled, thereby ensuring that the Newhouse empire remained intact.[82]

But upon the death of Si and Donald Newhouse, their heirs will apparently finally face the Tax Man. "A special arrangement" reached between the IRS and the Newhouse estate when the government opted not to appeal the Newhouse victory, means the full value of the Newhouse empire will be subject to estate taxes when the brothers die, Maier reported.[83] In accordance with US Tax Court document retention policies, the trial's entire record was destroyed in 2011, employees at the court said in mid-May 2013, and several attempts to learn more about the special agreement reached to govern the estate tax assessment upon the death of Si and Donald Newhouse were unsuccessful. However, given that the Newhouse brothers together are now worth an estimated $15.4 billion, any estate tax bill levied against their actual net worth could be a colossal obligation for the family's third generation to satisfy. The question remains as to how heavily those concerns are playing into decisions made by those now at the helm of Advance, part of that third generation in any family business often faced with the burden of estate and income taxes that can lead "to family friction and ultimately collapse," as noted in the lawsuit brought against the company by former *Press-Register* publisher Howard Bronson. The suit went on to say that Donald Newhouse reassured Bronson that "the Newhouse family had the tax issues worked out for three more generations," ensuring the company's continuity and stability.[84]

CHAPTER IX

The Ricky, Jim, and James Show

With Donald and Steven Newhouse largely sticking to their traditional "no comment" response when it came to answering questions about NOLA Media Group and the future of the *Times-Picayune*, the burden of responding to an angry public and skeptical news media fell to soon-to-be publisher and president Ricky Mathews, vice president of content and editor Jim Amoss, and to a lesser extent, director of state news and sports James O'Byrne.

The NOLA Media Group road show to rehabilitate the company's battered reputation began as soon as the layoffs were announced. Late on the morning of June 12, 2012, the day that employees were told whether they would be asked to stay or be terminated at the beginning of the fall, a video of Jim Amoss went live on NOLA.com. In the three-minute address, Amoss laid out the rationale for the draconian changes, but then made what many soon-to-be-laid-off employees thought was both an incongruous and insulting statement: "This is a difficult week at our paper. We have had to let go of some wonderful employees. It is a painful transition. We also will be hiring to increase coverage of areas we know are important to our readers."[1]

"If those employees were so wonderful, why let them go?" asked former St. Bernard Picayune section editor Kim Sensebe Gritter, a twenty-year veteran who lost her job as a result of the changes. "If they had come to me and said, 'We need you to take a big pay cut if you want to stay,' I would have taken it. Why not give us that option first?"[2]

A day later, Amoss appeared on the *PBS Newshour* with David Carr, the *New York Times* reporter who had broken the story in late May about the changes coming to the newspaper. A nervous-looking Amoss appeared unprepared and uncomfortable when anchor Judy Woodruff asked him an inevitable question: Would the newspaper be able to deliver the same quality news product with one-half of its previous staff? The uneasiness of Amoss's answer is startlingly apparent when watching the interview (which is available to view on the *Newshour* website). It's also one of those instances in which print cannot approach the power of video, but what follows is an exact transcription of his response: "Oh, that's, that's a misleading figure. Uhm, we had, uh, severances, layoffs yesterday, and uhm, and we, uh, are losing somewhere, uh, in the 40 percent-plus realm, but we also will be rehiring, so that when, uhm, all is said and done, uh, we will have a news operation that overall is about 14 percent to 15 percent smaller than now." As mentioned earlier, Amoss's assertion appears to be based on equating nearly 40 stringers and freelancers — some of whom contribute to the site and the newspaper infrequently — to full-time, experienced employees. The full-time headcount in mid-May 2013 clocked in at around 130, a nearly 26 percent reduction from the size of the staff before the layoffs.

During the PBS interview, Amoss also rejected Carr's contention that the purging of bench strength — in the form of experienced reporters, editors, and photographers who represented the news outlet's "muscle memory" as Carr put it — would lead to "the loss of a kind of civic common." "If I believed that, I wouldn't be sitting here," Amoss responded. "Everything that I will be focused on will be geared toward preserving that . . . Readers will just have to hold us accountable to that promise that I'm making."[3]

A day later, Amoss took to a much more familiar communications medium — writing — penning a front-page *Times-Picayune* commentary in which he again laid out the case for Advance's radical new approach against the backdrop of a deeply troubled and rapidly declining industry:

> Despite the economic challenges, our newspaper has remained a powerful brand with a loyal readership and unparalleled advertising reach in print and online. But equally clear is that we can't sustain the old business model in the face of irreversible print ad and readership trends. The demand for digital news content will continue to rise. And news organizations that do not position themselves to serve their digital audience risk a slow, irrelevant death. Our news organization has decided not to sit idly by as passive witnesses to our own decline.[4]

Four days later, in another front-page commentary in Sunday's newspaper that clocked in at nearly 1,800 words (or more than fifty-one column inches in newspaper parlance, longer than many page one Sunday articles), Ricky Mathews sprinkled his opinion piece with a reminder that he grew up on the Gulf Coast, including recollections of his days as a delivery boy for the paper he would one day lead to a Pulitzer Prize, the *Sun-Herald* in Biloxi, Mississippi; his lifelong love for New Orleans; and other personal attributes shared presumably to begin forging a connection with the *Times-Picayune*'s readers. He spent the bulk of the tract, however, arguing for "digital-first" and explaining why the drastic changes were necessary:

> Before we faced economic doomsday, we decided to build a new model, a combination of print and online that gives us a chance to achieve a sustainable business and content model. Our goal is to build a stable, thriving multimedia company that can make New Orleans and Louisiana proud. With the creation of NOLA Media Group, we will position ourselves to be able to serve our readers and advertisers for many years to come. We chose a path that we believe gives us the best chance of preserving the journalistic excellence of the *Times-Picayune*. The *Times-Picayune* and NOLA.com are here to stay. We have a commitment to this community. What this plan represents is an entrepreneurial investment in our future.[5]

In presenting their arguments, both men evoked Hurricane Katrina, and the resilience and courage the storm and its aftermath inspired: Mathews in talking about how he and his family weathered the hurricane in their Biloxi home; Amoss, as noted earlier, in how the storm unintentionally, but irrefutably, laid the path for the newspaper's digital transformation.

Conjuring the most devastating event in the city's long history to support a business decision that would cost hundreds of people their jobs and deprive the city of an important daily ritual did not, by and large, sit well with the newspaper's and NOLA.com's readers. "Ricky Mathews and Jim Amoss point to disasters of the past and predictions of the future to justify ending everyday production of the *Times-Picayune*," New Orleans resident Christina Albers wrote in a letter to the editor published in the newspaper. "People have seen through the Katrina appeal."[6] In the fourth of its six-part series, "The Murder of The *Times-Picayune*," the website Nola Anarcha delivered withering criticism of Mathews's commentary. "In his recent Pearl-Harbor-sized, above-the-fold, front-page *Times-Picayune* advertisement for himself, Ricky writes, 'The true story of our effort will be that we want the story that is told of our efforts to be that we embraced the amazing entrepreneurial spirit that has evolved since Hurricane Katrina.' If you can parse that f—ing mess, I doff my cap."[7]

Renée Peck, a former thirty-two-year veteran of the *Times-Picayune*, took a far softer approach in a column she wrote for NolaVie, the nonprofit lifestyle and culture website she co-founded after taking a company-sweetened early retirement in the first wave of buyouts in 2009. In the column, she talked about the "two-way street" of respect, reliability, and empathy that needs to exist between the newspaper and community if the *Times-Picayune* is to succeed with its "digital-first" strategy. At the end of a list of things the community expected from the newspaper and its website, she concluded, "We'll keep coming back if you will please stop talking about the way Hurricane Katrina bound us together, when you are tearing us apart."[8]

O'Byrne abruptly canceled a scheduled appearance before an influential neighborhood association the same day the layoffs occurred,[9] but he joined Mathews at a gathering of the city's fledgling tech community a week later. The two men apparently were unaware the audience would include Kevin Allman, editor of New Orleans' alternative weekly *Gambit*, whom some staffers speculated O'Byrne was trying to avoid when he cancelled the neighborhood association appearance. Allman promptly penned a dispatch about Mathews's and O'Byrne's presentation to the tech group. "I know that the layoff at the *Times-Picayune* seems significant," Allman reported O'Byrne as saying, "but it's important to realize that we're advertising for about fifty people in the new digital company. So you end up in a space where you're going from about 165 down to 140." The new headcount O'Byrne referenced was lower than the one Amoss repeatedly has used, but still exceeded what the full-time newsroom headcount would be once the layoffs were completed and new hires were made through the first half of 2013.

During the presentation, Mathews commented, "I've been talking till I don't have a voice anymore, explaining to people what we're doing." However, as Allman pointed out, Mathews had not addressed his new staff since Phelps had introduced him as the new publisher three months earlier and hadn't even been in the building on the day of the layoffs to support his managers charged with carrying them out. Mathews also told the tech gathering that he recently had met with New Orleans Mayor Mitch Landrieu for "about three hours, and he [Landrieu] got it immediately." Allman updated his online report hours later, after speaking to a source in Landrieu's office, who said the office "wouldn't characterize the meeting in those terms, either in the amount of time spent or in the mayor's takeaway."[10] (Mathews regularly returned to the office from meetings with community leaders and declared to employees "they understand my vision. They're on board," recalled one former employee who spoke on the condition of anonymity. "Save the Picayune" founder Anne Milling was one such prominent individual who Mathews told his staff had come to embrace the company's new direction after he met with her, the former employee said. Milling, however, laughed out loud during a March 2013 interview when asked whether she had ever told Mathews she understood his vision.)

A few days later, NOLA.com | *Times-Picayune* published an article reporting that most newsroom employees who had been asked to stay with the organization had agreed to do so, but noted that eight newsroom employees had rejected offers, many having secured new employment in the two weeks since the layoffs were communicated.[11] By the time this book went to press, that number had swelled to almost three dozen of the roughly ninety who had been asked to stay either originally or after having their terminations rescinded or regular contributor contracts offered. Those who left voluntarily cut across all functions and beats, from the state capital bureau to business, from the outdoors editor to the society columnist.[12] At least two newsroom staffers — part-time photographer Matthew Hinton and Special Sections manager Victor Andrews — declined to stay when they were offered contractual positions at substantially less pay, and with no benefits. More than a dozen of those the *Times-Picayune* had sought to retain defected to the *Advocate*, and in the case of Marshall, to investigative and public policy website the Lens. In addition, Jaquetta White, a New Orleans native who had departed to the *Nashville Tennessean* shortly after the changes were announced, returned to Louisiana, and the *Advocate*, in June 2013, as did former zone layout editor Jennifer Brown, via a five-month stint at the *Lafayette (La.) Daily Advertiser*. After months of indecision on the part of its celebrated restaurant critic and food industry reporter, Brett Anderson, the newspaper announced in June 2013 that Anderson would return after completing his Nieman Fellowship at the end of the summer.[13]

Although not as well publicized, other departments also encountered difficulty retaining employees, usually because they were offered part-time jobs in lieu of full-time ones. Roughly a dozen production employees were asked to stay on part-time to help produce the special *Black and Gold* New Orleans Saints Monday tabloid. However, only two employees accepted the employment offers, and one only after the position was made full-time, reported a longtime production employee who was laid off, but remained in touch with those still working in the newspaper's production operations. "There was simply a lack of trust in what your quality of life would be if you stayed," the former employee, who spoke on the condition of anonymity because of his concerns related to continuing severance payments, said about colleagues who rejected offers to stay. "Working in the press room can be physically challenging. And although the paper was being delivered three days a week, it took at least five days to print all of the sections. I think they felt that the workload and their schedules would just get crazier with fewer people." Others wanted to accept the financial cushion a severance provided while they explored other employment options they wished they had pursued earlier in their lives, the employee said. And a couple of others were simply very angry. "'Well, let's see, you didn't want me two weeks ago, but now that you need more people to make [Saints owner] Tom Benson happy, I'm good enough,'" is how some production employees felt, the former employee said.

The company's announcement of its impending move to One Canal Place was the organization's next attempt at positive PR, but it also failed to achieve the reactions the company undoubtedly hoped for. More than two dozen readers (including me) reacted to the NOLA.com report heralding the move. "Again, I will respectfully inquire as to how NOLA Media Group can financially manage to lease this prime space after all of the hoopla over not printing the *Times-Picayune* seven days a week because there isn't enough money to be made by doing so?" one reader noted. "Was it the savings from cutting back the number of staff that generated enough funds to be able to do this?"

Especially after they were regularly excoriated in early news media reports (mostly for the disastrous way they communicated the coming changes and terminated many of their employees), Mathews, Amoss, and O'Byrne began to adopt somewhat of a bunker mentality, in which public statements and news media interviews became the exception, rather than the rule. (Neither Mathews, Amoss, nor O'Byrne has ever responded to requests for comment or interviews from Allman, who has far-and-away led coverage of the saga.) "Nobody knows those guys anymore," said one veteran employee who continues to work for NOLA Media Group, and who spoke to me only on the condition of anonymity because of his fear of retribution. "Jim Amoss, Mark Lorando, I used to know those guys. As soon as this happened, they circled the wagons, and they seemed they were told how to behave to the masses. It was very non-emotional."

And while he has been willing to speak to business and community groups, Mathews deviated from the public persona he had cultivated in Mobile and had not given a single in-person interview to a New Orleans news media outlet besides NOLA.com | *Times-Picayune* at the time this book went to press. (He did, however, supply statements to WWL-TV and WDSU-TV for stories the stations did that spring.) "I'm really surprised at the way I hear he's sequestered himself in New Orleans," said a respected veteran reporter who previously worked under Mathews on the Gulf Coast, but who also spoke on the condition of anonymity because of the reporter's perceptions of Mathews's continued influence in the community. "That's just not his personality." Mathews and Amoss did continue to make limited presentations to industry and business groups, and to offer

Advocate publisher David Manship announces the launch of the newspaper's New Orleans edition in September 2012. The newspaper created the edition and initially hired a New Orleans staff comprised solely of former *Times-Picayune* employees who lost their jobs after the *T-P* announced its new "digital-first" strategy and moved to thrice-weekly publication. *Photo by* Advocate *staff photographer Richard Alan Hannon, courtesy of the* Advocate.

occasional responses to select news media, notably the *New York Times*, the *Wall Street Journal*, and the news site for the journalism think tank and continuing education organization the Poynter Institute.

Mathews and Amoss also continued to use the pages of their newspaper and website to try to influence public opinion about Advance's "digital-first" strategy. Throughout the remainder of the summer, NOLA Media Group detailed promotions and new hires, both in print and digitally, often while soon-to-be-laid-off employees continued to toil in the very jobs for which their successors were being named. The spirits of the beaten-down staff got a lift when, in September 2012, the *Advocate* announced that it would return to the New Orleans metro area in direct response to the *Times-Picayune*'s impending cutbacks. (The *Advocate* had shuttered its New Orleans bureau and laid off nearly fifty employees in May 2009, at the height of the Great Recession.) "From the moment that they announced that they were going to a three-day-a-week newspaper, we thought there would be tremendous opportunities for the *Advocate* to fill a void they're creating," Richard Manship, then-president and CEO of Capital City Press, owner of the newspaper, said in a July 2012 report in the newspaper.[14] Steven Newhouse responded by telling Poynter.org, "I say bring them on. Competition is great. We're not afraid at all. We're gonna have a really fantastic website and great print editions, and we'll let the readers decide."[15]

NOLA Media Group a few weeks later announced that it had signed a long-term lease for a new state capital bureau in downtown Baton Rouge, from which its expanded sixteen-member bureau would operate. NOLA Media Group executives insisted that the move had been in the works for six months and was not in response to the *Advocate*'s re-entry into the New Orleans market.[16] (The *Advocate* already had hired seven laid-off *Times-Picayune* employees.[17]) Launched in October 2012 to correspond with the *Times-Picayune*'s move to a three-day-a-week publishing schedule, the *Advocate* reported that by December its New Orleans edition had a circulation of 23,500, including 16,000 daily subscribers, despite serious delivery hiccups some area residents reported. "Both are strong [circulation] numbers for such a young paper, and it's hard to imagine that many or most of them aren't coming at the expense of the *Times-Picayune*," Ryan Chittum concluded on *CJR*'s website in December 2012.[18]

Earlier that month, O'Byrne and NOLA Media Group

vice president and business manager David Francis made an appearance on *Out to Lunch,* a business and public affairs show produced by New Orleans's National Public Radio affiliate, WWNO. In an episode titled "The Some-Times Picayune," O'Byrne and Francis painted a very upbeat assessment of NOLA Media Group. "We've been pleasantly pleased with what we've seen since October 1, when we launched the three-day-a-week newspaper," Francis said. "From a circulation standpoint, the passion . . . for the paper and the 175 years we've been producing it, has resulted in, actually, in an increase in our circulation. Those who were concerned about what this may mean for the community . . . have found themselves embracing us again. We saw people's attitudes and behaviors change, to the point that now we're very satisfied and we've exceeded our targets in circulation." Although Francis didn't specify what those internal circulation targets were, numbers the newspaper's brass reported to industry circulation and online readership auditing organization, the Alliance for Audited Media, released a few months later detailed the print publication's continuing circulation decline. Sunday print circulation fell more than 9 percent year over year, AAM figures through March 31, 2013 show. Because the newspaper no longer published daily, NOLA Media Group could not supply an average daily circulation figure that AAM has traditionally reported. However, its Wednesday circulation dropped almost 7 percent, and its Friday circulation fell nearly 8 percent.[19]

O'Byrne offered an equally glowing appraisal of the digital side of the business. While not quantifying the base on which the growth occurred, he said the company has enjoyed 20 to 25 percent upticks in digital revenues over the past four years, "and that trend has continued. It's been quite a pleasant surprise how well the launch has gone."[20]

Joey Hogh, an executive with the law office of Raymond J. Brandt and Brandt Management Limited, owner of the region's largest independent group of car dealerships and historically one of the largest advertisers in the newspaper, has a different perspective. After essentially eliminating "a very significant" annual print advertising budget with the *Times-Picayune* following the switch to a three-day-a-week publication schedule, "we're doing stuff with NOLA.com, but at a fraction of the cost of what we were doing with the print *Times-Picayune*. We upped [online advertising] some, but not much," Hogh said in a May 2013 interview. "They seemed to think this market was only important enough to publish three days a week, so we decided we didn't need to advertise in the paper anymore."[21]

Rick Haase, president of New Orleans-headquartered Latter & Blum, Inc., the largest real estate agency in the Gulf South and the *Times-Picayune*'s largest advertiser in the real estate category, concurred that the newspaper's retreat from print is accelerating the inevitable, but slow, withdrawal by advertisers. "The actions they have taken over the past months are driving us away from their print publication," Haase said in May 2013, adding that NOLA.com simply doesn't compete favorably with leading real estate websites. "We have always supported local businesses and will continue to do so, but if [NOLA Media Group] thought cutting its number of print editions was going to drive our print spend into the NOLA.com digital space, they made a serious error. We think that they are really hurting themselves." Haase pointed to two of the other biggest industry sectors that advertise in newspapers—jobs and automobiles—and noted that advertisers haven't moved from print to NOLA.com, but instead to Monster.com and AutoTrader.com. "When it comes to real estate, [print advertisers are] moving to Trulia, Zillow and Realtor.com," he said. "By trying to force people into their digital space, [NOLA Media Group] is instead forcing people completely away from their enterprise."[22]

H.D. Lanaux, whose five-generation upscale Langenstein's is the region's oldest independent grocer, said his businesses' decision to stop advertising in the newspaper in early July 2013 was more complex and evolutionary. The move came after surveys showed that only about 20 percent of customers saw the company's weekly *Times-Picayune* ads, but the decision ultimately was driven by cost. "I think the final straw was when they went to three-day distribution and they barely dropped their rates," Lanaux said. In response, Langenstein's suspended advertising in the newspaper beginning in early July through the end of 2013. During those six months, the company instead will focus on digital media advertising and direct marketing, including internally produced e-newsletters and digital ads customers can sign up to receive; social media; and community events at which Langenstein chefs prepare complimentary cuisine that serves as a culinary billboard of sorts. At year's end, the company plans to re-evaluate its sales and advertising expenditures and make any needed adjustments. The move appeared to make sense because "even the *Times-Picayune* seems to believe in the move to digital," Lanaux said, adding that the change to three-day-a-week publication probably only accelerated the inevitable for his business.

One issue related to the new publishing schedule that did affect the company had to do with ad deadlines. Langenstein's previously advertised in Thursday's newspaper, but it was forced to switch to Wednesday under the new publication schedule, which posed a problem marketing the higher-end fresh seafood and meat for which the grocer is known. Lanaux's team previously "really worked Mondays" calling suppliers to negotiate the best prices on the freshest products that would be available later that week, information that could still make it into Thursday ads. But the grocer now must submit ads to NOLA Media Group on Fridays at the latest, which significantly limited what higher-end perishable products could be advertised. Price, however, remained the biggest factor. "I've been with the *Times-Picayune* long enough that our decision does make me nervous because I've always considered it the sacred cow of advertising," he said. "But we'd have to lose a lot of business to compensate for the cost."[23]

The reduction in publishing frequency also influenced longtime major advertiser Ralph Brennan Restaurant Group to advertise "significantly less," executive vice president Charlee Williamson said. The company traditionally relied on the *Times-Picayune* more for promotions than brand advertising and found that advertising earlier in the week was most effective because that was when locals made weekend restaurant dining plans. The company previously favored Tuesdays as a major advertising day, to correspond with restaurant critic Brett Anderson's widely read reports in the newspaper's Living section. Since the switch to a Sunday-Wednesday-Friday publication schedule, however, Wednesday is the only day when advertising in the newspaper consistently makes sense for the company's five upscale restaurants. "Four days a week, people don't think about the newspaper as the leading source of news and information," Williamson said, noting that like Langenstein's, the changes at the newspaper accelerated her company's own digital jump, prompting it to begin relying primarily on an internally produced customer email list earlier than it likely would have.[24]

O'Byrne apparently jumped on an airplane shortly after his and Francis's WWNO interview because he was in Chicago the next day, making a presentation to the Inland Press Foundation's Executive Program for Innovative Change for senior newspaper executives. During his presentation, O'Byrne was more candid than anyone within NOLA Media Group publicly had ever been about the changes. Inland Press Association's publications editor Mark Fitzgerald, initially unaware of an expectation O'Byrne had that his comments were off-the-record, tweeted some of O'Byrne's remarks, which I saw and subsequently re-tweeted via the dashTHIRTYdash account and then used in a post on the blog I had set up for dashTHIRTYdash. Fitzgerald's tweets reported that O'Byrne shared the following insight into the newspaper's wrenching changes:

- Asked whether he had any "regrets on the *Times-Picayune* transition," O'Byrne cited the planning of the changes—which involved the secret, off-site meetings, exclusion of editors later laid off, and staff members reading first about the coming layoffs and changes in the *New York Times*. It was "arrogant to think we could keep a secret in a newsroom."

- Going from a daily to three-days-a-week has "not [been] painless, not seamless in any way."

- "It didn't help that we became so bland," in contrast with the *Times-Picayune's* "passionate reporting during Katrina."

- "The problem with seven-day papers is no one has time to read them." (However, a complaint some *Times-Picayune* subscribers have had is that they don't have time to read the two or three days of content crammed into the home-delivered Wednesday and Friday weekday editions, which, in addition to several days of news, sports, and living/entertainment reports, also includes several days of traditional daily features, such as cartoons, horoscopes, and puzzles.)

- "Being [the] only newspaper in town had no value for us. Being the place that people go for information—that had value for us."[25]

Within hours of the dashTHIRTYdash blog post, Fitzgerald deleted his earlier tweets,[26] leaving the blog post as the only publicly available account of O'Byrne's remarks.

A couple of months later, Amoss and Mathews teamed up to present at the Key Executives Mega Conference, sponsored by three industry organizations that, coincidentally, was meeting in New Orleans for the first time since NOLA Media Group's changes. Mathews's and Amoss's hour-long session, titled "On the Front End of Media Change in the Entrepreneurial City of New Orleans,"[27] detailed what was involved in transforming NOLA Media Group into a more digitally oriented organization. "This is a fifty-chapter book," Mathews told the gathering, according to Poynter.org. "The first chapter was we decided to make a bold change. This is chapter two. So far, so good, but we've got a lot to learn." Mathews said daily print circulation between the third quarter of 2012 (before the print change) and the fourth quarter of the year (after the change) increased 1 percent, while Sunday circulation was flat. "We're not kidding ourselves," he said. "We're trying to slow the decline." He and Amoss then touted what they characterized as dramatically climbing online and mobile figures.

"And let me dispel the notion that we have gutted our newsroom," Amoss said, citing a headcount of 181 before the changes (higher than the 173 newsroom employees the newspaper reported in its own article about the June 12, 2012 layoffs[28]), and 155 after the staff reduction, which, as noted earlier, appears to include the nearly forty part-time freelancers and high school prep sports stringers with which NOLA Media Group now contracts. Mathews and Amoss also highlighted NOLA Media Group's work during the two weeks leading up to and including the 2013 Super Bowl, which took place February 3 in New Orleans, only a couple of weeks before the conference. During that period, NOLA.com amassed 1.9 million page views of the more than 2,000 stories, photos, and videos it produced related to the event, Mathews reported. But NOLA.com isn't just about sports and entertainment, Amoss said: "Our embracing of the digital future is in no way a diminishment of the kind of journalism we've always been committed to as a news organization."[29]

Although the CBS news show *60 Minutes* had spent several days in New Orleans in July interviewing a number of people, including Amoss, New Orleans Mayor Mitch Landrieu, and "Save the Picayune" founder Anne Milling, for a planned segment about the newspaper, its broadcast wasn't confirmed until early January. Apparently making a pre-emptive strike against an anticipated critical report, Amoss again took to the pages of NOLA.com, with another prominent commentary published the day before the TV news magazine's report aired. "Four months ago [when *60 Minutes* traveled to New Orleans to report its story], our changes were still in the offing," Amoss wrote. "Readers had to accept on faith our assurances that we would maintain the journalistic excellence they have come to expect from us. That took a leap of faith . . . Now that we have more than three months under our belt, you have a basis for judging our performance." NOLA Media Group has since produced "stories and features that we believe bespeak our commitment to enterprising, in-depth journalism." Amoss detailed six major investigative and enterprise reports NOLA Media Group had produced in that time, and highlighted its state capital, arts, dining, entertainment, sports, and community coverage.

However, most of the nearly ninety reader comments posted to the commentary voiced skepticism. "It's hard to believe that the Newhouses are truly interested in quality when so many of the seasoned *Picayune* reporters were let go, and — your explanations notwithstanding — when owners think every few days is sufficient for a hard copy paper," wrote one commenter. "The tangible, print *T-P* was both part of the culture and the conveyor of the rest of the culture here, and the great unifier of the populace," another reader wrote. "Mr. Newhouse let us down, quality has suffered, the website should supplement, not replace, the flagship product, and — believe me — brand loyalty will be difficult to re-establish."[30]

One of the most compelling and perplexing questions of this entire saga centers on Amoss. One of six sons born into a prominent New Orleans family, he graduated *magna cum laude* from Yale University and studied European literature at Oxford University as a Rhodes scholar. He then returned home in 1974 and began his ascension to the top post in New Orleans journalism. He was an intern and reporter with the *States-Item* before it merged with the *Times-Picayune* in 1980. After a roughly three-month stint as bureau chief in St. Bernard Parish, Amoss was named city editor, then metro editor a year later, followed by another promotion, this time to associate editor, in 1988. A year later, he rose to the editorship of the newspaper under somewhat still mysterious circumstances. Amoss had been selected for a Nieman Fellowship at Harvard University, and he and his family had packed and were departing imminently for Cambridge, Massachusetts, when then-editor Charlie Ferguson stunningly retired, and Amoss was named to succeed him. To this day, only a handful of people know the reason for the completely unexpected departure of Ferguson, who was only fifty-three at the time. (As he consistently has with news reporters, Ferguson declined to comment for this book on the reason for his early retirement.)

Amoss's ascension heralded the beginning of the era in which the newspaper—and by extension, he—rose to national and international prominence. In addition to leading the *Times-Picayune* during the award of all four of its Pulitzer Prizes, Amoss in 1996 received the National Press Foundation's George Beveridge Jr. Editor of the Year Award (later renamed in honor of the *Washington Post*'s legendary editor, Ben Bradlee) from the National Press Foundation.[31] In 2006, the year following Katrina, he won just about every award bestowed upon a newspaper editor, including being named "Editor of the Year" by *Editor & Publisher* magazine, receiving the NPF's Chairman's Citation for the newspaper's coverage of hurricanes Katrina and Rita; the American Society of News Editors' Award for Editorial Leadership[32]; and the 2006-07 Anvil of Freedom Award from the Edward W. Estlow International Center for Journalism and New Media at the University of Denver.[33] That year also saw him named Jesuit High School's "Alumni of the Year," and receiving Gruner + Jahr's Henri Nannen Prize, Germany's equivalent of the Pulitzer Prize. (Amoss spent part of his childhood and teen years in Germany and Belgium, speaks fluent German and French, and has referred humorously to the relative lack of practical applicability to newspaper journalism of his senior thesis on German novelist Thomas Mann.[34]) That year also fell within his nine-year term as a member of the Pulitzer Prize Board, a stint that began in 2003 and ended as co-chair in 2011-12.[35]

In short, Amoss was at the pinnacle of his profession and was arguably one of the most respected and venerated natives of contemporary New Orleans. It has been fascinating to observe someone who has spent his career largely either speaking truth to power or encouraging his underlings to do so, behaving in the way he has during this difficult chapter in the history of his historic employer. "I think there's an enormous amount of disappointment about the changes going on in the *Times-Picayune*, and disappointment that Jim has thrown in with it," veteran reporter Bruce Nolan said in a profile of Amoss published in the summer of 2012 in the *American Journalism Review*. To Nolan's point, why did Amoss choose to support a business strategy that many in the industry think is deeply flawed at best, and perhaps even designed to ultimately deplete and perhaps discard the very organization to which he's devoted his career? Why, in the closing chapters of a storied career, did he choose to decimate his newsroom and fire so many people he worked with for decades, rather than retire, as his former boss, publisher Ashton Phelps, Jr., did? And if he somehow decided that Advance's "digital-first" plan was sound and best executed by him, why had he allowed it to be so bungled and poorly communicated?

Widely regarded as an intellectual, but emotionally inscrutable, leader—retired metro editor Jed Horne told *AJR* that Amoss is "'sphinx-like,'" and "not always forthcoming in conversations"—Amoss's public statements on his decision to stay have carefully trod the company line. They have contained little remorse or empathy over what was done to the lives of the hundreds of people who once worked for him and his newspaper. "Anytime you're engaged in a change of this scale, you'll make some good decisions and some not-so-good decisions," he told *AJR*, which is about as close to regret or contrition as he's expressed.

Unqualified support for Amoss is difficult to come by in New Orleans these days, although it is offered by a seemingly unlikely source: his predecessor, Ferguson, whose abrupt retirement almost twenty-five years ago cleared the way for Amoss's ascension. "They're very fortunate to have him as the face of this," Ferguson said in a March 2013 interview. "If Jim were not here, I don't know who would be the person out front, making the statements that need to be made."[36]

Some of his current and former co-workers have given him the benefit of the doubt, saying he stayed to preserve as much as he could. "I think he stayed in place with hopes that he could mitigate some of the worst repercussions in bloodshed and pain," Horne told *AJR* in the summer of 2012. "Somebody who assumes that role always runs the risk of enabling what they hope to avoid. It'll be the wisdom of hindsight as to whether he softened the blow or rolled over and let hatchet men inflict the pain and bring down the paper."[37] One of Amoss's longest and closest friends, Dean Baquet, who is a New Orleans native, *States-Item* and *Times-Picayune* alumnus, and now managing editor of news operations for the *New York Times*, declined to be interviewed for this book, but spoke to *AJR* for its profile of Amoss. "I get that he's taken a lot of heat in New Orleans," Baquet told *AJR*. "I don't know anything about the finances of the *Times-Picayune*, but I think when you got a guy who really loves the paper and the city, if he becomes involved in something as significant as these cuts, you have to believe they have to do something like this. He's not some corporate guy who would just do what they told him to do." Although Baquet asked *AJR*, "What would have been accomplished by [Amoss] retiring? I think the greater act of leadership is to do it yourself," when Baquet faced a similar quandary in his own career six years earlier, he chose the path Amoss rejected. As editor of the *Los Angeles Times*, Baquet resigned in November 2006 after publicly opposing more newsroom cuts he felt would mortally wound the publication. His stance sparked a bit of a revolt against the Tribune Company, which owns the California newspaper, when more than 600 newsroom employees signed a petition directed at Tribune backing their editor.[38]

More recent *Times-Picayune* staff assessments of Amoss have been more equivocal. "He's the captain that decided to go down with the ship," a reporter still working in the newsroom told *CJR* in March 2013. "He's a thinker. He's not a business guy. He's doing the best with what he's got." In that same article, Amoss said he had decided to stay because he's confident that Advance is committed to remaining in business long-term and determining "an intellectually rigorous way how to do so."[39]

A few former and continuing *Times-Picayune* staffers agree that Amoss indeed sees the digital-first challenge in this way. "I've gotten to know him better now since October [2012] than in all of my previous years with the paper," said one veteran staffer, who spoke on the condition of anonymity because of his fear of retribution for talking to me about the boss. "From a communications perspective, he sees this as fascinating and challenging. People have expressed that we're Steven Newhouse's guinea pigs, and I think [Amoss] sees himself as the Steve Jobs of the print and digital worlds." Nolan, who has known Amoss longer than anyone in the newsroom, has his own assessment. "Jim saw this as an opportunity to leave a lasting mark on the industry, and I think they persuaded him that this was a winning strategy," Nolan observed in March 2013. "They did one of two things: they appealed to his vanity or they appealed to his loyalty—or both. They probably portrayed it as 'this is an enormous leap, but the full resources of a deep-pocketed organization will be behind you, and you're the only person who can successfully bring it to fruition.' And I don't get that. But this is a case where everyone has to make his own decision and live with it."

Also surprising is how thin-skinned Amoss has been on the matter. This is especially astonishing because of the the high expectations the *Times-Picayune* has of its reporters to aggressively pursue stories—even when those inquiries and investigations make people's lives uncomfortable or even difficult, and in some cases, threatens their livelihoods. Now that the tables are turned, it's striking how seemingly unwilling they've been to take their lumps and acknowledge that this process has been so badly managed that they invited extra scrutiny during this particularly difficult and momentous chapter in the *Times-Picayune*'s history. (I've also found myself wondering if this experience has made Amoss and O'Byrne more sympathetic to targets of the newspaper's investigations who have complained of bias or unfair reporting.) In addition to Amoss's refusal to be interviewed by people he views as critical and/or biased, an interaction between Amoss and *CJR*'s Chittum also was telling.

As suggested earlier, Chittum worked on a lengthy article about NOLA Media Group for months and had spent a week in New Orleans reporting the story in December 2012. He tried unsuccessfully for seven weeks to secure interviews with Mathews and Amoss, but he received no response to any of his requests. In early 2013, Chittum again contacted Amoss, who to Chittum's surprise, was joined on the phone line by O'Byrne and director of metro content Mark Lorando. "They started into the whole spin job stuff — people like what they're doing, etc.," Chittum remembered in May 2013. "And I told them that wasn't the case, according to everyone I'd talked to on the street in New Orleans. They then cut off the interview after about five minutes, saying I needed to come down to New Orleans to see their new Canal Place newsroom, that 'I couldn't do the story fairly without seeing the new newsroom.' I told them I'd have to ask my editors, but that I seriously doubted that they'd send me [to New Orleans again] since we were running right up against deadline and we had a shoestring budget anyway. [*CJR* is a non-profit.] My editors declined to send me, and Amoss got back on the phone with me a few days later. I was actually surprised he did." When the two finally spoke, Amoss "told me the reason he hadn't called me back for so long was a post I had written last June [2012]," Chittum recalled in May 2013, referring to an online report he had penned titled "New Orleans meets the Hamster Wheel."[40] "He was 'appalled' by the hamster wheel graphic and the implication that's what the NOLA strategy entailed."[41] (In his report, Chittum cites *Times-Picayune* alumnus John McQuaid, who had used the "hamster wheel" description in a report he wrote two days earlier for Atlantic.com. The imagery was meant to draw an analogy with a hamster's never-ending journey on the wheel and the ceaseless demands NOLA.com journalists face in supplying content to an insatiable website.)

When Chittum's article went live March 1, 2013, on the *CJR* website, Amoss was the second reader to comment on it, with an angry and accusatory post that began, "It's a shame that Ryan Chittum refused our invitation earlier this year to visit our newsroom before writing a piece filled with bad assumptions, inaccuracies and preconceived notions," when Amoss knew full well that Chittum had tried to contact him for weeks, and most assuredly would have visited the new newsroom if Amoss had agreed to be interviewed during the week Chittum had been in New Orleans reporting the story.

Some employees, past and present, have begun to note an auto-pilot characteristic to Amoss's public interactions about NOLA Media Group and the changes that have gone on there. "Increasingly, his speech, his rhetoric, is more and more boilerplate, more and more corporate-speak, more and more disembodied, more and more robotic," Nolan, once one of Amoss's most loyal lieutenants, observed in March 2013. "It's almost as if he's throwing in the towel, like 'you're not going to believe this, so I'm not going to work very hard at convincing you.' It has that robotic quality to it. Who talks like that? Speak English, man."

That appeared to be the case during an interview Amoss did in mid-May 2013 on New Orleans TV talk show, *The 504.* Throughout the thirty-five-minute exchange with then-host Melanie Hebert, Amoss repeatedly returned to the themes of "remaining the largest news organization in this community," of being "digitally focused," and of "readers voracious for news" who were abandoning the newsprint product in favor of the digital one. But he refused to answer Herbert's question regarding the newspaper's latest circulation figures, instead directing her to look up the recent AAM report herself. When asked about the tremendous loss of experienced talent his organization has suffered since the changes began, he responded, again invoking Katrina: "On a personal level, these are people I rode in a newspaper truck with on August 29, 2005, so there's a ton of history and lots of bonds of friendship between us. On a professional level, the talent is still in my newsroom and there's new talent that's been added to it, so I feel very comfortable with what we have."

The reaction from former employees—both those who left voluntarily and those who were laid off—was swift. "Oh, my God, I'm ten minutes in and I am . . . I am . . . I am . . . speechless," former *Times-Picayune* columnist Chris Rose, a twenty-five-year veteran, wrote on the Friends of the *Times-Picayune* Editorial Facebook page. "Who is this guy? Did anyone ever know him? I am . . . oh, never mind. Did any of us know him at all? And does anyone know him now?"

Harking to Kovacs's comment to Amoss on the day after the first *New York Times* story about the changes, the ordeal seems to have cost Amoss dearly in the form of his reputation, at least among his many former *Times-Picayune* charges. "From day one, I've had a hard time getting my head around the idea that Jim Amoss would want to be involved in this," said a longtime veteran of both the newspaper's downtown and bureau operations who was laid off as part of the changes. "Before all of this happened, I probably had more respect for Jim Amoss than just about anyone I've ever met. I still think he's one of the most brilliant men I ever met, which makes it even more difficult to understand why he would want to be involved in this, why he'd want to do this so close to the end of his career. It boggles my mind that he'd want to be a part of this."[38] Equally puzzled is former zone layout editor Jennifer Brown, who is now executive editor of the *Advocate*, after being laid-off from the *Picayune* and then approached weeks later by two editors asking her instead to remain. "If Jim had said, 'Let's go jump off the Broad Street bridge because it will make a great story,' I would have followed him," Brown said almost a year after receiving the completely unexpected news that she was being terminated. "I still respect him as a leader, but I now feel like it's a Jekyll and Hyde situation. I don't even know what happened. I'm still puzzled by his acceptance of the way things have been executed."[42]

People in the industry are far kinder in their assessments. "I actually admire Jim a lot in all of this," said Joel Kaplan, associate dean for professional graduate studies at the S.I. Newhouse School of Public Communications at Syracuse University, a school endowed in 1964 by Sam Newhouse. "Clearly, when he was confronted with this situation, he could have said, 'This isn't for me, this isn't what I signed up for.' Or, he could have said, 'This isn't what I signed up for, but I have an allegiance to my colleagues and to this place, and I'm going to bring my expertise and my understanding to bear to try to make this work.' And I think he took the latter choice, and that he knew it was going to be a painful and difficult process."[43] Industry analyst Ken Doctor said this type of situation is among the lumps editors sign up for when they assume the top post. "He's trying to do his best," Doctor said. "Editors are put in a very difficult spot in these situations. He's doing the best he can with the hand he's been dealt." Even David Carr thinks Amoss's motives were noble. "I think the issue of what Jim is up to is a fascinating one," Carr said during a May 2013 interview. "I find it deeply mysterious that he stayed. I assign nothing but a pure motive to it. He thought he could keep or make things better. He stayed for all the right reasons."[44]

The motivations and utterances of O'Byrne, on the other hand, don't puzzle current and former colleagues nearly as much. "James is endlessly ambitious and he and Jim [Amoss] go all the way back to the St. Bernard Bureau, where Jim got his start in management, and James was one of his star reporters," said a longtime, deeply respected former staffer, who spoke on the condition of anonymity. "It's always been well known that O'Byrne always wanted to have as much power as possible,"said another former editorial employee, in a sentiment echoed privately by numerous former and current *Times-Picayune* colleagues. "And I think he'd tell you as much—he's always wanted to be in charge."

Although many don't expect a newspaper's business-side executives to abide by the same journalistic standards regarding truth as their editorial-side brethren must meet, Mathews has his own credibility issues—dating back to at least his arrival at Advance Publications in 2009.

In August of that year, when he was named publisher of Advance's *Mobile Press-Register* and the *Mississippi Press*, in Pascagoula, and president of the Alabama Media Group, which includes all three Advance newspapers in the state, the *Press-Register* announced his arrival with a front-page story. The story strongly implied—but did not explicitly state—that Mathews's predecessor, Howard Bronson, had voluntarily retired at age seventy-two. The story even included a quote from Bronson, remarking about how he and his wife looked forward to making Mobile their permanent home after living there primarily as a professional necessity during his seventeen-year stint as publisher.[45] The only problem is that Bronson, who did not respond to requests for an interview, didn't retire, and he didn't provide the newspaper with a quote. He had been summarily dismissed by the *Press-Register* from his $745,000-a-year job after refusing to retire at Donald Newhouse's behest, contending that he was covered by the company's job security Pledge and had been repeatedly reassured before accepting the job that he would be allowed to work as long as he pleased. According to extensive coverage of the episode by Mobile's alternative bi-weekly, *Lagniappe*, Bronson had been in pointed conversations with Donald and his nephew, Mark Newhouse, and they knew he was refusing to voluntarily retire. About a month after his forced retirement, he filed his $7.3 million breach of contract civil lawsuit against the newspaper and Advance,[46] an action the Newhouses and Mathews could have anticipated was a likely outcome of their unsuccessful negotiations with Bronson.

Lagniappe was quick to call Mathews on the misleading story. "The first story the *Press-Register* ran when Mathews came in was a lie, claiming his predecessor Howard Bronson had retired, when, in fact, he'd been fired," Rob Holbert, managing editor and co-publisher of *Lagniappe*, wrote about Mathews's arrival in Mobile. "That alone shows how little Mathews and the *P-R* brass understand what running a newspaper is about. Lying to your readers probably does far more damage to circulation than the worldwide web."[47]

And then there's the "piano story." About a year-and-a-half after Mathews was named publisher, the *Press-Register* ran a front-page story about William Jones, a resident of Tuscaloosa, a burg two-hundred miles north of Mobile primarily known as the home of the University of Alabama. Tuscaloosa and neighborhoods in and around Birmingham, and as far north as my former hometown of Huntsville, were devastated by deadly tornadoes that tore through the region in April 2011. "On this blazing afternoon in what remained of the shattered Rosedale neighborhood, William Jones was approached by a stranger," the April 2011 story teased. That stranger was Ricky Mathews. Again calling to mind his and his family's near-miss by Hurricane Katrina, "Mathews introduced himself to Jones and understood his pain," the story said, and wanted to help by restoring Jones's piano. The remainder of the article discussed in painstaking detail how the damaged piano was collected (by a special piece of machinery operated by one of Mathews's cousins), transported to a Birmingham man who restored it, and then returned to Jones's home.[48]

Holbert in May 2013 remembered the story vividly, more than three years later. "I was in the mood for an uplifting story that would restore my faith in humanity," he recalled sardonically, about opening his *Press-Register* that morning. "This story's talking about this poor soul who lost his piano in the rubble. And I get to the jump, and who comes to the rescue? Ricky Mathews. I just about spit out my oatmeal. I could not believe that the publisher of a newspaper would have a story like this written about himself, on the front page of the newspaper."

The piano story was one of thirty-three reports either written by or featuring Mathews that were published in the *Press-Register* or on al.com in the twenty-nine months between his August 2009 appointment and January 2012, two months before he was named incoming publisher of the *Times-Picayune*. Besides his efforts to have Mr. Jones's piano repaired, *Press-Register* readers learned about Mathews rubbing shoulders with media baron Rupert Murdoch while on a New York media tour with then-Alabama Gov. Bob Riley; exercising religiously to avoid the fate of his father, who died at forty-four of a heart attack; and winning an award from the Dauphin Island Sea Lab in Mississippi.[49] (One story included a reference to Mathews as "president and publisher of the *Press-Resister*," which made me wonder whether it was a typo or an act of quiet protest on the part of a defiant reporter.) Apparently accustomed to reading about Mathews in the pages of the *Press-Register* and al.com, a reader posted a cutting comment about the piano story: "Every time Ricky Mathews publishes a story about himself, an angel loses its wings. So, there are about a dozen flightless angels out there this year . . ."

In another story about the devastation caused by the tornadoes that damaged Jones's piano, Mathews wrote, "As I learned after Katrina, when folks don't have power, the printed newspaper becomes even more essential. On a normal day, we can tell a story better than other media, but if a storm takes out the power grid, everyone looks to us."[50] The passage made me wonder whether Mathews still feels the same about power outages that occur in Alabama on Mondays, Tuesdays, Thursdays, and Saturdays, the days that none of Advance's Alabama newspapers, the three largest in the state, publish print editions.

About a year later, *Press-Register* readers were greeted with another eyebrow-raiser, this time in the form of the headline on the story announcing the arrival of "digital first" and the termination of an undisclosed total number of[51] employees, including what turned out to be 50 of 70 who worked in the newsroom. The headline? "Exciting changes for our readers." *Press-Register* editor Mike Marshall acknowledged to Poynter.org that "he helped write the headline, which he characterized as an attempt to recast the story: 'Perhaps I got carried away, but basically the storyline all day long had been that the papers were cutting back to three publications, and lost was the story that we're building a digital future.'"[52] Mathews was not quoted in the story, but he was apparently still publisher of the newspaper at the time the report was published. [53]

Lagniappe's Holbert was at his take-no-prisoners best when zeroing in on the "exciting changes for our readers" headline. "Calling the coming firing of *P-R* employees and the loss of the city's daily newspaper 'exciting changes' is a lot like saying that getting hit in the face with a baseball bat is an exciting opportunity to work on a new look," Holbert opined in *Lagniappe*. He went on:

> They want us all to believe it's really just the Internet that's the problem. There have been suggestions by some that the citizens let the *P-R* down by not properly supporting the paper. But that's kind of like blaming people for not supporting a Golden Corral, even after they installed a fancy chocolate fountain. No one blames the citizens when they don't support a mediocre restaurant, and that applies as well to a mediocre newspaper. . . . Unfortunately, the people who will pay are the citizens who will have an even more timid watchdog and the people who really love newspapers and have been proud to work there. Newhouse can count his billions while Mathews moves to New Orleans and chops them to pieces

next. Sounds like another "exciting change" in the making.[54]

Holbert wasn't the only journalist outside of Advance outraged by the headline. "To call this an 'exciting change' is more than just an editing error; it amounts to a cruel joke on long-loyal readers and those who write for them honestly and directly," wrote Paul Greenberg, editorial page editor of the *Arkansas Democrat-Gazette*, in what became a nationally syndicated editorial. (The *Democrat-Gazette*, incidentally is one of the first US general-interest newspapers to successfully erect a paywall.) "It's hard to believe that any editor down in Mobile can believe the way this story was handled will add to the newspaper's credibility. It's an intangible quality—credibility—but it's easy to lose. And easy to tell—at a glance—when it's missing."[55]

Although it's generally been accepted in journalism circles for years that the *Press-Register* is, in fact, a mediocre newspaper, the *Times-Picayune* has enjoyed a much better reputation, especially in the past twenty-five years. And although the *Times-Picayune* went with a hard-hitting headline—"Newspaper Lays Off 200 Employees"[56]—when the extent of the workforce reduction was finally confirmed almost three weeks later, on the day after the *New York Times* broke the original story about the coming changes, all four Advance papers used neutral-to-misleading headlines, tinged with marketing-speak. While the *Press-Register* heralded "Exciting Changes for Our Readers," the *Birmingham News* went with "Changes coming to the *News*," and the *Huntsville Times* used a similarly innocuous "Changes Ahead at the *Times*." The *Times-Picayune's* headline? "Newspaper to Move Focus to Digital."[57]

Shortly after arriving at the newspaper, Mathews dissolved Phelps Jr.'s four-member *Times-Picayune* Advisory Board, of which philanthropist and "Save the Picayune" founder Anne Milling was a member, and replaced it with the nineteen-member NOLA. com | *Times-Picayune* Community Roundtable. Aside from being larger, the group is more diverse and includes prominent leaders from business, health care, education, and the arts, such as Ron Forman, president and CEO of Audubon Nature Institute; Alden McDonald Jr., president and CEO of Liberty Bank and Trust Co.; Charles Rice, president and CEO of Entergy New Orleans; and Susan Taylor, director of the New Orleans Museum of Art; and Norman Francis, president of Xavier University. (Francis is the only holdover from Phelps's earlier group, and the father of NOLA Media Group's vice president and business manager David Francis, who was promoted to executive vice president of NOLA Media Group, and associate publisher of NOLA.com | *Times-Picayune* in June 2013 [58]).Mathews also announced creation of the NOLA Access Initiative, a partnership between NOLA Media Group and the Greater New Orleans Foundation that invested up to $500,000 to provide New Orleans metropolitan communities with access to digital technology, including purchasing sixty-six iPads for New Orleans public libraries and a kiosk to allow patrons to use iPads at the main library.[59] The initiative also announced in late May 2013 a $20,000 grant to Columbia Parc at Bayou District, which is the former St. Bernard housing project, to provide students with internet access and supply more computers and software for training courses.[60]

CHAPTER X

Black, White, & Read All Over

You have to appreciate, or at least accept, that revelry and celebrations are a way of life in New Orleans to understand why it was important to host parties to mark the end of daily publication of the *Times-Picayune*. After all, in the words of that great contemporary New Orleans wordsmith and former *Times-Picayune* columnist, Chris Rose (which are immortalized on a local T-shirt), "We dance when there is no music. We drink at funerals. We talk too much, and live too large and, frankly, we're suspicious of those who don't." And although it's not something I'm pleased to be have been right about, I knew at the moment that longtime *Times-Picayune* staff writer John Pope interviewed me in late May 2012 about the end of the newspaper's daily publication that we would set aside a weekend to remember and commemorate.

Because of my concern for those losing their jobs—from both financial and emotional perspectives—I envisioned that final weekend as both a tribute and a helping hand. Via the Friends of the *Times-Picayune* Editorial Staff Facebook page, I connected with Babs Bryant Johnson, a member of a prominent New Orleans family who, after raising her three children, turned her attention to youth advocacy issues, especially reforming the New Orleans Recreation Department and establishing neighborhood playgrounds post-Katrina. Over the years, Babs had served on many fundraising event committees, so she immediately zeroed in on the idea of hosting a combination farewell and fundraiser for those losing their jobs. Recalling the wrenching use of "-30-"on the day the layoffs were announced, local author and marketing whiz

Kit Wohl had earlier suggested that we adopt that symbol as the name of our fundraising organization. Because just about every iteration of -30- already had been appropriated on the Internet, we went with "dashTHIRTYdash," and Kit quickly designed a logo. Babs then enlisted the help of the Contemporary Arts Center of New Orleans, which agreed to provide financial oversight for the efforts. DashTHIRTYdash Facebook and Twitter pages soon followed.

Even before we could formally set up the mechanism for the CAC to accept donations, local businesses were contacting us, wanting to know how they could help. The husband-and-wife co-owners of La Petite Grocery Restaurant, Justin and Mia Devillier (named one of New Orleans's Top 10 restaurants in both 2011 and 2012 by none other than the *Times-Picayune*) were the first, followed by Polly Watts, proprietor of the St. Charles Avenue Pub in the Lower Garden District. Justin and Mia offered to donate 30 percent of the dinner receipts on an evening we subsequently publicized primarily via social media and a plug by *Gambit*. In response, *Times-Picayune* staffers, alumni, and supporters streamed into the restaurant.

The only drama of the evening came courtesy of incoming NOLA Media Group president Ricky Mathews, who was directing the implementation of "digital first" and its associated layoffs, and the new company's vice president and business manager, David Francis. Apparently unaware of the benefit, the two arrived that evening for dinner, accompanied by another man. Sharp-eyed *Times-Picayune* St. Tammany Parish staff writer Christine Harvey was waiting at the bar for a friend and almost spit out her cocktail when she saw the trio, and she immediately posted their arrival on the Friends of the *Times-Picayune* Editorial Staff Facebook page. (Only days earlier, Harvey had become a public face of the mass layoff via a photograph on the front page of the June 13, 2012 edition of the newspaper showing her dissolved in tears after learning she would lose her job, and being comforted by fellow reporter Cindy Chang.) Mathews, Francis, and their companion left almost immediately, Harvey said, and when she asked the maître d' about their abrupt departure, he responded that Francis and Mathews "said they had an emergency and kind of giggled when they said it." Harvey assumed their selection of La Petite on the same evening as the dashTHIRTYdash benefit was coincidental and that as soon as they opened their menus and saw a flier promoting the benefit, they thought better of dining there, at least on that particular evening.[1]

A few nights later, Watts pledged all of the bar's proceeds to dashTHIRTYdash and recruited NOLA Brewing Co., and Crescent Crown Distributing, along with two additional neighborhood restaurants to participate. Those events were quickly followed by a brunch benefit at Slim Goodies Diner in the Irish Channel, during which owner Kappa Horne also collected additional direct donations to dashTHIRTYdash. And so it went throughout much of the summer. Ultimately, a dozen businesses—including Bywater's Euclid Record Store and Uptown's Plum Gift Stop—hosted benefits. Bars at the seven Ralph Brennan Restaurant Group properties created signature "Save the *Picayune*" cocktails, and donated all sales receipts from the drinks to the fund. Donations from individuals and businesses, such as the Greater New Orleans Foundation, Inc., the law firm Smith Stagg, LLC, and an anonymous $4,000 donation, enabled us to collect close to $25,000 within a couple of months.

Local jeweler Mignon Faget designed a stud pin that incorporated newsprint from issues of the *Times-Picayune* against a black grosgrain ribbon, and a set of Old-Fashioned glasses emblazoned with a "TP" reminiscent of the newspaper's masthead. Faget pledged 10 percent of the proceeds from sales of both items, and advertised the pin and dashTHIRTYdash in an ad in the newspaper just days after the changes were announced. NOLA.com | *Times-Picayune* "Social Scene" columnist Nell Nolan, former *Times-Picayune* editorial cartoonist Steve Kelley,

New Orleans jeweler Mignon Faget publicized her pin, created in protest to the changes coming to the *Times-Picayune,* via an ad in the newspaper. *Image courtesy of Mignon Faget.*

local fledgling actress Ashley Nolan, and the Mid-City Theatre produced a stage production whose nearly $4,000 in proceeds benefited dashTHIRTYdash. The money was donated in memory of Diana Pinckley, the local communications consultant who had been Anne Milling's chief social media lieutenant for the "Save the Picayune" effort, and *Times-Picayune* reporter John Pope's wife. She died after a long battle with cancer just days before the newspaper stopped publishing daily.

Babs and I turned our attention to planning the activities for the final weekend. Rock 'n' Bowl in Mid-City, which had hosted the early June rally to protest the changes, was a logical choice for a Friday night reunion, and owner John Blancher quickly agreed to accommodate us. Babs continued to search for an appropriate venue for a Saturday night dashTHIRTYdash fundraiser. After striking out with a number of venues and with the final weekend drawing closer, I contacted the Howlin' Wolf, a music hall I remembered from its Uptown days, but which had moved to larger quarters in the Warehouse District years earlier. Owner and general manager Howie Kaplan gave us *gratis* use of the facilities, a not insignificant gesture for a music venue on a Saturday night, in exchange for the bar receipts. With a venue secured, Babs went to work wrangling local restaurants to provide complimentary food, while I worked through Jason Patterson of Frenchmen Street music club Snug Harbor, to line up a slate of musicians who would agree to also perform for free.

The restaurants and eateries that ultimately provided cuisine included: a Mano, Cafe Atchafalaya, Galatoire's, Ralph's on the Park, Rio Mar Seafood, Liberty's Kitchen, Martin Wine Cellar Catering, and Whole Foods Market Arabella Station. David Torkanowsky, a keyboardist and a longtime host of a show broadcast on New Orleans's WWOZ community radio station, put together an "All-Stars Band" to accompany any musicians who could stop by for a set or two. Patterson, in turn, lined up longtime former Radiators guitarist Camile Baudoin; jazz pianist and vocalist Matt Lemmler; the Charmaine Neville Band; swing harmony group the Pfister Sisters; jazz saxophonist and bandleader Martin Krusche; and singer and guitarist John Rankin. Local production company Bernard Productions subsidized rental equipment the musicians needed for the evening. Admission would be a symbolic $30 for everyone except employees losing their jobs, and their guests, who were admitted free of charge.

My difficulties at trying to plan such an event from roughly 1,500 miles away apparently began to show, and fellow *Times-Picayune* alum Sheila Grissett, took pity on me and stepped in to help — in a bigger way than I am certain she ever envisioned when she first responded to one of my online pleas for assistance. On marathon phone calls we held most Saturdays and Sundays, we haggled over details and direction, conversations that weren't always easy, but which made for better events. Sheila and NOLA.com | *Times-Picayune* food editor Judy Walker recruited an army of primarily former and a few outgoing *Times-Picayune* staffers.[2]

As we continued with our planning, most of the community seemed to have resigned itself to the fact that New Orleans would soon become the largest American city without a daily newspaper. However, "Save the Picayune" founder Anne Milling remained defiantly confident that Advance's decision would be reversed, or that a new, white knight owner would arrive to keep the *Times-Picayune* a daily publication. Before I connected with Kaplan and the Howlin' Wolf, I phoned Milling in mid-July 2012, desperately hoping she would be willing to flex her considerable influence in the community and help deliver a location for the event that would commemorate the end of the daily newspaper. "We *will* save the daily *Times-Picayune*," she responded, with that touch of imperious edge she can deliver when she's been crossed. I quickly amended my request: "Well, we'll just have a big celebration then." Milling, of course, in the end was sadly wrong. She was still second-guessing herself months later over what could and should have been done differently to have convinced the Newhouses to take a different tack. But she and her husband, King, loyally joined the crowds at both events.

The Friday night Rock 'n' Bowl event attracted almost 200 current and former employees representing seven decades at the newspaper now living in ten states, from Hawaii to New York. Milling persuaded Ashton Phelps Jr. and his wife, Suzanne, to attend the Rock 'n' Bowl reunion, and they stayed for essentially the entire evening. With the exception of what sounded like canned quotes attributed to him that had made their way into a couple of *Times-Picayune* reports about the changes, Phelps had remained publicly quiet about the changes and only his closest intimates presumably knew how he actually felt about "digital first" and its far-reaching implications for *Times-Picayune* readers, employees, and advertisers. The only comment I uncovered that may have shed light into his personal feelings came in August 2012, when Phelps walked into the newsroom one day, and soon-to-be-laid-off veteran photographer John McCusker recalled asking him, "'Ashton, do you know when your last day is?'" Phelps, according to McCusker, tightly responded, "'They haven't told me anything, John.' If they could treat a man like Ashton like that, what could the rest of us hope for?"[3]

Regardless of how he felt about the changes and how he chose to handle his departure from the institution that literally had shaped his life from before his birth, Phelps's attendance at the Rock 'n' Bowl event seemed to mean a great deal to many staffers who had seen little of him during the long summer. Scores of employees greeted him and gathered for photos with him.

Determined to turn the Saturday night Howlin' Wolf event into a major fundraiser for dashTHIRTYdash, I had begun weeks earlier to work on online and silent auctions. Many people with far more experience with such events warned Sheila and me how much extra work we were in for—but I didn't listen (as much as

Sheila tried to get me to). The first order of business was to raid the (now primarily digital) rolodexes of everyone we knew to scare up whatever connections we had to notable New Orleanians or famous people in the news media who might be willing to donate items or experiences to the auction. Ultimately, we ended up uncovering direct or once-removed connections to some of the biggest names in news and talk, almost all of whom agreed to donate primarily VIP experiences for the high bidders.

CNN's Anderson Cooper (a New Orleans devotee since covering the aftermath of Katrina) offered VIP tickets to his talk show and a back-stage meet-and-greet, while the *Ellen DeGeneres Show* (DeGeneres is a New Orleans native) provided two VIP tickets to a taping of her show. *TODAY Show* host Hoda Kotb, who was a popular anchor on WWL-TV earlier in her career and has maintained ties to New Orleans, provided VIP tickets to the *TODAY Show* and backstage meet-and-greet with her and co-host Kathie Lee Gifford. ABC News's Rob Nelson, an alum of both the *Times-Picayune* and New Orleans's CBS affiliate, WWL-TV, got us four VIP passes to ABC's *Good Morning America* along with a studio tour and "face time" during the live outdoor weather shot. I befriended NBC News's *Meet the Press* executive producer and New Orleans native Betsy Fischer-Martin on Twitter, and she offered two sets of tickets to view a live taping of that Sunday morning news talk show staple. Native New Orleanian Cokie Roberts, a longtime National Public Radio political analyst and ABC News contributor, offered tickets to a live taping of ABC's *This Week* . . . Sunday morning political talk show, and lunch with her, the latter of which was promptly snapped up by the Loyola University's School of Mass Communication. New Orleans native, *States-Item* alumnus, and best-selling author Walter Isaacson offered an autographed set of all his books or lunch with him in Washington, DC. New Orleans native and former CNN morning anchor Soledad O'Brien offered coffee and a backstage viewing of her then-morning show. New Orleans milliner and costume designer Tracy Thomson created a silk-screened cotton print fabric of the first edition of the *Times-Picayune* with contemporary headlines collaged on top, from which she made limited-edition hats, bags, and handkerchiefs.

Several departing *Times-Picayune* illustrators, including veterans Kenny Harrison and Tony Champagne, donated artwork. Environmental and outdoors editor Bob Marshall, who had declined an offer to stay with NOLA Media Group, pledged an all-expenses-paid Lake Pontchartrain fishing tour that proved so popular, he ended up agreeing to host two additional tours, including one bought by Fischer-Martin for her husband. Legendary *Times-Picayune* sports columnist Pete Finney donated his Underwood typewriter, circa 1932, which he used to type his reports when he first came to a predecessor of the *Times-Picayune*, the *States*, on June 22, 1945. (It went for $300.) The *Times-Picayune*'s three most-recent editorial cartoonists, Steve Kelley, Walt Handelsman, and Mike Luckovich, all donated several original cartoons. Food editor Judy Walker created and donated a quilt whose panels came from scores of *Times-Picayune* T-shirts produced over the years. Countless other items of art and remembrances dominated the silent auction. Both auctions raised about $12,000 after expenses, and the Howlin' Wolf fundraiser drew more than three-hundred people and raised close to $20,000.[4]

Beyond the fundraising, the events provided a "community group hug," as outgoing columnist Stephanie Grace described it, and in addition to extensive local media coverage, the events received international and national media coverage, including by the *New York Times*, and the United Kingdom's *Guardian* newspaper and BBC Radio. It was exactly the proper send-off we had hoped for.

CHAPTER XI

Saint Georges Gonna Save Us Now?

John Georges—New Orleans billionaire, successful businessman, and not-so-successful political candidate—saw an opportunity created by the disastrous way the *Times-Picayune* handled its transition to a primarily digital news outlet. Georges had grown his family's $20 million business that supplied convenience stores with products ranging from Snickers candy bars to Tide detergent into a $1 billion enterprise now among the country's top convenience store wholesalers and Louisiana's largest video poker operator and distributor. Along the way, he had become proprietor of one of New Orleans's most famous restaurants (Galatoire's), member (by marriage) of one of its most prominent families (Coleman), and resident of its most exclusive street (Audubon Place).[1] He now wanted to apply some of that expertise to owning and operating a newspaper.

In 2007, during his unsuccessful campaign for governor, he began to think about the possibility of adding "newspaper publisher" to that list. "I rode every inch of the state, and talked to people in every parish in the state," he said in a May 2013 interview. "The experience added a whole new dimension to who I was."[2]

At six-feet-two-inches, the fifty-two-year-old Georges's physical presence is still reminiscent of his days as a linebacker on his high school football team. Aside from his successful business ventures and two unsuccessful political campaigns (in addition to running for governor, he placed a distant third in the 2010 New Orleans mayoral election), he is known for his philanthropy, which includes donating millions primarily to New Orleans non-profits, universities, museums, and civic groups. Ranked the thirtieth-wealthiest Greek in America by Greek-American newspaper the *National Herald*,[3] Georges is fluent in Greek and deeply proud of his heritage. (He regales reporters with how his father fought Nazis during the Greek Resistance,[4] and required John Georges and his siblings to study the language instead of going trick-or-treating on Halloween.[5]) In addition to serving as president of the New Orleans Greek Community during Katrina, he is a past member of the state Board of Regents, the governing board of higher education in Louisiana, and a past member of Tulane University's President's Council, along with holding past leadership roles in an assortment of educational and business boards.

Although the *Times-Picayune* had begun its long financial decline by then, at the time Georges began contemplating acquiring a newspaper, the *T-P* was still firmly an Advance Publications newspaper with a monopoly grip on the greater New Orleans market, and he had little hope of persuading the Newhouse family to sell. So, in late summer of 2011, he traveled eighty miles west to Baton Rouge and met with the Manship family, owners of the 171-year-old *Advocate*, then the second-largest daily newspaper in the state. Not as many people realize, however, that his protracted negotiations with the Manship family had been punctuated by a serious flirtation to instead acquire the *Times-Picayune*.

"I thought the *Picayune* would die a long, lingering death," Georges recalled in May 2013. "I didn't expect this 'widow maker' heart attack." When the *Times-Picayune* situation did explode into a full-blown community revolt, he sensed an opening. Working through Tommy Boggs and former Louisiana Sen. John Breaux at the Washington, DC-based Patton Boggs lobbying firm, Georges made entreaties to Advance Publications's Si Newhouse about Advance's willingness to sell the *Times-Picayune*. "They were interested in talking to me," Georges recalled. "But between the time my representatives talked to Si and we could schedule a meeting, the fury in New Orleans erupted and inflamed the situation. Less than two weeks later, Steven [Newhouse's] position hardened, and he killed it. I would have paid two times what Warren Buffett would have paid because I'm the hometown boy."

Once the *Times-Picayune* was ruled out as an acquisition possibility, Georges returned his attention to the *Advocate*, but the *T-P's* volatile situation had created a hiccup there as well. "The Manships told me, 'We've been approached by a group in New Orleans about starting a New Orleans edition, so we're going to have to take a break, and we'll have to talk after we launch in New Orleans,'" he said. "So, I went away for the month of August and monitored the New Orleans situation from the outside, but I knew I was going to have to come in and finish it."

The *Advocate* quickly hired a skeleton staff composed entirely of laid-off *Times-Picayune* staffers for the new edition, and rather quickly built a circulation of more than 23,000 in New Orleans, including 16,000 daily subscribers. Negotiations between Georges and the Manships resumed toward the end of 2012. Then in late January 2013, the website of Baton Rouge ABC affiliate WBRZ-TV, also owned by the Manships, broke the news that the family was in discussions to sell the *Advocate* to a "private individual."[6] A day later, the *Greater Baton Rouge Business Report* reported that Georges was the suitor.[7] Negotiations dragged on, with the *Advocate's* publisher, David Manship, telling the *Greater Baton Rouge Business Report* in late March that a decision was strictly up to Georges. The family's asking price was more than $50 million, Manship told the *Business Report*, and then he incredibly added, "I'm telling you it's high. It's not worth what we're asking for it."[8] In late March 2013, the Manships and Georges announced they had signed a letter of intent to have Georges acquire the newspaper.[9]

Although NOLA Media Group refused to concede that they were preemptive strikes, it made a number of significant announcements related to the Baton Rouge market as the rumors of Georges's pending acquisition circulated during the winter of 2012 and spring of 2013. First came NOLA Media Group's expanding Baton

Rouge bureau, and its move into new downtown offices.[10] Then in April 2013, the company heralded the launch of *BR*, a new free weekly tabloid distributed to grocery, drug, and convenience stores throughout Baton Rouge. In a nearly 1,000-word article on NOLA. com introducing *BR*, NOLA Media Group's director of state news and sports James O'Byrne became the latest executive to evoke Katrina in promoting the company or its products, writing that the link between New Orleans and Baton Rouge became "forever stronger in the days, weeks and months" after the storm, when thousands of New Orleanians evacuated to Baton Rouge. "New Orleans and its citizens were in desperate need," O'Byrne wrote, "And no community opened its arms wider after Katrina than Baton Rouge. My family and I benefitted from this community's overwhelming generosity and kindness."

As had been the case with other recent NOLA Media Group announcements, reader reaction was as swift and derisive. "Hey! Great! NOLA.COM is making a Baton Rouge magazine!" one reader wrote on NOLA.com. "Oh, and the *Baton Rouge Advocate* is making a New Orleans paper because the NOLA.com Group decided to cut the *Times-Picayune* to three days a week. Hey, how about this idea, why doesn't the NOLA.com group focus on *New Orleans* and the *Baton Rouge Advocate* focus on *Baton Rouge*??? Like they used too, that would be a novel idea, instead of pushing your *local* readers aside to fight over the city 60 miles away." Harking to O'Byrne's disdainful "Inkosaurus" nickname for the newspaper's print edition, another reader wrote, "It's not *BR*, it's BS. O'Byrne, I thought print was the 'dinosaur.' But no, you have to be petty and try and hit back at the *Advocate*. How about you stop playing around and give us back our seven-days-a-week paper. You know, the one that you 'can't afford' in your new penthouse offices."[11]

Less than a week later, *Times-Picayune* editor Jim Amoss announced the launch of *TPStreet*, the newsstand tabloid that NOLA Media Group would begin producing on the three weekdays the *Times-Picayune* no longer published. In a nod to the region's first honest-to-goodness newspaper war since the *States-Item* merged with the *Times-Picayune* in 1980, Georges a few hours later announced he had completed acquisition of the *Advocate*. (Although the price was not disclosed, it was rumored to be between $25 million and $50 million.) "John believes in Louisiana and knows the *Advocate* can fuel its growth," Richard Manship said at a news conference the next day. "Not a three-day-a-week paper, but a seven-day-a-week paper."[12] Although the acquisition appeared almost quixotic to some, Georges focused on the confluence of extraordinary developments that had led him to acquire the state's other major newspaper.

"Conventional wisdom, which I don't follow, is that nobody has come into a competing city with a newspaper and survived," he said only a few weeks after the purchase was finalized. "To me, it's the perfect storm: the third [Newhouse] generation taking over. The city of New Orleans, which lost a lot of population and lost a lot of advertisers [post-Katrina]. The loss of the legacy publisher who probably retired five years too early. This rush to digitization. And the loss of the monopoly hold." Georges also couldn't resist taking another jab at his *T-P* competitors. "[Former newspaper editor-turned-analyst] Alan Mutter told me the future of newspapers is entrepreneurs. I don't know Mr. Mathews. I know Mr. Amoss, and he's no entrepreneur."

Georges's experiences as a political candidate also gives him a unique understanding of Louisiana's two largest cities, perspective that will help him successfully lead the *Advocate*, both in his hometown of Baton Rouge and in its new territory of New Orleans, he said. "Baton Rouge is [Governor] Bobby Jindal, LSU football and Raising Cane's" fast food restaurants, he added. "New Orleans is [Mayor] Mitch Landrieu, Popeye's [fast food] and the Saints. And I understand both."[13]

In a move that may have sent chills down the spines of Advance and NOLA Media Group executives, Georges also announced

New Orleans businessman John Georges talks about his acquisition of the *Advocate* at a May 2013 news conference. Pictured, left to right, are: East Baton Rouge Mayor-President Kip Holden; *Advocate* Publisher David Manship; Georges and his wife, Dathel; and Louisiana Gov. Bobby Jindal. *Photo by* Advocate *staff photographer Bill Feig, courtesy of the* Advocate.

that he had hired ousted veteran *Times-Picayune* co-managing editors Peter Kovacs and Dan Shea, naming Kovacs editor of the publication, and Shea its chief operating officer and general manager. "We fought the Battle of New Orleans once before; some think we are going to fight it again in the newspaper," Georges said three weeks later in an interview with National Public Radio. In the same report, Shea also referenced the seemingly tough odds they faced. "The notion of going into another newspaper's market and convincing their readers to read yours is a fool's errand—except when you so break the bonds of your brand with your readers, and it's created this once-in-a-lifetime opportunity."[14]

By late July, Kovacs and Shea had poached additional *Times-Picayune* talent, including city editor Gordon Russell and news editor Martha Carr. (Police and criminal courts reporter Ramon Antonio Vargas was the latest defection as this book went to press, becoming the third reporter the *Advocate* will assign to cover the Saints.) Vargas also became the thirty-fourth former or current *Times-Picayune* editorial employee hired by the *Advocate*. Former high-profile *T-P* veterans James Gill and Stephanie Grace also had joined as contributing columnists, followed by a number of reporters and editors. Earlier in the day on which the *Advocate* announced Vargas's defection, NOLA.com countered by publishing a report that it had re-hired Littice Bacon-Blood, a former seventeen-year veteran who had been laid off in the "digital first" changes, to cover the River Parishes, a three-parish region between New Orleans and Baton Rouge where the *Picayune* had long operated a bureau before closing it as part of the 2012 workforce reduction. Bacon-Blood's re-hiring came about a week after the *Advocate* poached *Times-Picayune* business reporter Ricky Thompson (who also had been laid off and then re-hired during the previous chaotic summer) to cover the region. (Signaling that the newspaper war was on, every time the *Advocate* made a new hire from the *Picayune*, it promptly published an article heralding the addition, and as the *Times-Picayune* strove to regain the upper-hand, it also trumpeted internal promotions and external hires.)

Russell was the highest-profile defection (named "managing producer of enterprise" after the NOLA Media Group transition), who had moved to editing from reporting, although his Twitter profile confessed that he continued to like to "dabble in reporting." He had long been rumored as someone the *Advocate* sought to poach, and in early May 2013, he made the jump. He declined to be interviewed for this book, but he spoke to *Columbia Journalism Review* immediately after tendering his resignation at the *Times-Picayune*. "I don't agree with the direction that the *Picayune*'s going in," Russell told *CJR* while driving to Baton Rouge for his first meeting as an *Advocate* employee. "There's an increasing emphasis on quantity over quality, and speed and breaking news—but small news. I love breaking news as much as the next guy, but it feels a little like being on a hamster wheel. I love the *Picayune*. I've worked there almost fifteen years. I feel like it's in my blood and my DNA. There are a lot of terrific people who work there — terrific people and terrific journalists. That makes this a little bittersweet."[15]

As news spread of Georges's acquisition, some expressed reservations about a former gubernatorial and New Orleans mayoral candidate with unknown political aspirations owning the state's now-largest daily newspaper. Georges dismissed such concern by also invoking Katrina. "I think my movement into politics was really a Katrina phenomenon, a desire to build a better community," he said in our late May 2013 interview. "I worked in business for forty-one years of my life, from eleven years old on, and I ran for governor for three months. I don't have a burning political agenda. I have a Louisiana agenda, and a successful business agenda. Being publisher of a daily newspaper might be a better way to serve the community." If anything, his campaigns, particularly for the governorship, enhanced his business prowess, he said. "The benefit for me is that I developed a public profile."

So, why would a New Orleanian with no experience in publishing, choose a newspaper as his method for serving the community? Despite the sting Georges must have felt when his hometown newspaper did not endorse him in either of his runs for public office, and published a somewhat unflattering profile of him during the 2010 mayoral campaign, he insists this is business, not personal. "We are not spiteful," Georges told the *Greater Baton Rouge Business Report*. "This is a business opportunity, a business we think we can run well."[16]

But owning the state's largest daily newspaper also provides other benefits to an ambitious and immensely self-assured businessman like Georges, the *Business Report* concluded:

> It gives him credibility and prestige that neither the wholesale business, nor video poker, nor politics were ever able to confer. His voice will matter now. His counsel will be sought. He will be courted and schmoozed by every powerful person in the state, sooner or later. What's more, he will have a forum for his platform should he choose to run again for office. Should he not, he will

be in a position to help crown the next king. It is a win-win, an enviable position, which is where Georges likes always to be—in the driver's seat, out in front, calling the shots. "You always want to be a star," he said. "Not a comet."[17]

"I think I'm in the odd position of making history," Georges said in our interview. "I can tell you that an effort to buy a newspaper in the heart of Louisiana turned into a battle for the soul of New Orleans, and the war to preserve print journalism." He also flatly dismissed rumors that his purchase of the *Advocate* was highly leveraged and could crash into financial flames *a la* Chicago real estate kingpin Sam Zell's highly debt-financed acquisition of the Tribune Company. Tribune emerged from bankruptcy December 31, 2012, after four years of court supervision, during which it helped to draw attention to the financial state of the newspaper industry and the executives who helped put it there: "There's effectively no debt," Georges declared to me about his acquisition of the *Advocate*. "I have a line of credit if I need it, but there's no debt." And in what may have been the true opening salvo in his war against bottom-line-oriented Advance, he added: "Maybe I win, maybe I don't, but I can tell you that I have a very long-term outlook and a very high threshold for pain."

Those are two traits Georges better have as he heads into this battle, newspaper analyst and author Ken Doctor said. "The big question is, can the *Advocate* substantially eat into the *Picayune*'s ad revenues?" Doctor asked in a May 2013 interview. "The advertising is going to be tough, and it's going to be a long-term pursuit, if it works at all. They've got to improve the content, they've got to get the readers, and they've got to take readers away from the *Picayune*. It's a long-term proposition." *CJR*'s Chittum agreed. "It will take a lot of investment by Georges to make a true run at the *Picayune*, which despite its enervation, still has a newsroom of roughly 130," he wrote on the magazine's website.[18]

Predictably, Georges's new general manager and COO Shea

had only high praise for Georges in the very early days of his ownership of the *Advocate*. "He's been remarkably hands-off. He calls me and asks, 'What can I do to help?'" Shea said during a mid-May 2013 appearance on *The 504* local TV talk show, the night before Amoss's less-than-flattering appearance. Shea then took a veiled swipe at Advance, contrasting what it has done in New Orleans with what the *Advocate* intends to do: "You can't ask for a better owner [than Georges], as opposed to one who hands you a playbook and says, 'We're going to change everything about what people want in New Orleans.'" Although it's far too early to make a credible assessment of how hands-off Georges ultimately will be, Shea said he and new editor Peter Kovacs were assured of complete editorial independence from any agenda Georges may have, and "that's a promise he made to us and that's a promise we'll hold him to."[19]

Georges's entrée into the New Orleans newspaper market also likely complicates and perhaps even spoils Advance's potential longer-term plans for the *Picayune,* and the June 2013 arrival of *TPStreet* appeared to confirm that appraisal. "It throws another roadblock up for what I've argued is the Newhouses' liquidation strategy in New Orleans, and the [Newhouse] family has already squandered much of the enormous goodwill the *Picayune* had . . . with their actions over the last year," *CJR's* Ryan Chittum wrote in early June. "The *Advocate* has a big built-in advantage in state politics and in LSU sports. It will also not have a hard time poaching talent from the *Picayune* and its layoff pool." And if Georges is primarily in the game for the prestige and power that owning the state's largest daily newspaper offers, profits—or lack thereof—may not matter. "We're not talking about a lot of money for someone who has hundreds of millions," Doctor added.

And the *Advocate*'s financial accomplishments only have to be modest for him to deem it a triumph, Georges said. "We don't have to come in and take all of the *Picayune*'s business to be successful," he told me. "If we take 15 percent or 20 percent of their pie, we'll be in great shape. I'm not looking at a financial statement. I'm looking at how to win a game." Taking another not-so-subtle shot at New York-based Advance and the Newhouse family, Shea told then-host Hebert on his *The 504* appearance, "We're seeking a market niche of people who want a seven-day, home-delivered local paper that reflects Louisiana values, that is run by Louisianans, not by an out-of-state chain. We believe there's still a substantial and profitable newspaper audience in New Orleans and all we want to do is give them what they want. [Advance and NOLA Media Group] have their business model. History is going to decide this."

Georges said he had five goals for the *Advocate*: Win over the existing employees; reassure the Baton Rouge community that it remains a priority; improve the New Orleans product (including the addition of everything from New Orleans-area obituaries to offering New Orleans-oriented columnists and entertainment coverage); reintroduce the New Orleans edition to the community after those changes are made; and develop and execute a strong digital strategy. He already was well on his way to achieving the first three as this book went to press. "People may pick up the newspaper today and ask, 'Where are all these changes?'" Shea said during his *The 504* appearance. "It's a big shift. Virtually every week over the summer, you'll see changes, and by mid-summer, you'll see a truly *New Orleans Advocate*."

At the end of May 2013, Georges's team addressed one of the chief complaints about its New Orleans edition: the lack of local obituaries. Readers made it clear that they wanted to see local obituaries in the newspaper, and "our job was to give the readers of New Orleans what they want with their seven-day-a-week newspaper," Sheila Runnels, the *Advocate*'s advertising vice president, said in the story announcing the new service. (Signaling the importance to newspapers of the long-standing obituary category, a sharp-eyed *Times-Picayune* critic a few weeks earlier noticed a house ad in the pages of that newspaper, "Real

Time Death Notices on NOLA.com Now Updated Throughout the Day." Michael Tisserand posted a photo of the ad on the "Friends" Facebook page along with the quip, "Glad they didn't go with the original promo: You toast 'em, we post 'em.")

The *Advocate* in early June 2013 also announced formation of a New Orleans advisory board, with a star inaugural member, Anne Milling. Milling had led the "Save the Picayune" effort the previous year and had been a long-serving member on Ashton Phelps Jr.'s advisory board, which new publisher Ricky Mathews disbanded in advance of creating his own, larger citizens' roundtable. Newly crowned *Advocate* editor Peter Kovacs took the opportunity to deliver another barb to his former longtime employer, Advance and the *Times-Picayune*. "We plan to succeed by relentlessly listening to the people of New Orleans, and this board will help us do that," Kovacs said in an *Advocate* article announcing the board's creation. "We are a Louisiana company so we have no one to answer to except the people of Louisiana."[20]

What's next in the New Orleans newspaper saga that has continued to take new twists and turns more than a year after employees and the community read about the news in the *New York Times*? Invoking another sports analogy, Georges offered this evaluation: "I feel like I have the advantage: The competitors are out of state, they lost their local credibility, they're moving in a different direction and trying to leave New Orleans behind. It would be like going in to Green Bay and taking away the football team. [Advance and NOLA Media Group] misjudged the desires of their customers, and success in business is understanding your customers and understanding their needs—today and in the future. But they'll come back. I don't think they're dead; I just think they're wounded and confused right now."

CHAPTER XII

"Time to Turn in my License"

Not long after the devastation of June 12, 2012, when some two-hundred *Times-Picayune* employees and an undisclosed number of freelancers and contractors learned they would no longer have jobs after September 30, veteran reporter and editor Bruce Nolan, and his wife, Emily, celebrated their fortieth wedding anniversary with a long-anticipated cruise on Europe's Rhine River. While on what should have been a worry-free celebration of the couple's long marriage, Nolan thought about his upcoming layoff and "how I could go back and give it my all for the remaining weeks we all had there," he recalled in the March 2013 interview I conducted with him. But his return to the newspaper, his employer for forty-one years, was stark and ugly:

> I got back to the place and there was no pride, the demoralization was complete. The dress code had fallen apart. People were looking for jobs. But most of all, there was no chance to die with grace and dignity. We just staggered across the finish line. On the last day for everybody, the newsroom was virtually empty. That was it. There was no structure to the final day. There were no exit interviews. I came in and literally had nothing to do. I sat and looked around for a little while, and then I realized it's time for me to go.[1]

After returning to New Orleans and the *Times-Picayune*, Nolan worked through that difficult summer, only to be approached by editor Jim Amoss weeks before he was scheduled to be laid off from his job and asked to stay. Already at retirement age and having invested significant psychic energy into the difficult process of leaving a job he loved, Nolan chose instead to depart. "It was just too late," he would write in a heartrending essay he posted to the private "Friends of the *Times*-Picayune Editorial" Facebook page. "By then, I had devoted too much energy to preparing for separation and the years to come."

Nolan subsequently granted permission to longtime news media blogger Jim Romenesko to republish the essay on Romenesko's popular blog.[2] It encapsulated Nolan's long career, beginning at twenty-four, and ending on that sad September day. The essay highlighted a handful of major events he covered for the newspaper, including a sniper assault in downtown New Orleans in 1973, catching Pope John Paul's eye during the pontiff's historic 1987 US visit, and interviewing volunteers who traveled to New Orleans to help rebuild the city after Hurricane Katrina in 2005. After each remembrance, he repeated the essay's title: "I had a license to be there."

"It's true that after forty-one years, the end at the *Times-Picayune* is ragged and traumatic," the essay continued. "Half the newsroom has been laid off in service to a head-long publishing experiment that feels poorly thought-out and risky in the extreme. People are badly hurt and anxious. A few are hopeful. Each receives a constant stream of encouragement from friends, as I have, that there is not only life after the *Times-Picayune*, but actual happiness as well."

Nolan has since spoken candidly about his enviable position of being "financially secure" and at an age and time in his life where retirement was a viable and acceptable alternative for him. However, for scores of other employees, retirement was not an option—not psychologically, and certainly not financially.

In consultation with Carey Stapleton, a University of New Orleans PhD student who also works for the UNO Survey Center, I conducted a non-scientific survey in late May 2013 of current NOLA Media Group employees and those who lost or chose to leave their jobs as a result of the "digital-first" changes. The survey asked respondents fifteen-some-odd questions regarding the changes and their lives since then. I publicized the survey through the private Facebook page and through a confidential email sent to roughly one-hundred former and current employees whom I either personally knew or who had received assistance through dashTHIRTYdash. Ultimately, 124 primarily former NOLA.com | *Times-Picayune* employees took the survey (only seventeen current employees participated), out of roughly six hundred individuals who were employed by the company at the time of the changes. Given the low number of current employees who participated and the results from the ones who did, it is likely that most people who participated were negatively predisposed toward the company. Because of the way the data was collected, the survey is not statistically valid, but merely a snapshot in time of the thoughts and feelings of non-scientifically selected current and former employees. Some of the most provocative findings were:

• **Of those who left the newspaper, less than half had found full-time jobs at the time of the survey.**

❏ *Of those who had not yet found full-time jobs, almost 70 percent continue to look for work, and one-third are supplementing whatever income, if any, they have by freelancing.*

❏ *Some respondents indicated in optional open-ended responses that they are suffering financially.* "I had to sell the home I loved in order to survive," one respondent wrote. "I have applied for dozens of jobs and rarely get even verification that my resume was received. I have had several interviews, but in most cases, I am either over- or under-qualified. I feel lonely and hopeless most of the time and would rather be dead if I didn't have the few responsibilities I do have." Another wrote, "It has been a very difficult time, financially and emotionally. It has been very hard to move forward in finding another job, and feeling good about myself as a person."

❏ *About half of those who have a new, full-time job still work in the news media, but the layoff forced a significant number of respondents to leave the profession.*

❏ *Respondents fifty years old and older were less likely to have found new jobs, compared with those under fifty.* Only 29 percent of respondents fifty and older have secured new employment, compared with 58 percent of those under fifty. Open-ended comments provided by older employees who lost their jobs indicated that they felt their age was a determining factor in getting laid off. "I just made fifty on May 16, 2013," one former employee wrote. "I truly believe my age and income was a major factor in being replaced with a twenty-eight year old. [Editor] Jim Amoss, shame on you!"

❏ *Editorial employees have had the most success finding jobs among all of the newspaper's departments.* A little more than two-thirds of editorial employees who responded have found new jobs.

• **Most respondents who have found new full-time work earn less than they did at the *Times-Picayune.*** Of respondents who were laid off and have new jobs, about two-thirds make less now than they did at the newspaper. "My life, career-wise, is worse," one wrote. "I spent more than a decade at the *Times-Picayune*. After I was severed, I found a full-time job, but my department is dismantling, so I might lose this job, too. I make about half what I made at the *Times-Picayune*, which is stressful for my family. I was forced to find a less-expensive school for my children because of the salary cut. My current job is much less stressful and more nine-to-five than the *Times-Picayune*, but there are none of the rewards of working in daily journalism."

• **Most respondents left NOLA.com | *Times-Picayune* involuntarily, but 27 percent left of their own accord.** The most-cited reason for choosing to leave was the way the changes were handled or the reality that the work environment was no longer pleasurable.

• **Almost no one thought the changes leading to "digital first" were handled well.** *Of respondents who were former employees,* *almost all disagreed that the changes were handled well, while 85 percent of current employees felt that way.* "June 12, 2012, was the beginning of a jolting, heart-breaking life change for dozens of dedicated veterans of the *Times-Picayune*," one former employee wrote. "As the end drew near, as I showed up for work for more than three months knowing I had no future there, I had to accept that I had been deleted and there was no 'undo' key." Another said: "The way the layoffs were handled was a huge lesson in what *not* to do. The decision-makers were heartless, cowardly liars." Another wrote, "June 12th was the day where I felt mass murderers had entered the building and I had to relive the carnage daily through September 30th."

• Employees who remained with the company were far more likely to believe that a dramatic change was necessary than those who left.

❏ *Employees who stayed with the company felt the changes were driven more by greed on the part of the Newhouse family, and few believed the newspaper's financial performance required such a radical move.* "Unlike the first and second generations of Newhouses, the third generation has no interest at all in working for their money," one respondent wrote. "They want to squeeze every little dime they can from the business and take the money and run." Another respondent who had left the company and has landed a new job said, "I am blessed to no longer be associated with the *Times-Picayune*. I can't fathom knowingly putting my talents, time and energy into a company that totally abandons its purpose to serve the public and allows *greed* to be its compass. Agreed, it is a business, but it was one with a higher moral responsibility to the community. If money were the *only* factor, the owners should never have gotten into the business of providing such an important public service. There are plenty of other ways to make money."

Although many of the stories were grim, other respondents have found happiness post-*Times-Picayune*. "I am extremely happy in my new job and life and often wonder why I didn't leave sooner," one former employee wrote. "I am working at a place where my skills are appreciated and admired — something I rarely felt at the *T-P*."

While several employees who provided open-ended responses held the Newhouses responsible for the pain associated with the changes, an equal number singled out Amoss for blame. "I had always admired and respected Jim Amoss, and it was difficult for me to accept that my feelings were misguided and that the sentiments weren't shared by him," one respondent wrote. "I was hesitant to speak to him about why I was being laid off, but I did send him an email. He never responded."

Several former employees I interviewed independent of the survey have struggled significantly since losing their jobs.

The husband-and-wife duo of Ana and Jorge Courtade had worked for fifteen years in the newspaper's packaging center, assembling the newspaper for distribution to carriers, newsstands, and boxes. Both immigrants and naturalized citizens (Ana Courtade is from Mexico, Jorge Courtade from El Salvador), the couple had put a son and daughter through college, and a third child, a daughter, attends parochial school in New Orleans. They lost their home in Katrina but rebuilt it with the help of the Friends of the *Times-Picayune* Relief Fund created by four newspaper alumnae to help employees hurt by Katrina and its aftermath. Then came the layoff. Exactly four months later, Jorge Courtade was diagnosed with terminal liver cancer. He died six weeks later, at age fifty-nine. Rather than immediately looking for a new job after leaving the *Times-Picayune,* Ana Courtade, fifty-two, instead spent her husband's final weeks caring for him. "All the dreams and things we were having in our minds, we know they will never happen," she said in March 2013. "And now, with his passing, all life has changed forever, and it will never be the same."[3] Ana Courtade secured a new job in April with the help of a former *Times-Picayune* colleague, but left it only a couple of weeks later after it aggravated a chronic health condition she has. As of late

June 2013, she had not secured another job.

Senior NOLA.com copyeditor Cathy Hughes (with whom I contracted to copyedit this book) also has faced some of life's most heartbreaking challenges. She and her husband divorced, then months later, Hurricane Katrina flooded her Lakeview home. She also battled a serious illness, "and through most of that, the *Times-Picayune* was there."

Until September 30, 2012.

When her severance ended February 18, 2013, Hughes, at fifty-three, knew she faced some tough choices. "I want to stay in my house very much, but I've come to understand that that's optional," she said in March 2013. "So, if I have to sell it and get a modest apartment, I can last in New Orleans for quite a while."[4] At the time this book went to press in mid-May 2013, she was freelancing, while continuing to look for a full-time job, and investing money and energy into learning the latest digital publishing and social media skills.

Cass DeLatte's father was a *Times-Picayune* pressman, and died during his thirty-eighth year working for the newspaper. "He used to tell me, 'I'll be there forever,'" Cass DeLatte's wife, Lisa, remembered during a March 2013 interview. "The worst day of my life was packing up my lockers and walking out for that last day," Cass DeLatte said. "I passed my Daddy's old office as I left and I cried." While Cass has landed another position, he earns less than half what he made working at the newspaper, with no benefits except for medical insurance after a nine-month waiting period. A lifelong speech impediment leaves him less-than-confident during job interviews, and a previously undiagnosed break in the bone that attaches his arm and elbow caused severe physical pain and required surgery in April, which forced him to take a medical leave from his new job. But the emotional pain is almost as bad. "I don't feel like a man or the provider of my family anymore," he said, acknowledging that he's struggled with clinical depression since losing his job.[5]

The superior benefits the *Times-Picayune* historically provided to its employees meant St. Bernard Community News editor Kim Sensebe Gritter worked while her husband stayed home and cared for the couple's children, an eleven-year-old son, and an eight-year-old daughter with special needs. After she was laid off from the newspaper, Sensebe Gritter's husband landed a job, while she stayed home and provided their children's primary care. But she still struggles with the psychological scars of losing a job she loved. "You know those plastic dividers that separate your items on the grocery store conveyor belt from the person behind you?" she asked. "Some of the dividers at my local grocery say '*The Times-Picayune*' on them. I was in the check-out line, and I saw one of them, and I broke down. The tears started coming, and I couldn't stop. The cashier came around and gave me a hug and the man behind me said he was going to go home and cancel his subscription."[6]

Longtime River Parishes prep sports reporter Lori Lyons faces similar struggles. "One of the hardest things about this is to let go," she wrote on the Facebook page. "I was a newshound before the *T-P* hired me. I am a newshound still. And it's hard seeing news happen and not have a way to report it—other than my Facebook and Twitter feeds. And it's hard to be unemployed, knowing I could have done the work as well, or better."

I approached about a dozen current employees in an effort to talk to them about life at NOLA Media Group today. Environmental reporter Mark Schleifstein was the only one who spoke to me on the record, and most of the other employees I contacted declined to speak to me even on background.

As both former and current employees prepared to chart their path in a world much different than the one offered for more than 175 years by the *Times-Picayune* of New Orleans, Louisiana, Nolan's essay offered these parting words:

Time to turn in the license.
I took care to honor it. In return, it provided me a better career than I
had a right to expect.
Time for others to use it.
I'm grateful for having been able to borrow it.
-30-

Epilogue

Shortly after I began work on this book, a brief news report, not really more than a blurb, was picked up by news industry website Poynter.org, which despite its brevity, spoke volumes to employees of Advance newspapers across the country who already had lost their jobs, or feared doing so. "Si Newhouse's net worth is $8.1 billion and his brother Donald is worth $7.3 billion, *Forbes* estimates in its new list of world billionaires," Poynter's Andrew Beaujon reported in early March 2013. "Both men's wallets have thickened, at least by *Forbes*'s count, since September, when it said they were worth $7.4 billion and $6.6 billion, respectively."[1] September 30, 2012 was, of course, when the carnage that had begun three years earlier at eight Newhouse-owned newspapers in Michigan commenced across the country.

As I tried to make sense of this saga and to keep up with the sometimes daily developments related to the radical remaking of the Newhouse newspaper empire, I often joked with people familiar with what's gone on in New Orleans that there's nothing like trying to write a book in real time. Significant events continue to happen more than a year after the *Times-Picayune*'s management and Advance Publications were hastily forced by a *New York Times* story to share with their employees and the world what was in store for the 175-year-old, Pulitzer Prize-winning newspaper — and for at least seven additional Advance Publications from Mobile, Alabama, to Portland, Oregon. Some regions like Pennsylvania's Lehigh Valley, seemingly accepted the changes in stride, while New Orleans and Cleveland, fought back. However, the old saying, "Never argue with a man who buys ink by the barrel" seemed to apply during this very modern saga—even if the very livelihoods of those arguing were at stake. With the exception of the fierce grassroots campaign in New Orleans, a local advertising and social media campaign in Cleveland, and incisive commentary by alternative media in Mobile and Birmingham, Alabama; Syracuse, New York; and Portland, Oregon, community objections to the changes were largely subdued.

From that May 2012 evening during which I first read the *New York Times*'s story that my former employer, the venerable *Times-Picayune* of New Orleans, Louisiana—chronicler of deadly yellow fever epidemics, the rise and fall of politicians from Huey Long to David Duke, and the devastation of hurricanes Camille, Betsy and Katrina—would be diminished, I saw this issue as so much more than a daily newspaper moving into the digital age. I viewed it as a fierce and remarkable grassroots battle that America's most unique city would wage against a multi-national media company and its billionaire controlling family-in-transition, and a romantic, yet battered, industry struggling to pull itself out of free fall.

For me, it was also about yet another American employer morally violating a bond with its employees, and robbing them of their livelihoods, often in the final chapters of their working lives when it's generally difficult to secure new, meaningful work. In the case of Advance Publications' newspapers, I also saw this mistreatment as even more grievous because it involved the revocation of an extraordinary Pledge an employer exhorted its employees to rely on for decades—and the resulting carnage that played out in newsrooms, pressrooms, and back offices across the country when that pact was rescinded. Only now, as former employees of Advance newspapers begin to exhaust their severance *en masse*, will New Orleans and other communities across the country begin to fully feel the toll these decisions will exact. Yes, I understand that making people disposable has become an accepted way of conducting business in America, but I also believe that it doesn't mean we should like it—and that we shouldn't try to do better and call it into question when we see it in particularly outrageous forms.

This saga also has been about the apparent combination of hubris and gullibility on the part of an internationally lauded newspaper editor who seemingly swallowed a corporate line with little critical consideration of the true underlying dynamics, and, as a result, tragically lost the respect of many on his staff. It's also about the arrogance and disdain of a previously shrewdly generous and successful monopoly, and the executives who miscalculated the strengths and weaknesses of its operations, and failed, after half a century, to understand one of its most successful markets.

And then there's the centuries-old question this episode renews: does the news media — with the special privileges afforded to it by the US Constitution, numerous state laws, and landmark legal cases — also have special responsibilities that demand different standards of operations and ethics than other businesses? Does Advance owe the markets in which it operates newspapers a different level of consideration and care than, for example, a hedge fund? "It's a cynical plan," consumer news analyst Ken Doctor told me in May 2013, about Advance's "digital first" strategy. "They are shrinking from their community mission. From a short-term profits perspective, it works, but from a democracy and civic impact point of view, it doesn't."

Amid Advance's disastrous handling of the *Times-Picayune* transition, other New Orleans media have emerged or flourished. Of note, of course, is the *Advocate*'s expansion from Baton Rouge into the city, but a range of other outlets — including investigative and public policy website the Lens; hyperlocal Uptown Messenger and its offshoot, Mid-City Messenger; and expanding and emboldened public radio station WWNO — are now nipping at the once-invincible heels of the region's once-daily newspaper. What remains to be seen is whether this renewed concern for and commitment to New Orleans's civic common can replace — or even expand — upon the role the *Times-Picayune* previously played. And as parochial and behind-the-times as New Orleans is often viewed, it's ahead of this game when compared to other Advance markets, where it's unlikely that another John Georges will emerge to force resurrection of halted newspaper editions or to ensure a level of commitment that only competition can. And it's still unclear what the final outcome will be in New Orleans. "Our hope is that we will be treated to an invigorating old-time press war between the *Advocate* and the *Times-Picayune,* but of course, it could end up being two dinosaurs fighting over the last mud hole on an overheated planet," retired *Times-Picayune* metro editor Jed Horne told the *New York Times'*s David Carr in May 2013.[2]

"The name 'the *Times-Picayune'* used to mean one thing—civic constancy, and a very special and significant role within a very unique American city," Carr told me in May 2013 about the previous year in the life of the newspaper. "Now, it means another thing entirely—the dysfunction of the industry at large, and specifically, the lack of understanding of the market the newspaper was serving. I can't think of another story I've covered in the media where the marble has rolled off the table quite as ferociously as this one. I find it kind of breathtaking."[3] During a panel discussion at the American Society of News Editors annual conference in late June 2013,[4] *Times-Picayune* editor Jim Amoss commented, "Maybe we should have listened sooner than we did," the closest he's publicly sounded to regretful since the beginning of this sad, yet extraordinary chapter.

Based on their at-least partial retrenchment from the full-on "digital-first" assault they launched in New Orleans and Alabama in 2012, Advance Publications and its controlling Newhouse family seem to have learned some painful lessons at the expense of the once-mighty *Times-Picayune.* It remains to be seen whether they ultimately will arrive at the same conclusion that Warren Buffett, Aaron Kushner, and other emerging newspaper owners now accept: serving the public interest at profit margins lower than the wildly lucrative decades of the recent past may be the only way the industry can survive.

Notes

Author's Note

1. Cheryl Wagner, *Plenty Enough Suck to Go Around: A Memoir of Floods, Fires, Parades and Plywood* (New York: Citadel Press, 2009), 2.

Chapter 1

1. David Carr, "New Orleans Paper Said to Face Deep Cuts and May Cut Back Publication," Media Decoder, *New York Times*, 23 May 2012, http://mediadecoder.blogs.nytimes.com/2012/05/23/new-orleans-paper-said-to-face-deep-cuts-and-may-cut-back-on-publication/?smid=pl-share.

2. Dan Shea, interview with the author, 14 March 2013.

3. Kevin Allman, "*Times-Picayune* Employees in Shock as Extent of Newhouse Cuts Begins to Emerge," *Gambit* | Best of New Orleans.com, 24 May 2012, http://www.bestofneworleans.com/blogofneworleans/archives/2012/05/24/times-picayune-employees-in-shock-tonight-as-extent-of-newhouse-cuts-begins-to-emerge.

4. Allman, "After the News: Today at *The Times-Picayune*," *Gambit* | Best of New Orleans.com, 24 May 2012, http://www.bestofneworleans.com/blogofneworleans/archives/2012/05/24/after-the-news-today-at-the-times-picayune.

5. Errol Laborde, interview with the author, 13 March 2013.

6. Anne Milling, interview with the author, 15 March 2013.

7. Cass and Lisa DeLatte, interview with the author, 16 March 2013.

8. Carr, "Audio: Veteran *Times-Picayune* Reporter on How Staff Heard the News," Media Decoder, *New York Times*, 25 May 2012, http://mediadecoder.blogs.nytimes.com/2012/05/25/audio-veteran-times-picayune-reporter-on-how-staff-heard-the-news/.

9. Amoss's response was not part of the recording provided by the *New York Times*, but was transcribed from an audio recording of the staff meeting made by a former *Times-Picayune* reporter. Both the transcription and audio recording were shared with the author on the condition that the identity of the reporter would not be disclosed.

10. Bruce Nolan, interview with the author, 19 March 2013.

11. Andrew Beaujon, *"Press-Register* Editor on 'Exciting changes' Headline: 'Perhaps I got carried away,'"* Poynter.org, 25 May 2012, updated 28 May 2012, http://www.poynter.org/latest-news/mediawire/175225/press-register-editor-on-exciting-changes-headline-perhaps-i-got-carried-away/.

12. Rebecca Theim, "NOLA.com Editor on Messy Digital Announcement: 'Arrogant to think we could keep a secret in a newsroom,'" DashTHIRTYdash. org, 12 December 2012, http://dashthirtydash.org/2012/12/12/arrogant/.

13. "The Friends of the *Times-Picayune* Editorial" Facebook page is a private group that requires admission by an administrator, who when this book went to press was Dennis Persica, a longtime former editor at the newspaper. All members are required to secure permission from anyone posting information to the page before publicly disclosing it. In abiding by that rule, the author sought and secured permission from all individuals whose "Friends" Facebook posts are quoted in this book.

14. Evan Christopher, "Riffing on the Tradition: Thank You, Mr. Buffett," NolaVie.com, 1 June 2012, http://www.nolavie.com/2012/05/riffing-on-the-tradition-open-letter-to-mr-warren-buffett-re-the-times-picayune-81243.html.

15. Tom Benson, "Tom Benson's Letter of Support for a Daily Newspaper in New Orleans," Official Site of the New Orleans Saints, 27 May 2012, http://www.neworleanssaints.com/news-and-events/article-1/Tom-Bensons-Letter-of-Support-for-a-Daily-Newspaper-in-New-Orleans/8a88a5e1-2d35-408c-840d-3c447d283c91.

16. Paul Murphy, "Citizens' Group Forms to Save Daily *Times-Picayune* Newspaper," WWL-TV, 4 June 2012, http://www.wwltv.com/news/Times-Picayune-Citizens-Group-Forms-To-Save-Daily-Newspaper-157059965.html.

17. Alex Rawls, "The *T-P* Rally & America's Petri Dish," MySplitMilk.com, 11 June 2012, http://myspiltmilk.com/t-p-rally-americas-petri-dish.

18. Rudy Matthew Vorkapic, "The Future of the *Times-Picayune* Newspaper," *New Orleans Levee*, 13 July 2012, http://nolevee.com/?p=1894.

19. Allman, "'Save the *Picayune*' Rally Draws Hundreds," *Gambit | Best of New Orleans.com*, 5 June 2012, http://www.bestofneworleans.com/blogofneworleans/archives/2012/06/04/save-the-picayune-rally-draws-hundreds.

20. Murphy, "Citizens' Group Forms to save Daily Times-Picayune Newspaper."

Chapter 2

1. Bruce Nolan, *"Times-Picayune* Publisher Ashton Phelps Jr. to Retire this Year," NOLA.com | *Times-Picayune*, 27 March 2012, http://www.nola.com/business/index.ssf/2012/03/times-picayune_publisher_ashto.html.

2. Thomas Ewing Dabney, *One Hundred Great Years: The Story of The Times-Picayune From Its Founding to 1940,* (Baton Rouge: Louisiana State University

Press, 1944).

3. "Samuel I. Newhouse, Publisher, Dies at 84," *New York Times*, 30 August 1979, http://select.nytimes.com/gst/abstract.html?res=F50711F6345D12728D DDA90B94D0405B898BF1D3 (subscription required).

4. "The Newspaper Collector," *Time*, 27 July 1962: 54-59.

5. "Ashton Phelps, 69, Is Dead; New Orleans News Executive," *New York Times*, 22 March 1983, http://www.nytimes.com/1983/03/22/obituaries/ ashton-phelps-69-is-dead-new-orleans-news-executive.html.

6. Carol Felsenthal, *Citizen Newhouse: Portrait of a Media Merchant*, (New York: Seven Stories Press, 1998), 148.

7. "1980: New Orleans' Two Major Newspapers Merge," NOLA.com | *Times-Picayune*, 23 December 2011, http://www.nola.com/175years/index. ssf/2011/12/1980_new_orleans_becomes_a_sin.html.

8. Bruce Nolan, "*Times-Picayune* Publisher Ashton Phelps Jr. to Retire This Year," NOLA.com | *Times-Picayune*, 27 March 2012, http://www.nola.com/ business/index.ssf/2012/03/times-picayune_publisher_ashto.html.

9. Micheline Maynard, "3 Numbers in the Battle to Save the New Orleans *Times-Picayune*," Forbes.com, 25 May 2012, http://www.forbes.com/sites/ michelinemaynard/2012/05/25/3-numbers-in-the-battle-to-save-the-new-orleans-times-picayune/.

10. Jennifer Saba, "New Study Charts Readership Reach—Guess Who's No. 1?" *Editor & Publisher*, 2 June 2009, http://www.editorandpublisher. com/Article/New-Study-Charts-Readership-Reach-Guess-Who-s-No-1- (subscription required).

11. Richard H. Meeker, *Newspaperman: S.I. Newhouse and the Business of News*, (New York and New Haven: Ticknor & Fields, 1983), 252.

12. Richard Pollak, ed. "The 10 Worst," *(MORE)*, 4, no. 5 (May 1974): 20.

13. Jack Nelson, "New Orleans *Times-Picayune* Series on Racism," Pew Research Center's Project for Excellence in Journalism Case Studies, 15 February 2003, http://www.journalism.org/node/1784 and http://www.unc. edu/~pmeyer/racism.html.

14. Felsenthal, 440.

15. *W. Howard Bronson v. the Mobile Press-Register, Inc., et. al.*, 02-CV-2009-901831.00 (C.C. Mobile, AL 2009).

16. Holbert, Rob, "Bronson's suit ends in undisclosed settlement," *Lagniappe*, 19 April 2011, http://classic.lagniappemobile.com/article. asp?articleID=4415&sid=1.

17. *The Times-Picayune, From A to Z: The Times-Picayune Employee Benefits for Permanent and Term Full-Time Employees*, Employee Booklet, (New Orleans, 1991).

18. Maggie Mahar, "All in the Family: How the Newhouses Run Their Vast Media Empire," *Barron's National Business and Financial Weekly*, 27 November 1989, available on 69, 48, ProQuest.

19. Richard Meeker, telephone interview with the author, 16 April 2013.

20. Aaron Mesh, "Black and White and Red All Over," *Willamette Week*, 26 June 2013, http://www.wweek.com/portland/article-20836-black_and_white_and_red_all_over.html.

21. Rob Holbert, "Observations from Bronson Trial," *Lagniappe*, 19 April 2011, http://classic.lagniappemobile.com/article.asp?articleID=4433&sid=18.

22. Ashton Phelps, Jr., memo to employees, 23 June 2008.

23. Ashton Phelps, Jr., memo to employees, 26 December 2008.

24. Ashton Phelps, Jr., memo to employees, 16 November 2011.

25. Ashton Phelps, Jr., memo to employees, 19 January 2012.

26. "New Digitally Focused Company Launches this Fall with Beefed Up Online Coverage; The *Times-Picayune* Will Move this Fall to Three Printed Papers a Week," NOLA.com | *Times-Picayune*, 24 May 2012, updated 5 June, 2012, http://www.nola.com/business/index.ssf/2012/05/nolamediagroup.html.

27. The author ran a search on "Ricky Mathews" on al.com and reviewed all of the listed stories to arrive at these numbers.

28. Joseph Serna, "Hurricane Sandy Death Toll Climbs Above 110, N.Y. Hardest Hit," *Los Angeles Times*, 3 November 2012, http://articles.latimes.com/2012/nov/03/nation/la-na-nn-hurricane-sandy-deaths-climb-20121103.

29. Allison Plyer, "Facts for Features: Hurricane Katrina Impact," Greater New Orleans Community Data Center, 10 August 2012, http://www.gnocdc.org/Factsforfeatures/HurricaneKatrinaImpact/index.html.

30. Linda Deutsch, "New Orleans *Times-Picayune* Trying to Report, Survive," Associated Press, 16 January 2006, http://www.editorandpublisher.com/Article/New-Orleans-Times-Picayune-Trying-to-Report-Survive (subscription required).

31. Brian Thevenot, "Apocalypse in New Orleans," *American Journalism Review*, (October/November 2005), http://www.ajr.org/article.asp?id=3959.

32. "Post-Hurricane Katrina Population Estimates: New Orleans and Houston," n.d. http://www.demographia.com/db-katrinano.htm.

33. Keach Hagey, "*Times-Picayune* Is Singing the Blues to Angry Readers," *Wall Street Journal*, 9 September 2012, http://online.wsj.com/article/SB10000872396390443589304577638023262616192.html?mg=id-wsj#articleTabs%3Darticle.

34. Warren Buffett, 2012 Shareholders' Letter for Berkshire Hathaway, Inc., 1 March 2013, http://www.berkshirehathaway.com/letters/2012ltr.pdf.

35. Newspaper Association of America, "The American Newspaper Media Industry Revenue Profile 2012," 8 April 2013, http://www.naa.org/Trends-and-Numbers/Newspaper-Revenue/Newspaper-Media-Industry-Revenue-Profile-2012.aspx.

36. Nat Ives, "What Print Cuts at *Times-Picayune* Mean for Papers," *Advertising Age*, 28 May 2012, http://adage.com/article/media/print-cuts-times-picayune-papers/235006/.

37. "The State of the News Media 2013: An Annual Report on American Journalism," Pew Research Center Project for Excellence in Journalism, 18 March 2013, http://stateofthemedia.org/.

38. Jim Amoss, "The Message for Our Organization Is Clear: Adapt, or Fade Away," NOLA.com | *Times-Picayune*, 13 June 2012, http://www.nola.com/opinions/index.ssf/2012/06/post_153.html.

39. Felsenthal, 433.

40. Mark Holan, "'Newhouse Pledge,' Job Security, Now Relics of Once-Thriving Newspaper Industry," Poynter.org, 23 September 2009, http://www.poynter.org/latest-news/top-stories/98490/newhouse-pledge-job-security-now-relics-of-once-thriving-newspaper-industry/.

41. Dave Astor, "Newhouse News Service to Close," *Editor & Publisher*, 30 July 2008, http://www.editorandpublisher.com/Article/UPDATED-Newhouse-News-Service-to-Close (subscription required.)

42. Joe Strupp, "Advance Announces Company-wide Furloughs," *Editor & Publisher*, 23 March 2009, http://www.editorandpublisher.com/Article/Advance (subscription required).

43. Ashton Phelps, Jr., letter to employees, 7 December 2009.

44. Ashton Phelps, Jr., memo to all full-time employees, 25 August 2011.

45. Ashton Phelps, Jr., letter to employees, 5 August 2009.

46. Mark J. Perry, "Free-fall: Adjusted for Inflation, Print Newspaper Advertising Revenue in 2012 Was Lower than in 1950," American Enterprise Institute, 8 April 2013, http://www.aei-ideas.org/2013/04/free-fall-adjusted-for-inflation-print-newspaper-advertising-in-2012-was-lower-than-in-1950/.

47. Toon Van Beeck, "Ten Key Industries That Will Decline, Even After the Economy Revives," *Commercial Insights | Sales and Marketing,* ABA Center for Commercial Lending & Business Banking, May 2011, http://www.ibisworld.com/Common/MediaCenter/DyingIndustries.pdf.

48. "BLS Spotlight on Statistics: Media and Information," Bureau of Labor Statistics, January 2013, http://www.bls.gov/spotlight/2013/media/data_cew_establishments.htm.

49. "2013 Census" and "American Society of Newspaper Editors 2012 Census: Table A—Minority Employment in Daily Newspapers," American Society of News Editors, 4 April 2012, http://asne.org/content.asp?pl=140&sl=129&contentid=129 and http://asne.org/content.asp?pl=121&sl=284&contentid=284.

50. Rick Edmonds, "ASNE Census Finds 2,600 Newsroom Jobs Were Lost in 2012," Poynter.org, 25 June 2013, updated 26 June 2013, http://www.poynter.org/latest-news/business-news/the-biz-blog/216617/asne-census-finds-2600-newsroom-jobs-were-lost-in-2012/.

51. Richard Pérez-Peña, "At Newhouse Newspapers, a Change in a No-Layoffs Policy." Media Decoder, *New York Times*, 5 August 2009, http://mediadecoder.

blogs.nytimes.com/2009/08/05/at-newhouse-newspapers-a-change-in-a-no-layoffs-policy/.

52. Mesh, "Black and White and Red All Over."

53. Katherine Sayre, "Former *Press-Register* Publisher Howard Bronson's Civil Trial Ends in Settlement," al.com | *Press-Register*, 9 April 2011, http://blog.al.com/live/2011/04/former_press-register_publishe_1.html.

54. Douglas McCollam, "Up and Down on the Bayou: A Snapshot of The *Times-Picayune* Five Years after Katrina," *Columbia Journalism Review*, 1 July 2010, http://www.cjr.org/behind_the_news/timespicayune_five_years_later.php?page=all.

55. Chris Rose, "Stop the Presses: Life and Death at the *Times-Picayune*," *Oxford American*, 27 August 2012, http://www.oxfordamerican.org/articles/2012/aug/27/new-south-journalism-sometimes-picayune/.

56. Nolan, interview with the author.

57. Mark Lisheron, "Big Time in the Big Easy," *American Journalism Review*, July/August 1997, http://www.ajr.org/article.asp?id=682.

58. Harry Shearer, "The Sometimes Picayune: Want to Damage New Orleans (Again)? Decimate its Newspaper," *Columbia Journalism Review*, 6 June 2012, http://www.cjr.org/behind_the_news/the_sometimes_picayune.php?page=all.

59. Jacob Fenton, "Broadband Adoption Map: South Lags Behind, Rural Areas Improve," Investigative Reporting Workshop, American University School of Communication, 23 March 2012, http://investigativereportingworkshop.org/investigations/broadband-adoption/htmlmulti/broadband-adoption-map/.

Chapter 3

1. *Times-Picayune* newsroom employees, letter to Jim Amoss and Lynn Cunningham, 1 June 2012.

2. Kevin Allman, "*Times-Picayune* Meetings Now Unscheduled for Monday and Tuesday," *Gambit* | Best of New Orleans.com, 1 June 2012, http://www.bestofneworleans.com/blogofneworleans/archives/2012/06/01/times-picayune-meetings-now-unscheduled-for-monday-and-tuesday.

3. Cathy Hughes, interview with the author, 17 March 2013.

4. Renée Peck, "'A Bloodbath, No Other Word for It,'" NolaVie, 12 June 2012, http://nolavie.com/2012/06/a-bloodbath-no-other-word-for-it-70436.html.

5. Ray Massett, general manager, *Times-Picayune*, letter to Greg A. Anders, state rapid response coordinator, Louisiana Workforce Commission, New Orleans, 15 June 2012.

6. Kathy Anderson and Doug Parker, interview with the author, 17 March 2013.

7. Ryan Chittum, "The Battle of New Orleans," *Columbia Journalism Review*, 1 March 2013, http://www.cjr.org/feature/the_battle_of_new_orleans.

php?page=all.

8. John Pope, "NOLA Media Group Announces Ad Sales Leadership Team," NOLA.com | *Times-Picayune*, 5 August 2012, http://www.nola.com/business/index.ssf/2012/08/nola_media_group_announces_ad.html.

9. Patti Pitt, telephone interview with the author, 7 May 2013.

10. Erik Wemple, "*Times-Picayune* Food Critic Says Nieman Fellowship Prompted his Layoff," A Reported Opinion Blog on News Media, *Washington Post*, 12 June 2012, http://www.washingtonpost.com/blogs/erik-wemple/post/times-picayune-restaurant-critic-laid-off/2012/06/12/gJQA3dywXV_blog.html.

11. Brett Anderson. Twitter posts, 12 June 2012, 1:35 p.m. and 2:27 p.m.; and 13 June 2012, 3:11 p.m., https://twitter.com/BrettAndersonTP.

12. "Brett Anderson Invited to Return After Nieman Fellowship," NOLA.com | *Times-Picayune*, 15 June 2013, http://www.nola.com/dining/index.ssf/2012/06/brett_anderson_invited_to_retu.html.

13. "Death by 400 Cuts," *Weld for Birmingham,* 19 June 2012, http://weldbham.com/blog/2012/06/19/death-of-400-cuts-advances-retreat-the-lifelines-of-those-bylines/.

14. Wade Kwon, "*Birmingham News* Fires More than 100 Employees," Media of Birmingham (blog), 12 June 2012, http://mediaofbirmingham.com/2012/06/12/birmingham-news-fires-more-than-100-employees/.

15. Ed Griffin-Nolan, "Post-Mortem," *Syracuse New Times*, 3 February 2013, http://www.syracusenewtimes.com/newyork/article-6446-post-mortem.html.

16. Griffin-Nolan, "When Newspapers Are the News," *Syracuse New Times*, 20 February 2013, http://www.syracusenewtimes.com/newyork/article-6454-when-newspapers-are-the-news.html.

17. Ted Sherman and Kelly Heyboer, "*Star-Ledger* Announces Layoffs of 34 Employees, Including 18 Newsroom Staff," nj.com | *Star-Ledger*, 17 January 2013, http://www.nj.com/news/index.ssf/2013/01/star-ledger_announces_layoffs.html.

18. Robert L. Smith, "*Plain Dealer* Staff Launches Campaign to Save the Daily Paper," Cleveland.com | *Plain Dealer*, 9 November 2012, http://www.cleveland.com/business/index.ssf/2012/11/plain_dealer_staff_launch_a_ca.html.

19. Erick Trickey, "*Plain Dealer* Union Members Drink 7-Day Lager, Mull Bitter Agreement," *Cleveland Magazine* blog, 7 December 2012, http://www.clevelandmagazine.blogspot.com/2012/12/plain-dealer-union-members-drink-7-day.html.

20. Julie Moos, "Cleveland *Plain Dealer* Union Gets New Deal That Protects Staff from Future Layoffs, Raises Pay 8%," Poynter.org, 7 December 2012, http://www.poynter.org/latest-news/mediawire/197469/cleveland-plain-dealer-union-gets-new-deal-that-protects-staff-from-future-layoffs-raises-pay-8/.

21. Rollie Dreussi, telephone interview with author, 3 May 2013.

22. "TNG Local 1: the Northeast Ohio Newspaper Guild," n.d., http://tnglocal1.org/mainpages/home.htm.

23. Erik Wemple, "*Cleveland Plain Dealer* Staffers Find Out if They're 'Separated From Employment,'" A Reported Opinion Blog on News Media, *Washington Post*, 31 July 2013, http://www.washingtonpost.com/blogs/erik-wemple/wp/2013/07/31/cleveland-plain-dealer-staffers-find-out-if-theyre-separated-from-employment/.

24. Vanessa Wong, "Layoffs: *Plain Dealer* Journalists Get Axed Over the Phone," *Bloomberg Businessweek*, 1 August 2013, http://www.businessweek.com/articles/2013-08-01/plain-dealer-journalists-feel-pain-of-being-laid-off-by-phone.

25. Abe Zaidan, "The *PD* Hit List. Anybody You Know?" GrumpyAbe.com, 31 July 2013, http://grumpyabe.blogspot.com/2013/07/the-pd-hit-list-anybody-you-know.html

26. Industry news site Poynter.org compiled a list of some of the tweets from *Plain Dealer* staffers on the day the layoffs were announced, which was incorporated into its news report at http://www.poynter.org/latest-news/mediawire/219751/plain-dealer-eliminated-the-jobs-of-approximately-50-journalists/#.Uflc5v3hZRg.twitter.

27. Robert L. Smith, "The Plain Dealer Executes Newsroom Layoffs as Era of Daily Delivery Nears End," Cleveland.com | *Plain Dealer*, 31 July 2013, http://www.cleveland.com/business/index.ssf/2013/07/plain_dealer_executes_newsroom.html.

28. Dylan McClemore, "Mass Layoffs or 'Job Notifications'? Advance's Attempt to Spin its Deep South Newspaper Guttings," DylanMcClemore.com, 13 June 2012, http://dylanmclemore.com/2012/06/13/mass-layoffs-or-job-notifications-advances-attempt-to-spin-its-deep-south-newspaper-guttings/.

29. James Arruebarrena, telephone interview with the author, 3 May 2013.

30. "Exhibit A: The *Times-Picayune*, Department, Title, Age, Selected for Layoff?" 12 June 2012.

31. *W. Howard Bronson v. the Mobile Press-Register, Inc.*, et. al.

32. Amoss, "Major Changes Had to Be Done, More to Come," interviewed by Melanie Hebert, *The 504*, WUPL-TV and WWL-TV, 17 May 2013, http://www.wwltv.com/on-tv/wupl/T-P-editor--207957051.html.

33. Rick Edmonds, "Cutting Print Is a Money-Loser for *Times-Picayune*, but Cutting Staff Makes Changes Slightly Profitable," Poynter.org, 18 June 2012, http://www.poynter.org/latest-news/business-news/the-biz-blog/177005/cutting-print-is-a-money-loser-for-times-picayune-but-cutting-staff-makes-changes-slightly-profitable/.

34. Kelly Nelson, recruitment partner, NOLA Media Group Recruitment Team (contractor with Decision Toolbox), email to Catherine Hughes, 11 December 2012.

35. Lori Lyons, telephone interview with the author, 12 April 2013.

36. Megan Braden-Capone, Facebook instant message interview with the author, 4 May 2013.

37. Matthew Hinton, email interview with the author, 2 April 2013.

38. Victor Andrews, Facebook message interview, 24 April 2013.

39. New Orleans Bureau, "Nell Nolan, N.O.'s Leading Social Columnist, to Join the *Advocate*," *Advocate*, July 22, 2013, http://theadvocate.com/news/6564047-123/nell-nolan-nos-leading-social.

40. Kyle Whitmire, "New Orleans Rallies around *Times-Picayune*, but Where's the Outrage in Birmingham?" *Weld for Birmingham*, 5 June 2012, http://weldbham.com/secondfront/2012/06/05/new-orleans-rallies-around-times-picayune-but-wheres-the-outrage-in-birmingham/.

41. Allman, "The Fight to Save the *Times-Picayune*," *Gambit* | Best of New Orleans.com, 18 September 2012, http://www.bestofneworleans.com/gambit/the-fight-to-save-the-times-picayune/Content?oid=2072666.

42. John Archibald, "Why No Protest in Birmingham?" *Birmingham News*, 5 June 2012, http://blog.al.com/archiblog/2012/06/why_no_protest_in_birmingham.html.

43. Holbert, "Media Frenzy — By Rob Holbert," *Lagniappe*, 10 January 2012, http://classic.lagniappemobile.com/article.asp?articleID=5100&sid=18.

44. Holbert, telephone interview with the author, 13 May 2013.

Chapter 4

1. Mark Schleifstein, "Covering the Coast," *GW Magazine*, Fall 2010, http://www.gwu.edu/~magazine/archive/2010_fall/feature2.html.

2. James O'Byrne, "Bicycling Into the Heart of the Flood: A Hurricane Katrina Remembrance," NOLA.com | *Times-Picayune*, 28 August 2010, updated 29 August 2011, http://www.nola.com/katrina/index.ssf/2010/08/bicycling_into_the_heart_of_th.html.

3. Lisa Guernsey, "Hurricane Forces New Orleans Newspaper to Face a Daunting Set of Obstacles," *New York Times*, 5 September 2005, http://www.nytimes.com/2005/09/05/business/media/05picayune.html.

4. "*Times-Picayune* Editor Jim Amoss, a Voice for New Orleans," *Fresh Air*, NPR, 4 January 2006, http://www.npr.org/templates/story/story.php?storyId=5126000.

5. Guernsey, "Hurricane Forces."

6. David Meeks, "Lessons in Rebuilding: A House and a Newspaper," *Nieman Reports: Nieman Foundation for Journalism at Harvard*, Fall 2007, http://www.nieman.harvard.edu/reports/article/100155/Lessons-in-Rebuilding-A-House-and-a-Newspaper.aspx.

7. Thevenot, "Apocalypse in New Orleans."

8. Rusty Costanza, interview with the author, 15 March 2013.

9. Guernsey, "Hurricane Forces."

10. Shea, email interview, 9 May 2013.

11. Rose, "Stop the Presses," 2012.

12. Rose, *One Dead in Attic* (New Orleans: Chris Rose Books, 2005).

13. "*T-P* Resumes Printing," NOLA.com | *Times-Picayune*, 1 September 2005, http://www.nola.com/katrina/index.ssf/2005/09/t-p_resumes_printing.html.

14. G. Sherman, "Newhouses Right *Times-Picayune* As It Bails Water," *New York Observer*, 12 September 2005, http://observer.com/2005/09/newhouses-right-itimespicayunei-as-it-bails-water.

15. Robert Niles, "NOLA.com Blogs and Forums Help Save Lives after Katrina," Online Journalism Review, 13 September 2005, http://www.ojr.org/050913glaser/.

16. Sig Gissler, interview with the author, 3 May 2013.

17. Beverly Spicer, "The Ordeal of Ted Jackson and the New Orleans *Times Picayune*," The Digital Journalist, December 2005, http://digitaljournalist.org/issue0512/jackson_intro.html.

18. "City Not Safe for Anyone." NOLA.com | *Times-Picayune*. 1 September 2005, updated 13 August 2010, http://www.nola.com/katrina/index.ssf/2005/09/city_not_safe_for_anyone.html.

19. Thevenot, "Apocalypse in New Orleans."

20. Susan Saulny, "After Long Stress, Newsman in New Orleans Unravels," *New York Times*, 10 August 2006, http://www.nytimes.com/2006/08/10/us/10orleans.html?_r=0.

21. John McCusker, interview with the author, 18 March 2013.

22. John Pope, "Johanna Schindler, Director of Communications at UNO, Dies at 53," NOLA.com | *Times-Picayune*, 8 March 2010, http://www.nola.com/news/index.ssf/2010/03/johanna_schindler_director_of.html.

23. "The 2006 Pulitzer Prize Winners: Commentary," n.d., http://www.pulitzer.org/citation/2006-Commentary.

24. Barry Yeoman, "The Redemption of Chris Rose," *Columbia Journalism Review*, January/February 2008, http://barryyeoman.com/2008/01/chris-rose/.

25. Rose, interview with the author, 31 May 2013.

26. Pope, "Personal Circumstances Intersect with Professional Obligations," *Nieman Reports: Nieman Foundation for Journalism at Harvard*, Fall 2007, http://www.nieman.harvard.edu/reports/article/100153/Personal-Circumstances-Intersect-With-Professional-Obligations.aspx.

27. Michael Perlstein, "Covering Katrina: On Taking it Personally," in *The Mind of a Journalist*, ed. Jim Willis, (Los Angeles: Sage, 2010).

28. Nolan, "New Orleans and *The Times-Picayune*," *The Story*, American Public Media, 21 June 2013, http://www.thestoryonline.org/stories/2012-06/new-orleans-and-times-picayune.

29. "Faster, Faster–Please" (editorial), *Times-Picayune*, 2 September 2005, http://www.nola.com/katrina/index.ssf/2005/09/editorial_faster_faster_--please.html.

30. "An Open Letter to the President" (editorial), *Times-Picayune*, 4 September 2005, http://www.nola.com/katrina/pages/090405/a15.pdf.

31. "Is New Orleans Worth Reclaiming?" (editorial), *Waterbury Republican-American*, 31 August 2005, http://www.freerepublic.com/focus/f-news/1474336/posts.

32. "Yes, We Are Worth It" (editorial), *Times-Picayune*, 2 September 2005, http://www.nola.com/katrina/pages/090205/a15.pdf.

33. Jarvis DeBerry, "A Forceful Voice About the City's Survival," *Nieman Reports: Nieman Foundation for Journalism at Harvard*, Fall 2007, http://www.nieman.harvard.edu/reports/article/100154/A-Forceful-Voice-About-a-Citys-Survival.aspx.

34. O'Byrne, Schleifstein, and Susan Feeney, "Journalism Driven By Passion," *Nieman Reports*, Fall 2007, http://www.nieman.harvard.edu/reports/article/100149/Journalism-Driven-By-Passion.aspx.

35. Feeney, "The Friends of The *Times-Picayune* Relief Fund." *Nieman Reports: Nieman Foundation for Journalism at Harvard*, Fall 2007, http://www.nieman.harvard.edu/reports/article/100201/The-Friends-of-The-Times-Picayune-Relief-Fund.aspx.

36. Brian Thevenot, "To Love This City Back to Life," *American Journalism Review*, August/September 2006, http://www.ajr.org/article.asp?id=4155.

37. Curtis Brainard, "Calling Katrina: New Orleans *Times-Picayune*'s 2005 Hurricane Coverage Included in NYU's 'Top 10 Works of the Decade,'" *Columbia Journalism Review*, 6 April 2010, http://www.cjr.org/the_observatory/calling_katrina.php?page=all.

38. Sherman, "Newhouse Rights *Times-Picayune* as it Bails Water."

39. Carr, "A Flood Begets a Paper Ark," *New York Times*, 30 April 2007, http://www.nytimes.com/2007/04/30/business/media/30carr.html.

40. Jennifer Saba, "*Times-Picayune* Circ Down Nearly 30% Over Four Years," *Editor & Publisher*, 28 April 2008, http://www.editorandpublisher.com/Article/-Times-Picayune-Circ-Down-Nearly-30-Over-Four-years (subscription required).

41. Allison Plyer, "Facts for Features: Hurricane Katrina Recovery," Greater New Orleans Community Data Center, 3 February 2013, http://www.gnocdc.org/Factsforfeatures/HurricaneKatrinaRecovery/index.html.

42. "Total Circ: The *Times-Picayune*," Alliance for Audited Media, Circulation averages for the six months ended 30 September 2012, http://abcas3.auditedmedia.com/ecirc/newstitlesearchus.asp.

Chapter 5

1. Jeff Adelson, Bruce Alpert, Bill Barrow, Cindy Chang, Claire Galofaro,

Stephanie Grace, David Hammer, Michelle Krupa, Laura Maggi, Brendan McCarthy, Becky Mowbray, John Pope, Rich Rainey, Paul Rioux, Mark Schleifstein, Andrew Vanacore, and Jaquetta White, letter to Jim Amoss, Mark Lorando, Lynn Cunningham, 19 June 2012.

2. David Hammer, email interview with the author, 21 April 2013.

3. Errol Laborde, interview with the author, 13 March 2013.

4. Emmett Mayer III, email interview with the author, 22 April 2013.

5. "*Oregonian* Asks Staffers to Scab at Paper in Ohio," *Northwest Labor Press*, 17 December 2004, http://www.nwlaborpress.org/2004/12-17-04Oreg.html.

6. Jennifer Brown, telephone interview with the author, 10 May 2013.

7. Brown, text interview with the author, 30 June 2013.

8. Kari Dequine Harden, telephone interview with the author, 30 May 2013.

Chapter 6

1. Allman, "*Times-Picayune* Citizens' Group Formally Asks Newhouse Family to Sell the Paper," *Gambit* | Best of New Orleans.com, 9 July 2012, http://www.bestofneworleans.com/blogofneworleans/archives/2012/07/09/times-picayune-citizens-group-formally-asks-newhouse-family-to-sell-the-paper.

2. Dylan Byers, "Newhouse: 'No' on *Times-Picayune* Sale," Politico.com, 10 July 2012, http://www.politico.com/blogs/media/2012/07/newhouse-spurns-request-to-sell-timespicayune-128512.html.

3. Erik Wemple, "*Times-Picayune* Publisher Spews Standard Workforce-Reduction Garbage." A Reported Opinion Blog of the News Media, *Washington Post*, 24 May 2012, http://www.washingtonpost.com/blogs/erik-wemple/post/times-picayune-publisher-spews-standard-workforce-reduction-garbage/2012/05/24/gJQAfy4FnU_blog.html.

4. Vorkapic, "Daily *Times-Picayune* Newspaper Dead at 175," *New Orleans Levee*, 8 October 2012, http://nolevee.com/?p=2263.

5. Jules Bentley, "The Murder of *The Times-Picayune*: Part One," NOLA Anarcha, 9 July 2012, http://nolaanarcha.blogspot.com/2012/07/murder-of-times-picayune-part-one.html.

6. Bentley, "The Murder of *The Times-Picayune*: Part Two," NOLA Anarcha, 10 July 2012, http://nolaanarcha.blogspot.com/2012/07/murder-of-times-picayune-part-two.html.

7. Allman, "Spotted in *The Times-Picayune* Newsroom: Lou Grant," *Gambit* | Best of New Orleans.com, 10 June 2012, http://www.bestofneworleans.com/blogofneworleans/archives/2012/06/10/spotted-in-the-times-picayune-newsroom-lou-grant.

8. "Jindal Laments Changes at *Times-Picayune*," WDSU.com, 1 July 2012, http://www.wdsu.com/news/politics/Jindal-laments-changes-at-Times-Picayune/-/9853324/15364302/-/146jm0q/-/index.html#ixzz2PLRY89UQ.

9. David Vitter, "Vitter Urges Newhouse to Sell the *Times Picayune*," 26 July

2012, US Senator David Vitter of Louisiana Website, http://www.vitter.senate.gov/newsroom/press/vitter-urges-newhouse-to-sell-the-times-picayune.

10. Benson, Letter to Steven Newhouse, 25 July 2012, http://images.bimedia.net/documents/BENSON+LETTER.pdf.

11. Mike Hoss and Dominic Massa, "Benson Offers to Buy *Times-Picayune*; Paper Not for Sale, Say Advance Officials," WWL-TV, 26 July 2012, http://www.wwltv.com/news/Benson-Times-Picayune-163863846.html.

12. Rebecca Theim, "New Orleans' 2013 Mardi Gras parades take aim at radical changes, layoffs at *Times-Picayune*," dashTHIRTYdash.org, 8 February 2013, http://dashthirtydash.org/2013/02/08/2013-mardi-gras-tp-satire/.

Chapter 7

1. Steve Newhouse, "Steve Newhouse Explains Michigan Transition, *Times-Picayune* Future," Poynter.org, 3 August 2012, updated 6 August 2012, http://www.poynter.org/latest-news/business-news/183948/steve-newhouse-explains-michigan-transition-times-picayune-future/.

2. Amoss, "The Message for Our Organization Is Clear: Adapt, or Fade Away," NOLA.com | *Times-Picayune*, 13 June 2012, http://www.nola.com/opinions/index.ssf/2012/06/post_153.html.

3. Laurel Champion, "Letter from Ann Arbor News Publisher Laurel Champion," MLive.com, 23 March 2009, http://www.mlive.com/news/ann-arbor/index.ssf/2009/03/letter_from_ann_arbor_news_pub.html.

4. Dan Gaydou, "Letter from Publisher Dan Gaydou: Announcing the MLive Media Group," MLive.com, 2 November 2011, http://blog.mlive.com/updates/2011/11/letter_from_our_publisher_anno.html.

5. Lindsay Kalter, "The Ann Arbor Precedent," *American Journalism Review*, August/September 2012, http://ajr.org/Article.asp?id=5377.

6. Micheline Maynard, "What New Orleans Can Expect When Its Newspaper Goes Away," Forbes.com, 24 May 2012, http://www.forbes.com/sites/michelinemaynard/2012/05/24/what-new-orleans-can-expect-when-its-newspaper-goes-away/.

7. Amoss, "Message for Our Organization Is Clear: Adapt, or Fade Away."

8. Howard Kurtz, "Why Warren Buffett Still Buys Newspapers as the Industry Sinks," Daily Beast, 4 June 2012, http://www.thedailybeast.com/articles/2012/06/04/why-warren-buffett-still-buys-newspapers-as-the-industry-sinks.html.

9. Ken Doctor, "The Newsonomics of Aaron Kushner's Virtuous Circles," Nieman Journalism Lab, 31 January 2013, http://www.niemanlab.org/2013/01/the-newsonomics-of-aaron-kushners-virtuous-circles/.

10. Dena Levitz, "MXC Session Coverage: Why Invest in Newspapers?" Newspaper Association of America MediaXchange website, 16 April 2013, http://mediaxchange.naa.org/why-invest-in-newspapers.

11. Rem Rieder, "Against All Odds, a New Newspaper War Erupts," *USAToday*, 24 July 2013, http://www.usatoday.com/story/money/columnist/rieder/2013/07/24/money-columnist-rieder-newspaper-war/2578511/.

12. Martin Langeveld, "The Coming Death of Seven-Day Publication," Nieman Journalism Lab—A Project of the Nieman Foundation at Harvard, 21 December 2012, http://www.niemanlab.org/2012/12/the-coming-death-of-seven-day-publication/.

13. Tom Rosenstiel, Mark Jurkowitz, and Hong Ji, "The Search for a New Business Model: How Newspapers Are Faring Trying to Build Digital Revenue," Pew Research Center's Project for Excellence in Journalism, 5 March 2012, http://www.journalism.org/analysis_report/industry_looking_ahead.

14. Clive Mathieson, "Fairfax Chief Greg Hywood Sizes Up the End of Papers," *Australian*, 1 May 2013, http://www.theaustralian.com.au/media/fairfax-chief-greg-hywood-sizes-up-the-end-of-papers/story-e6frg996-1226632738646 (subscription required).

15. "Editor's Choice: The Top 21," *Columbia Journalism Review*, November/December 1999, 16. The magazine polled editors of newspapers in all fifty states and former presidents of the American Society of Newspaper Editors to compile the rankings.

16. *Oregonian, "The Oregonian* and the Pulitzer Prize," 8 April 2013, http://www.oregonlive.com/editors/index.ssf/2013/04/the_oregonian_and_the_pulitzer.html.

17. Matthew Kish, "Q&A: *Oregonian* Publisher N. Christian Anderson III," *Portland Business Journal*, 20 June 2013, http://www.bizjournals.com/portland/news/2013/06/21/qa-oregonian-publisher-chris-anderson.html?page=all

18. Aaron Mesh, "Stop the Presses: The *Oregonian* May Not Be a Daily Newspaper Much Longer," *Willamette Weekly*, 8 August 2012, http://www.wweek.com/portland/article-19535-stop_the_presses.html.

19. Mesh, "Black, White and Red All Over."

20. Dave Miller, "*Oregonian* Publisher Talks About The Changes," Oregon Public Radio, *Think Out Loud*, 21 June 2013, http://www.opb.org/thinkoutloud/shows/oregonian-publisher-talks-about-changes/.

21. Mesh, "*The Oregonian* Is Already Hiring New Reporters," *Willamette Week*, June 24, 2013, http://wweek.com/portland/blog-preview-30355-the-oregonian-is-already-hiring-new-reporters.html.

22. Mesh, "More Than 35 Newsroom Staff Laid Off at *The Oregonian*."

23. OregonLive.com, "Oregonian Media Group to Launch with Digital, Print Products," June 20, 2013, http://www.oregonlive.com/news/index.ssf/2013/06/oregonian-media-group.html#incart_river_default.

24. Doctor, "The Newsonomics of Advance's Advancing Strategy and its Achilles' Heel," Nieman Journalism Lab, 27 June2013, http://www.niemanlab.org/2013/06/the-newsonomics-of-advances-advancing-strategy-and-its-

achilles-heel/.

25. Mesh, "Black and White and Red All Over."

26. John Hunt, Twitter post, 21 June 2013, 1:38 p.m., https://twitter.com/JHuntweet.

27. Ryan White, "How Is This News?" RyanWhite.Tumbler.com, 21 June 2013, http://ryanwwhite.tumblr.com/post/53530454660/thanks-or-the-hopefully-not-too-long-or-for-long.

28. CharlieInDC twitter post, 21 Jun 13, 3:25 p.m., https://twitter.com/CharlieInDC.

29. Mesh, "Stop the Presses: The *Oregonian* May Not Be a Daily Newspaper Much Longer."

30. John McQuaid, "Why a Weak Website Can't Replace a Daily Newspaper in New Orleans," Atlantic.com, 12 June 2012, http://www.theatlantic.com/national/archive/2012/06/why-a-weak-website-cant-replace-a-daily-newspaper-in-new-orleans/258393/.

31. Carr, "The Fissures Are Growing for Papers," *New York Times*, 8 July 2012, http://www.nytimes.com/2012/07/09/business/media/newspapers-are-running-out-of-time-to-adapt-to-digital-future.html?pagewanted=all&_r=0

32. Carr, telephone interview with the author.

33. Carr, "Newspaper Monopoly That Lost Its Grip."

34. Jason, Fry, "Sad News Out of New Orleans," ReinventingTheNewsroom.wordpress.com, 24 May 2012, http://reinventingthenewsroom.wordpress.com/2012/05/24/sad-news-out-of-new-orleans/.

35. Kalter.

36. Geoff Larcom, telephone interview with the author, 4 March 2013.

37. Newhouse, "Steve Newhouse Explains Michigan Transition, *Times-Picayune* Future."

38. Dan Gaydou, "Surging Past One-Year Mark, MLive Media Group Builds on Journalism, Grows Readership and Engagement," MLive.com, 23 June 2013, http://www.mlive.com/opinion/index.ssf/2013/06/headline-worthy_success_surgin.html#incart_river_default.

39. Jim Romenesko, "Advance Publications Memo: 'Our New Companies Are Performing Well,'" JimRomenesko.com, 25 July 2013, http://jimromenesko.com/2013/07/25/our-new-companies-are-performing-well-writes-advance-publications-local-digital-strategy-chief/.

40. Ken Doctor, telephone interview with the author, 11 May 2013.

41. Alliance of Audited Media, Snapshot Report; Audit Reports and Newspaper Publisher's Statements for the *Times-Picayune, Huntsville Times, Birmingham New* and *Mobile Press-Register*, 31 March 2012 and 31 March 2013, and AnnArbor.com, 30 September 2009 and 31 March 2013.

42. The Alliance for Audited Media granted me access to its online "Media Intelligence Center," which contains current and some historical reports for all

member newspapers. The analysis of "credit and arrears allowance," "targeted verified circulation," and "average unpaid circulation" comes from individual AAM publishers' statements and audit reports I accessed from the center.

43. Ken Schultz, telephone interview with the author, 11 June 2013.

44. These calculations were made by the author using figures detailed in the semi-annual reports the AAM requires member newspapers to file, specifically the March 2012 and March 2013 reports.

45. Michael Tisserand, email interview with the author, 21 April 2013.

46. Rob Holbert, "Media Frenzy," *Lagniappe*, 6 March 2013, http://classic.lagniappemobile.com/article.asp?articleID=6210&sid=18.

47. Marcus Wohlsen, "The 10 San Francisco Tech Companies You Wish You Worked For," *Wired*, 30 October 2012, http://www.wired.com/business/2012/10/best-san-francisco-tech-companies/?viewall=true.

48. An analysis of Quantcast data available for the first half of 2012 and 2013 shows all of the websites of Advance newspapers generally saw flat or decreased figures for both unique visitors and page views during those periods year over year—except for MLive.com and al.com. NOLA.com had a 12 percent decline in unique visitors, to a total of 13.7 million in the first half of 2013, while its page views were roughly flat, at 139 million. PennLive.com's unique visitors declined 12 percent, to about 7.9 million, and page views fell 9 percent during the same period, to 74.2 million. Syracuse.com had a 19 percent decline in unique visitors, to about 9.4 million, and a 7 percent drop in page views, to about 105.3 million. Cleveland.com saw unique visitors fall 12 percent, to about 18 million, while page views dropped 8 percent, to about 150 million. OregonLive's unique visitors dropped 9 percent to slightly more than 16 million, while page views fell nearly 4 percent to almost 121 million. Cleveland.com's unique visitors dropped about 12 percent, to almost 18 million, while page views fell 8 percent, to almost 151 million. On the other end of the spectrum, al.com saw a slight decline in its unique visitors, to about 18.8 million, but its page views grew nearly 7 percent, to almost 193 million. MLive.com saw unique visitors increase almost 5 percent, to 24 million, while page views climbed 14 percent, to about 220 million.

49. Kollath Wells, "*Times-Picayune* Publisher: 'This Is Chapter Two,'" Poynter.org, 19 February 2013, updated 20 February 2013, http://www.poynter.org/latest-news/top-stories/204743/times-picayune-publisher-this-is-chapter-two/.

50. AAM does not require member newspapers to report website traffic, but instead offers them the option of including web traffic in the semi-annual reports they must file with the organization to maintain membership in good standing. Approximately 170 newspapers currently do so, including many of Advance's newspapers. In addition to the NOLA.com figures cited in the text, other Advance newspaper websites reported the following figures: al.com's unique visitors climbed almost 23 percent year over year, to 37.7 million, while page views increased 16 percent, to 579.8 million. PennLive's unique visitors

were up 17 percent, to 16.3 million, while its page views grew 4 percent, to 234 million. OregonLive's numbers showed strong growth: a 21 percent increase in unique visitors, to almost 33 million, and a 31 percent increase in page views, to 357 million. Cleveland.com's unique visitors grew 21 percent, to almost 33 million, while page views climbed 14 percent, to almost 429.5 million. AnnArbor.com | MLive and Syracuse.com did not include web usage figures in their corresponding AAM reports.

51. Romenesko, "Advance Publications Memo: 'Our New Companies Are Performing Well.'"

52. Beaujon, "Newhouse on New Orleans Changes: 'There's Every Reason to Be Upset and Angry, But . . .'", Poynter.org, 3 August 2012, http://www.poynter.org/latest-news/mediawire/183922/newhouse-theres-every-reason-to-be-upset-and-angry-but/.

53. This information attributed to Doctor is drawn from 5 July 2013 and 22 July 2013 email interviews with the author, and Doctor's 27 June 2013 Nieman Journalism Lab article titled,"The Newsonomics of Advance's Advancing Strategy and Its Achilles' Heel."

54. Keach.

55. Rosenstiel, et. al.

56. Peter C. Beller,"Building the Great Newspaper Paywall," 5 July 2012, eByline's The News Hook, http://ebyline.biz/2012/07/building-the-great-newspaper-paywall/.

57. Tess Stynes, "Circulation Up at *Journal, Times*," *Wall Street Journal*, 1 May 2012, http://online.wsj.com/article/SB10001424127887324482504578454693739 428314.html (subscription required).

58. Christine Haughney, "Asset Sales Help Lift Profit at New York Times Company, but Ad Revenue Declines," *New York Times*, 7 February 2013, http://www.nytimes.com/2013/02/08/business/asset-sales-help-quarterly-profit-at-times-company.html?smid=pl-share.

59. "News Adventures: After Years of Bad Headlines the Industry Finally Has Some Good News," *Economist,* 8 December 2012, http://www.economist.com/news/business/21567934-after-years-bad-headlines-industry-finally-has-some-good-news-news-adventures.

60. Carr, "Pay Wall Push: Why Newspapers Are Hopping Over the Picket Fence," Media Decoder, *New York Times*, 7 December 2012, http://mediadecoder.blogs.nytimes.com/2012/12/07/pay-wall-push-why-newspapers-are-hopping-over-the-picket-fence/?smid=pl-share.

61. Henry Blodget, "These Numbers Show Why the *New York Times* Is Firing More Journalists," BusinessInsider.com, 3 December 2012, http://www.businessinsider.com/why-new-york-times-is-firing-more-journalists-charts-2012-12#ixzz2TSffV6Oj.

62. Carlie Kollath Wells, "Publishers Say Paywalls, Price Hikes Are Working

for Newspapers," Poynter.org, 20 February 2013, http://www.poynter.org/latest-news/mediawire/204794/publishers-say-paywalls-price-hikes-are-working-for-newspapers/.

63. Doctor, "The Newsonomics of Aaron Kushner's Virtuous Circles."

64. Beaujon, "Newhouse on New Orleans Changes: 'There's Every Reason to Be Upset and Angry, But …'"

65. Miller, "*Oregonian* Publisher Talks About The Changes."

66. Doctor, "The Newsonomics of Advance's Advancing Strategy and Its Achilles' Heel."

67. Theim, "NOLA Media Group Reps Paint Glowing Picture of *Times-Picayune* Digital Transition," dashTHIRTYdash (blog), 12 December 2012, http://dashthirtydash.org/2012/12/10/out-to-lunch/.

68. Rick Edmonds, "The Business Case For and Against Advance's Strategy for the Future of News," Poynter.org, 7 August 2012, updated 10 August 2012, http://www.poynter.org/latest-news/business-news/the-biz-blog/184002/the-business-case-for-and-against-advances-strategy-for-the-future-of-news/.

Chapter 8

1. Campbell Robertson, "New Orleans Struggles with Latest Storm, Newspaper Layoffs," *New York Times*, 12 June 2013, http://www.nytimes.com/2012/06/13/us/new-orleans-struggles-with-latest-storm-newspaper-layoffs.html?smid=pl-share.

2. Deirdre Carmody, "At Condé Nast, Newhouse Maintains Loose Reins with a Tight Grip," *New York Times*, 27 July 1992.

3. Brett Will Taylor, "Hello? Steve Newhouse? It's WTF calling," NOLAVie.org, 14 June 2012, http://nolavie.com/2012/06/love-nola-hello-steve-newhouse-its-wtf-calling-78390.html.

4. "Mr. Newhouse's Noise," *Gambit* | BestOfNewOrleans.com, 18 June 2013, http://www.bestofneworleans.com/gambit/mr-newhouses-noise/Content?oid=2024458.

5. Steve Newhouse, "Steve Newhouse Explains Michigan Transition, *Times-Picayune* Future."

6. Alan Mutter, telephone interview with the author, 30 April 2013.

7. John Morton, telephone interview with the author, 8 May 2013.

8. Doctor, telephone interview with the author.

9. Amoss, "An Update on NOLA Media Group," Nola.com | *Times-Picayune*, 5 January 2013; updated 8 January 2013, http://www.nola.com/business/index.ssf/2013/01/update_on_nola_media_group.html#incart_m-rpt-2.

10. Chittum, "An Eye on the *Times-Picayune's* Numbers," Audit, CJR.org, 22 February 2013, http://www.cjr.org/the_audit/an_eye_on_the_times-picayunes.php?page=all.

11. Kollath Wells, "*Times-Picayune* Publisher: 'This Is Chapter Two.'"

12. The author accessed unique-visitor statistics as compiled by QuantCast. com for each of the twelve months in 2012 for NOLA.com at http://www. quantcast.com, and totalled and averaged the monthly figures for an average monthly unique visitor count.

13. Jason Berry, "Rolling the Dice at *The Times-Picayune*," *The Nation*, 11 June 2012, http://www.thenation.com/article/168330/rolling-dice-times-picayune#.

14. Chittum, "The Battle of New Orleans."

15. Sherman, "*Star-Ledger* Publisher Says Newspaper Will Close if Unions Don't Give Concessions."

16. Holbert, "Testimony Ends in Bronson Suit," *Lagniappe*, 8 April 2011, http://classic.lagniappemobile.com/article.asp?articleID=4395&sid=1.

17. Holbert and Pete Teske, "Defense Witnesses Called in Bronson Suit," *Lagniappe*, 7 April 2011, http://classic.lagniappemobile.com/article. asp?articleID=4391&sid=1.

18. Steve Fishman, "Si Newhouse's Dream Factory," *New York Magazine*, 31 May 2009, http://nymag.com/news/media/57076/.

19. Jefferson Grigsby, "Newhouse, After Newhouse," *Forbes*, 29 October 1979, 110-15.

20. Felsenthal, 432-33.

21. Carr, "*Portfolio* Magazine Shut, a Victim of Recession," *New York Times,* 27 April 2009, http://www.nytimes.com/2009/04/28/business/media/28mag. html.

22. Stephanie Clifford, "Condé Nast's Executive on Why the Company Closed Four Magazines," Media Decoder, *New York Times*, 5 October 2009, http:// mediadecoder.blogs.nytimes.com/2009/10/05/conde-nasts-townsend-on-why-the-company-closed-four-magazines/.

23. Fishman, "Si Newhouse's Dream Factory."

24. "Brighthouse Networks: Property Solutions." Brighthouse.com., n.d., http://properties.brighthouse.com/BottomNav/AboutUs.aspx.

25. Fishman

26. Keith J. Kelly, "Townsend Stays Put: Condé Nast CEO Re-ups in Multiyear Deal," *New York Post*, 4 July 2013, http://www.nypost.com/p/news/business/ townsend_stays_put_x5HJxtVProZSvDK4n07iRM.

27. John K. Hartman, "Shoptalk: Cutting News to Line Pockets?" *Editor & Publisher*, 20 June 2013, http://www.editorandpublisher.com/Columns/ Article/Shoptalk--Cutting-News-to-Line-Pockets.

28. Kat Stoeffel, "The Sunset of Si," *New York Observer*, 1 August 2012, http:// observer.com/2012/08/the-sunset-of-si-as-the-conde-nast-chairman-fades-away-his-glossy-kingdom-is-losing-some-sparkle/?show=all.

29. Shea, personal interview with the author.

30. Morton, email interview with the author, 10 May 2013.

31. Chittum, "The Battle of New Orleans."

32. Jack Shafer, "The Great Newspaper Liquidation," Reuters.com, 5 June 2012, http://blogs.reuters.com/jackshafer/2012/06/05/the-great-newspaper-liquidation/.

33. Dan Mitchell, "Profits Aren't the Only Consideration for Newspapers," CNN Monday: A Service of CNN, *Fortune,* & *Money,* 7 June 2012, http://tech.fortune.cnn.com/2012/06/07/profits-arent-the-only-consideration-for-newspapers/.

34. Warren Buffett, 2012 Shareholders' Letter for Berkshire Hathaway, Inc., 3 March 2013, http://www.berkshirehathaway.com/letters/2012ltr.pdf.

35. Littice Bacon-Blood and Kevin Gill, "Paper's New Owner to Beef up New Orleans Edition," Associated Press report via CNBC.com, 2 May 2013, http://www.cnbc.com/id/100700843.

36. Jaquetta White, "*Times-Picayune* Lays Off Nearly One-Third of Its Staff," NOLA.com | *Times-Picayune,* 12 June 2012, http://www.nola.com/business/index.ssf/2012/06/times-picayune_employees_to_le.html.

37. Sam Kennedy, "*Express-Times* Will No Longer Print in Easton," *Morning Call,* 24 April 2013, http://articles.mcall.com/2013-04-24/news/mc-easton-express-times-moves-printing-20130424_1_express-times-website-publisher-lou-stancampiano-other-advance-newspapers.

38. Sherman and Heyboer, "*Star-Ledger* Announces Layoffs."

39. Although several local websites aggregated Vezza's quote from the 17 January 2013 NJ.com | *Star-Ledger* article (at http://www.nj.com/news/index.ssf/2013/01/star-ledger_announces_layoffs.html), it no longer appeared in the online version of the NJ.com report when the author first reviewed the story in June 2013. Vezza did not respond to a July 2013 email inquiring about the quotation.

40. Ted Sherman, "*Star-Ledger* Publisher Says Newspaper Will Close if Unions Don't Give Concessions," *Star-Ledger,* 26 June 2013, http://www.nj.com/sussex-county/index.ssf/2013/06/star-ledger.html#incart_river.

41. Sherman, "*Star-Ledger* Puts its Building on the Market, Says It Is Seeking to Lease Space," *Star-Ledger,* 4 July 2013, http://www.nj.com/business/index.ssf/2013/07/star-ledger_puts_its_building.html.

42. Ed Shown, telephone interview with the author, 28 June 2013.

43. Sherman and Heyboer, "*Star-Ledger* Announces Layoffs."

44. "Layoffs Announced at Easton *Express-Times,* Newark *Star-Ledger,*" Associated Press via PennLive.com, 16 January 2013, http://www.pennlive.com/midstate/index.ssf/2013/01/easton_express_times_layoffs.html.

45. Keith J. Kelly, "Newark's *Star-Ledger* Threatens to Close Unless Unions Agree to Concessions," *New York Post,* 26 June 2013, http://www.nypost.com/p/news/business/newark_star_ledger_threatens_concessions_V27rUdMq3m2gXVwk6bcdKP.

46. Doctor, "The Newsonomics of Advance's New Orleans Strategy," Nieman

Journalism Lab, 4 October 2012, http://www.niemanlab.org/2012/10/the-newsonomics-of-advances-new-orleans-strategy/.

47. Edmonds, "Cutting Print Is a Money-loser for *Times-Picayune*, but Cutting Staff Makes Changes Slightly Profitable."

48. Alan D. Mutter, "What's Next for Newspapers?" Reflections of a Newsosaur, 12 July 2012, http://newsosaur.blogspot.com/2012/07/whats-next-for-newspapers.html.

49. Terry Eggers, interview with Tom Beres, Mary Anne Sharkey, and Dennis Eckart, *Between the Lines*, WKYC-TV, 23 December 2012, http://www.wkyc.com/news/article/274465/45/Between-the-Lines-PD-publisher-discusses-papers-futureough.

50. Griffin-Nolan, "When Newspapers Are the News."

51. *Plain Dealer* Staff, "Dear Readers: Information about the *Plain Dealer's* Delivery Schedule," Cleveland.com | *Plain Dealer*, 21 May 2013, www.cleveland.com/metro/index.ssf/2013/05/dear_readers_information_about.html.

52. Robert L. Smith, "*Plain Dealer* to Remain Daily, but 7-day Home-delivery Will End: Newsroom Briefed about PD Changes," Cleveland.com | *Plain Dealer*, 4 April 2013, updated 5 April 2013, http://www.cleveland.com/business/index.ssf/2013/04/plain_dealer_to_remain_daily_b.html#incart_m-rpt-2.

53. Maggie Calmes, "What Is the *Black and Gold Report*, and How Can I Get It?" NOLA.com, 26 September 2012, updated 28 September 2012, http://blog.nola.com/faq/2012/09/what_is_the_black_and_gold_rep.html.

54. "The *Times-Picayune* Will Print and Deliver New Orleans Saints Coverage after Every Game this Year," NOLA.com | *Times-Picayune*, 26 July 2012, updated 27 July 2012, http://www.nola.com/saints/index.ssf/2012/07/the_times-picayune_will_print.html.

55. "Early Sunday Edition to Hit Newsstands Saturday Mornings Beginning Oct. 6," NOLA.com | *Times-Picayune*, 5 October 2012, http://www.nola.com/business/index.ssf/2012/10/early_sunday_edition_to_hit_ne.html.

56. Amoss, "NOLA.com | The *Times-Picayune* to Launch Newsstand Tab," 30 April 2013, NOLA.com, http://blog.nola.com/updates/2013/04/nolacom_the_times-picayune_to.html.

57. Christine Haughney, "*Times-Picayune* Plans a New Print Tabloid," *New York Times*, 30 April 2013, http://www.nytimes.com/2013/05/01/business/media/times-picayune-plans-a-new-print-tabloid.html.

58. Doctor, interview with the author.

59. Chittum, "The *Advocate* vs. The *Times-Picayune*," The Audit, CJR.org, April 30, 2013, http://www.cjr.org/the_audit/the_advocate_vs_the_times-pica.php?page=all.

60. Doctor, "The Newsonomics of Advance's Advancing Strategy and Its Achilles' Heel."

61. Amoss, "Major Changes Had to Be Done, More to Come."

62. John McQuaid, Twitter post, 30 April 2013, 12:31 pm, https://twitter.com/johnmcquaid.

63. Allman, "*Times-Picayune* to Begin Printing on Days It Doesn't Print in Order to Provide 'Front-to-back Newspaper Reading Experience,'" *Gambit* | Best of New Orleans.com 30 April 2013, http://www.bestofneworleans.com/blogofneworleans/archives/2013/04/30/times-picayune-to-begin-printing-on-days-it-doesnt-print-in-order-to-provide-front-to-back-newspaper-reading-experience.

64. Bill McHugh, email interview with the author, 21 February 2013.

65. McHugh, "What a Daily *Times-Picayune* Will Cost You," DumpThePicayune.com, 18 May 2013, http://www.dumpthepicayune.com/what-a-daily-picayune-will-cost-you-now/.

66. Carr, "Newspaper Monopoly That Lost Its Grip."

67. Amoss, "Major Changes Had to Be Done, More to Come."

68. McHugh, "Is the *Times-Picayune* Brand Being Killed Off?" DumpThe Picayune.com, 12 November 2012, http://www.dumpthepicayune.com/is-the-times-picayune-brand-being-killed-off/.

69. Allman, "NOLA Media Group Meets with the New Orleans Tech Community," *Gambit* | Best of New Orleans.com. http://www.bestofneworleans.com/blogofneworleans/archives/2012/06/21/nola-media-group-meets-with-the-new-orleans-tech-community.

70. "NOLA Media Group Leases Top Floors of Canal Place Office Tower," NOLA.com | *Times-Picayune*, 24 August 2012, http://www.nola.com/business/index.ssf/2012/08/nola_media_group_leases_top_fl.html.

71. Kollath Wells, "New *Times-Picayune*'s Newsroom Features 'Hotel Seating,'" BusinessJournalism.org, 19 February 2013, http://businessjournalism.org/2013/02/19/new-times-picayunes-newsroom-features-hotel-seating/.

72. Cheron Brylski, interview with the author, 21 May 2013.

73. Kollath Wells, "New *Times-Picayune*'s Newsroom Features 'Hotel Seating.'"

74. Schleifstein, interview with the author, 15 March 2013.

75. Dawn Kent, "Prices for *Birmingham News* and Mobile *Press-Register* Buildings Top $21 Million," al.com, 25 January 2013, http://blog.al.com/wire/2013/01/birmingham_news_building_price.html.

76. Lee Roop, "Alabama Media Group Signs Lease to Move *Huntsville Times* Offices Downtown in Early 2013," Alabama Business News, 5 December 2012, http://bamabusinessnews.com/alabama-media-group-signs-lease-to-move-huntsville-times-offices-downtown-in-early-2013-updated-2/.

77. Kennedy, "*Express-Times* Will No Longer Print in Easton."

78. Tim Knauss, "Syracuse Media Group's Move Signals Shift to Digital-First Focus for News and Ads," Syracuse.com | *Post-Standard*, 20 January 2013, http://www.syracuse.com/news/index.ssf/2013/01/digital-first_syracuse_

media_g.html.

79. David Lassman, "New Headquarters of Syracuse Media Group," Syracuse.com | *Post-Standard*, 14 May 2013, http://photos.syracuse.com/post-standard/2013/05/new_headquarters_of_syracuse_m_64.html.

80. John Luciew, "Advance Central Services Pennsylvania and print Publications Hub also Moving to New Offices," PennLive.com, 16 June 2013, updated 18 June 2013, http://www.pennlive.com/midstate/index.ssf/2013/06/advance_central_services_penns.html#/0.

81. Chittum, "The Advance Publications name game: The old Newhouse Pledge and the company's corporate shuffle,"*The Audit*, CJR.org, 19 June 2013, http://www.cjr.org/the_audit/the_oregonian_readies_the_guil.php?page=all.

82. This assessment comes from both Thomas Maier, *Newhouse: All the Glitter, Power & Glory of America's Richest Media Empire & the Secretive Man Behind It*, (Boulder Colorado: Johnson Books, 1997), 386, and Alison Frankel, "How the Newhouses Crushed the IRS," *American Lawyer,* May 1990: 40-49.

83. *W. Howard Bronson v. the* Mobile Press-Register, *Inc., et. al.*

Chapter 9

1. Amoss, "*Times-Picayune* Editor Jim Amoss on Announced Changes," video, NOLA.com | *Times-Picayune*, 12 June 2012, http://videos.nola.com/times-picayune/2012/06/times-picayune_editor_jim_amos.html.

2. Kim Gritter, interview with the author, 21 May 2013.

3. Carr and Amoss, interviewed by Judy Woodruff, "*Times-Picayune* Editor on Commitment, Accountability Amid Cutbacks," *PBS NewsHour,* 13 June 2012, http://www.pbs.org/newshour/bb/media/jan-june12/nolapaper_06-13.html.

4. Amoss, "The Message for Our Organization Is Clear."

5. Ricky Mathews, "NOLA.com and the *Times-Picayune* Are Here to Stay," NOLA.com | *Times-Picayune*, 17 June 2013, http://www.nola.com/opinions/index.ssf/2012/06/the_times-picayune_and_nolacom.html.

6. Christina Elbers, "Paper Is Better for New Orleans Community: A Letter to the Editor," NOLA.com | *Times-Picayune*, 27 June 2012, http://www.nola.com/opinions/index.ssf/2012/06/paper_is_better_for_new_orlean.html.

7. Bentley, "The Murder of The *Times-Picayune*: Part Four," NOLA Anarcha, 12 July 2012, http://nolaanarcha.blogspot.com/2012/07/murder-of-times-picayune-part-four.html.

8. Peck, "Viewpoint: 'We Are One City,'" NolaVie.com, 18 June 2013, http://nolavie.com/2012/06/viewpoint-we-are-one-city-95567.html.

9. Allman, "The Axe Prepares to Fall at the *Times-Picayune*," *Gambit* | Best of New Orleans.com, 11 June 2012, http://www.bestofneworleans.com/blogofneworleans/archives/2012/06/11/the-axe-prepares-to-fall-at-the-times-picayune.

10. Allman, "NOLA Media Group Meets with the New Orleans Tech Community."

11. White, "Most *Times-Picayune* Workers Accept Offer to Work for Successor Companies," NOLA.com | *Times-Picayune*, 29 June 2012, http://www.nola.com/business/index.sf/2012/06/many_times-picayune_workers_ac.html.

12. *Times-Picayune* newsroom staffers who had voluntarily left at the time this book went to press included: state capital political reporter Jeff Adelson; Special Sections manager Victor Andrews; state politics and health care reporter Bill Barrow; zone layout editor Jennifer Brown; news editor Martha Carr; special projects reporter Cindy Chang; sports reporter John DeShazier; reporter Claire Galofaro; political columnists James Gill and Stephanie Grace; investigative reporter David Hammer; photographer Matthew Hinton; City Hall reporter Michelle Krupa; health care reporter Laura Maggi; outdoors and environmental reporter Bob Marshall; graphic artist Emmett Mayer III; criminal justice reporter Brendan McCarthy; business reporter Becky Mowbray; religion reporter Bruce Nolan; society columnist Nell Nolan; Living section clerk Glen Pinera; city editor Gordon Russell; reporter Paul Rioux; courts and criminal justice reporter John Simerman; sports reporter Kevin Spain; InsideOut editor Stephanie Stokes; sports editor Doug Tatum; photographer Scott Threlkeld; business reporter Ricky Thompson; reporter Andrew Vanacore; police and criminal courts reporter Ramon Antonio Vargas; and business reporter Jaquetta White.

13. NOLA.com | *Times-Picayune*, "Brett Anderson to Return as Restaurant Critic for NOLA.com | *Times-Picayune*," NOLA.com | *Times-Picayune*, 13 June 2013, http://www.nola.com/dining/index.ssf/2013/06/brett_anderson_to_return_as_re.html.

14. Skip Descant, "*Advocate* Plans Localized Edition for New Orleans," *Advocate*, 28 July 2012, http://theadvocate.com/news/business/3423596-123/advocate-laying-plans-for-new.

15. Beaujon, "Newhouse on New Orleans Changes: 'There's Every Reason to Be Upset and Angry, but . . .'"

16. "NOLA Media Group Signs Long-Term Lease in Downtown Baton Rouge," NOLA.com | *Times-Picayune*, 3 October 2012, http://www.nola.com/business/index.ssf/2012/10/nola_media_group_signs_long-te.html.

17. Former *Times-Picayune* employees initially hired to staff the *Advocate's* new New Orleans edition included seven: bureau chief Sara Pagones (a former *T-P* editorial writer who would become St. Tammany bureau chief in May 2013 when NOLA.com news editor Martha Carr defected to the *Advocate* and assumed the top editing spot in the *Advocate's* New Orleans operations), reporters Kari Dequine Harden and Danny Monteverde, photographer John McCusker, classified advertising manager Sara Barnard, community news editor Annette Naake Sisco, and bureau assistant Edwin Curry. They were later joined by former *T-P* co-managing editors Peter Kovacs and Dan Shea, advertising manager Yvette Dellucky and St. Tammany community news editor Sharon Edwards, along with the fifteen full- and part-time employees who ultimately

defected to the *Advocate*, either directly from the *Picayune*, or from other outlets to which they went in the interim.

18. Chittum, "The Louisiana Newspaper War," Audit, CJR.com, 21 December 2012, http://www.cjr.org/the_audit/the_louisiana_newspaper_war.php.

19. Alliance for Audited Media.

20. Theim, "NOLA Media Group Reps Paint Glowing Picture of *Times-Picayune* Digital Transition," dashTHIRTYdash.org, 10 December 2012, http://dashthirtydash.org/2012/12/10/out-to-lunch.

21. Joey Hogh, telephone interview with the author, 13 March 2013.

22. Theim, "NOLA Media Group Reps Paint Glowing Picture."

23. H.D. Lanaux, telephone interview with the author, 3 July 2013.

24. Charlee Williamson, personal and email interviews with the author, 19 March, 30 June, and 9 July 2013.

25. Theim, "NOLA.com Editor on Messy Digital Announcement: 'Arrogant to Think We Could Keep a Secret in a Newsroom.'"

26. Mark Fitzgerald, email interview with the author, 21 May 2013.

27. Key Executives Mega-Conference, conference program, New Orleans, Louisiana, 17-20 February 2013, http://www.mega-conference.com/Program.pdf.

28. White, "*Times-Picayune* Lays Off Nearly One-Third of Its Staff."

29. Kollath Wells, "*Times-Picayune* Publisher: 'This Is Chapter Two.'"

30. Amoss, "An Update on NOLA Media Group."

31. "Benjamin C. Bradlee Editor of the Year Award," National Press Foundation, n.d., http://nationalpress.org/awards/detail/benjamin_bradlee_editor_of_the_year_award/archives/.

32. "News Leadership 2006: ASNE Recognizes Gulf Coast Editors for Leadership," American Society of Newspaper Editors, 9 March 9 2006, http://asne.org/content.asp?pl=104&sl=15&contentid=112.

33. Eastlow International Center for Journalism and New Media, "Previous Anvil of Freedom Winners," n.d., http://www.estlow.org/index.php?option=com_content&task=view&id=93&Itemid=91.

34. Michaelle Bond, "The Embattled Editor," *American Journalism Review* | AJR.org, June/July 2012, http://ajr.org/Article.asp?id=5367.

35. Columbia University Office of Communications and Public Affairs, "Three Journalism Leaders Elected to Head Pulitzer Prize Board," ColumbiaNews, 12 May 2011, http://www.pulitzer.org/2011_board_chairs.

36. Charlie Ferguson, interview with the author, 18 March 2013.

37. Bond, "The Embattled Editor."

38. James Rainey, "*Times* Editor Is Out After Fighting Cuts," *Los Angeles Times*, 8 November 2006, articles.latimes.com/2006/nov/08/business/fi-baquet8.

39. Chittum, "The Battle of New Orleans," 1 March 2013.

40. Chittum, "New Orleans Meets the Hamster Wheel," CJR.org, 14 June 2013,

http://www.cjr.org/the_audit/new_orleans_meets_the_hamster.php?page=all.

41. Chittum, email interview with the author, 13 May 2012.

42.Brown, telephone interview with the author.

43. Joel Kaplan, telephone interview with the author, 23 May 2013.

44. Carr, telephone interview with the author, 20 May 2013.

45. George Talbot, "Ricky Mathews Named President, Publisher of *Press-Register*," al.com | *Press-Register*, 18 August 2009, http://www.al.com/news/press-register/metro.ssf?/base/news/1250586943198880.xml&coll=3.

46. Holbert, "Bronson Takes on *P-R*," *Lagniappe*, 22 September 2009, http://classic.lagniappemobile.com/article.asp?articleID=2642&sid=18.

47. Holbert, "Damn the Torpedoes by Rob Holbert," *Lagniappe*, 29 May 2012, http://classic.lagniappemobile.com/article.asp?articleID=5483&SID=3.

48. Izzy Gould, "April 27, 2011 Storms: Restored Piano Symbolizes Second Chance for Tuscaloosa Resident," video, al.com, 6 November 2011, http://blog.al.com/live/2011/11/april_27_2011_storms_refurbish.html.

49. The author ran a search on "Ricky Mathews" on al.com and reviewed all of the listed stories to arrive at these numbers.

50. Ricky Mathews, "A Sea of Destruction: Recovery Will Be a Marathon, Not a Sprint (Ricky Mathews)," al.com | *Press-Register*, 8 May 2011, http://blog.al.com/press-register-commentary/2011/05/a_sea_of_destruction_recovery.html.

51. Although the *Press-Register* didn't publicly disclose how many total employees lost jobs because of the "digital-first" changes there, Advance disclosed that 400 of its Alabama employees were notified June 12, 2012 of their September 30 terminations. The *Birmingham News* said 107 were losing jobs there, and Poynter.org reported that 102 lost their jobs at the *Huntsville Times*. It seems unlikely that the balance of the 400 layoffs occurred at the *Press-Register*. The newsrooms were particularly hard-hit, with *Birmingham News* managing editor Chuck Clark telling Poynter.org (http://www.poynter.org/latest-news/top-stories/177191/what-the-future-of-news-looks-like-in-alabama-after-advance-cuts-staff-there-by-400/) that 67 of 112 newsroom employees there lost their jobs, while 38 of 53 *Huntsville Times* editorial employees were terminated and about 50 of 70 editorial employees were laid off at the *Press-Register*.

52. Beaujon. "*Press-Register* Editor on 'Exciting Changes' Headline: 'Perhaps I Got Carried Away.'"

53. Although it already had been announced that Mathews would be the next publisher of the *Times-Picayune*, the story announcing that appointment noted that no transition date between Mathews and Phelps had been set and that "Mathews will remain in his current roles in Alabama and Mississippi until he announces his successor." The website al.com did not list a new publisher for the newspaper as of mid-May, and an employee answering the phone at the *Press-Register*'s advertising department (repeated calls to the newsroom

went to a general voice mail box) said the newspaper would no longer have a publisher, but instead would be overseen by then-Alabama Media Group president Cindy Martin, who is based in Birmingham. Martin did not respond to an email sent in mid-May 2013 inquiring about whether that description was accurate. About a month later, she was promoted to senior vice president of business development for Advance Digital, although she continues to work in Birmingham.

54. Holbert, "Damn the Torpedoes."

55. Paul Greenberg, "Exciting Changes, or: How Not to Report the News," Tribune Media Services, 31 May 2012, http://articles.chicagotribune.com/2012-05-31/opinion/sns-201205311830--tms--pgreenbgtp--u-a20120531-20120531_1_newspaper-bad-news-front-page.

56. PDF of the front page of the *Times-Picayune*, 13 June 2012, NOLA.com | *Times-Picayune*, http://media.nola.com/pages/other/MetroA1 June132012.pdf.

57. Julie Moos and Steve Myers, "How *Times-Picayune*, Alabama Newspaper Changes Played on Their Front Pages," Poynter.org, 25 May 2012, updated 28 May 2012, http://www.poynter.org/latest-news/mediawire/175181/how-times-picayune-alabama-newspaper-changes-played-on-their-front-pages/.

58. "Meet the *Times-Picayune*/NOLA.com Community Roundtable: Editorial," NOLA.com | *Times-Picayune*, 9 December 2012, updated 20 December 2012, http://www.nola.com/opinions/index.ssf/2012/12/meet_the_times-picayunenolacom.html.

59. "NOLA Media Group Launches $500,000 Effort to Boost Community Access to Digital Technology, Information," NOLA.com | *Times-Picayune*, 24 September 2012, http://www.nola.com/business/index.ssf/2012/09/nola_media_group_launches_5000.html.

60. "Nola Access Initiative Chooses Columbia Parc for $20,000 Technology Grant," NOLA.com | *Times-Picayune*, 21 May 2013, http://www.nola.com/business/index.ssf/2013/05/nola_access_initiative_chooses.html.

Chapter 10

1. Christine Harvey, Facebook interview with the author, 26 May 2013.

2. Those volunteers included: retired travel editor Millie Ball; outgoing marketing manager Brenda Bell; retired features writer Chris Bynum; longtime newsroom assistant and TP Store manager Edwin Curry; outgoing political columnist Stephanie Grace; former city editor Mary Heffron Arno; retired books editor and host of New Orleans public radio station WWNO's "The Reading Life" Susan Larson; former *T-P* features writer, development professional, and NolaVie co-founder Sharon Litwin; former InsideOut editor and NolaVie co-founder Renée Peck (and her husband, Stewart, a prominent local attorney who became our trusted "money man" the night of The Howlin' Wolf event); and former features writers Katy Read and Suzanne Stouse. They were joined

by Sheila's daughter, Erin McAlister, an investigator in the Medicaid Fraud Control Unit for the state; communications maven Cheron Brylski; and retired philanthropy executive Jackie Sullivan.

3. McCusker, interview with the author.

4. Most of the fundraising efforts on behalf of dashTHIRTYdash were chronicled earlier by the author at the organization's blog, http://www. dashTHIRTYdash.org.

Chapter 11

1. Stephanie Riegel, "Baton Rouge's New Power Broker: John Georges," *Greater Baton Rouge Business Report*, 13 May 2013, http://www.businessreport. com/article/20130513/BUSINESSREPORT0401/130519966.

2. John Georges, interview with the author, 28 May 2013.

3. Constantine S. Sirigos, "50th Wealthiest Greeks in America," *National Herald*, 27 March 2012, https://s3.amazonaws.com/2013backup/tnhcontent/ pdf/inserts/2012/Insert_3_2012_5516.pdf.

4. David Hammer, "John Georges Is a Big Spender Searching for His Voice in Mayoral Race," *Times-Picayune*, 14 January 2010, http://www.nola.com/ politics/index.ssf/2010/01/post_261.html.

5. Riegel, "Baton Rouge's New Power Broker: John Georges."

6. A.E. Stevenson, "Possible Sale in the Works for the *Advocate*," WBRZ-TV, 25 January 2013, http://www.wbrz.com/news/possible-sale-in-the-works-for-the-advocate-.

7. Riegel, "News Alert: John Georges Potential *Advocate* Buyer," *Greater Baton Rouge Business Report*, 26 January 2013, http://www.businessreport. com/daily-report/1262013/News_alert-John_Georges_potential_Advocate_ buyer#ixzz2UeclMFhw.

8. Staff report, "*Advocate* Deal Up to Georges, Publisher Says," *Greater Baton Rouge Business Report*, 21 February 2013, http://businessreport.com/daily-report/PM/2212013/Advocate_deal_up_to_Georges_publisher_says.

9. Staff report, "Georges Signs Letter of Intent to Buy the *Advocate*," 25 March 2013, http://theadvocate.com/home/5450322-125/georges-signs-letter-of-intent.

10. "NOLA Media Group Signs Long-Term Lease in Downtown Baton Rouge," NOLA.com | *Times-Picayune*, 3 October 2012, http://www.nola.com/ business/index.ssf/2012/10/nola_media_group_signs_long-te.html.

11. James O'Byrne, "*BR*, a Free Weekly Publication from NOLA.com, Launches Wednesday," NOLA.com | *Times-Picayune*, 24 April 2013, http:// www.nola.com/business/baton-rouge/index.ssf/2013/04/br_a_free_weekly_ publication_f.html.

12. Timothy Boone, "John Georges 'Extremely Proud' to Own the *Advocate*," *Advocate*, 2 May 2013, http://theadvocate.com/home/5860899-125/georges-extremely-proud-to-own.

13. Georges, interview with the author.

14. Eve Troeh, "Two Newspapers Battle It Out for the New Orleans Market," National Public Radio, 29 May 2013, http://www.npr.org/2013/05/29/186900885/two-newspapers-battle-it-out-for-the-new-orleans-market.

15. Chittum, "The *Advocate* Raids the *Picayune*," Audit, CRJ.org, 8 May 2013, http://www.cjr.org/the_audit/the_advocate_raids_the_picayun.php?page=all.

16. Riegel, "Baton Rouge's New Power Broker: John Georges."

17. Ibid.

18. Chittum, "The *Advocate* vs. the *Times-Picayune*."

19. Shea, "Former *T-P* Editor: The *Advocate* Will Give the City a Daily Newspaper," interviewed by Melanie Hebert, *The 504*, WUPL-TV and WWL-TV, 16 May 2013, http://www.wwltv.com/on-tv/wupl/Former-T-P-editor-The-Advocate-will-give-the-city-a-daily-newspaper-207810411.html?ref=prev.

20. New Orleans bureau, "*Advocate* Assembles Advisory N.O. Panel," *Advocate*, 3 June 2013, http://theadvocate.com/news/neworleans/6126713-148/advocate-assembles-advisory-no-panel.

Chapter 12

1. Nolan, personal interview with the author.

2. Bruce Nolan, "I Had a License to Be There," JimRomenesko.com, 28 September 2012, http://jimromenesko.com/2012/09/28/a-times-picayune-veterans-farewell/.

3. Ana Courtade, telephone interviews with the author, 25 March 2013 and 31 May and 30 June 2013.

4. Hughes, interview with the author.

5. Cass and Lisa DeLatte, interview with the author, and Lisa DeLatte, telephone interview with the author, 3 June 2013.

6. Kim Sensebe Gritter, telephone interview with the author, 21 May 2013.

Epilogue

1. Andrew Beaujon, "Buffett, Newhouses, Murdoch on *Forbes* List of Billionaires," Forbes.com, 4 March 2013, http://www.poynter.org/latest-news/mediawire/206056/buffett-newhouses-murdoch-on-forbes-list-of-billionaires/.

2. Carr, "Newspaper Monopoly That Lost Its Grip."

3. Carr, telephone interview with the author.

4. Rem Rieder, "One Newspaper Cuts to Survive; Another Invests to Thrive," *USA Today*, 25 June 2013, http://www.usatoday.com/story/money/columnist/rieder/2013/06/25/rem-rieder-newspapers/2457629/.

Bibliography

Adelson, Jeff, and Bruce Alpert, Bill Barrow, Cindy Chang, Claire Galofaro, Stephanie Grace, David Hammer, et al. Letter to Jim Amoss, Mark Lorando, and Lynn Cunningham, 19 June 2012.

Advocate staff report. "Georges Signs Letter of Intent to Buy the *Advocate.*" *Advocate,* 25 March 2013, http://theadvocate.com/home/5450322-125/georges-signs-letter-of-intent.

Alliance for Audited Media. "Total Circ: The *Times-Picayune.*" Circulation averages for the six months ended 30 September 2012. http://abcas3.auditedmedia.com/ecirc/newstitlesearchus.asp.

———. Newspaper Statements and/or Audit Reports for all newspapers named, 30 July 2009–March 2013.

Allman, Kevin. "*Times-Picayune* Employees in Shock as Extent of Newhouse Cuts Begins to Emerge." *Gambit* | Best of New Orleans.com, 24 May 2012. http://www.bestofneworleans.com/blogofneworleans/archives/2012/05/24/times-picayune-employees-in-shock-tonight-as-extent-of-newhouse-cuts-begins-to-emerge.

———. "After the News: Today at the *Times-Picayune.*" *Gambit* | Best of New Orleans.com, 24 May 2012. http://www.bestofneworleans.com/blogofneworleans/archives/2012/05/24/after-the-news-today-at-the-times-picayune.

———. "'Save the *Picayune*' Rally Draws Hundreds." *Gambit* | Best of New Orleans.com, 5 June 2012. http://www.bestofneworleans.com/blogofneworleans/archives/2012/06/04/save-the-picayune-rally-draws-hundreds.

———. "Spotted in the *Times-Picayune* Newsroom: Lou Grant." *Gambit* | Best of New Orleans.com, 10 June 2012. http://www.bestofneworleans.com/blogofneworleans/archives/2012/06/10/spotted-in-the-times-picayune-newsroom-lou-grant.

———. "The Axe Prepares to Fall at the *Times-Picayune.*" *Gambit* | Best of New Orleans.com, 11 June 2012. http://www.bestofneworleans.com/blogofneworleans/archives/2012/06/11/the-axe-prepares-to-fall-at-the-times-picayune.

———. "NOLA Media Group Meets with the New Orleans Tech Community."

Gambit | Best of New Orleans.com, 21 June 2012. http://www.
bestofneworleans.com/blogofneworleans/archives/2012/06/21/nola-
media-group-meets-with-the-new-orleans-tech-community.

———. "*Times-Picayune* Citizens' Group Formally Asks Newhouse Family to Sell
the Paper." *Gambit* | Best of New Orleans.com, 9 July 2012. http://www.
bestofneworleans.com/blogofneworleans/archives/2012/07/09/times-
picayune-citizens-group-formally-asks-newhouse-family-to-sell-the-paper.

———. "The Fight to Save the *Times-Picayune.*" *Gambit* | Best of New Orleans.
com, 18 September 2012. http://www.bestofneworleans.com/gambit/the-
fight-to-save-the-times-picayune/Content?oid=2072666.

———. "*Times-Picayune* to Begin Printing On Days It Doesn't Print in Order to
Provide 'Front-to-Back Newspaper Reading Experience.'" *Gambit* | Best
of New Orleans.com, 30 April 2013. http://www.bestofneworleans.com/
blogofneworleans/archives/2013/04/30/times-picayune-to-begin-printing-
on-days-it-doesnt-print-in-order-to-provide-front-to-back-newspaper-
reading-experience.

American Society of Newspaper Editors. "News Leadership 2006: ASNE
Recognizes Gulf Coast Editors for Leadership." American Society of
Newspaper Editors Website, 9 March 2006. http://asne.org/content.
asp?pl=104&sl=15&contentid=112.

———. "American Society of Newspaper Editors 2012 Census: Table A — Minority
Employment in Daily Newspapers." American Society of Newspaper Editors
Website, 4 April 2012. http://asne.org/content.asp?pl=140&sl=129&content
id=129.

Amoss, Jim. "The Message for Our Organization Is Clear: Adapt, or Fade Away."
NOLA.com | *Times-Picayune*, 13 June 2012. http://www.nola.com/opinions/
index.ssf/2012/06/post_153.html.

———. "Times-Picayune Editor Jim Amoss, a Voice for New Orleans." Interview
by Terry Gross. *Fresh Air*, NPR, 4 January 2006.

———. "Times-Picayune Editor Jim Amoss on Announced Changes." Video.
NOLA.com | *Times-Picayune*, 12 June 2012. http://videos.nola.com/times-
picayune/2012/06/times-picayune_editor_jim_amos.html.

———. "An Update on NOLA Media Group." NOLA.com | *Times-Picayune*, 5
January 2013, updated 8 January 2013. http://www.nola.com/business/
index.ssf/2013/01/update_on_nola_media_group.html#incart_m-rpt-2.

———. "NOLA.com | The *Times-Picayune* to Launch Newsstand Tab." NOLA.com
| *Times-Picayune*, 30 April 2013. http://blog.nola.com/updates/2013/04/
nolacom_the_times-picayune_to.html.

———. "Major Changes Had to Be Done, More to Come." Interview by Melanie
Hebert. *The 504*. WUPL-TV and WWL-TV, 17 May 2013. http://www.wwltv.
com/on-tv/wupl/T-P-editor--207957051.html.

Anderson, Brett. Twitter posts, 12 June 2012 1:35 p.m. and 2:27 p.m., and 13 June

2012 3:11 p.m. https://twitter.com/BrettAndersonTP.

———. Email response to author, 16 May 2013.

Anderson, Kathy, and Doug Parker. Interview with author, 17 March 2013.

Andrews, Victor. Facebook message interview with author, 24 April 2013.

Archibald, John. "Why No Protest in Birmingham?" *Birmingham News*. 5 June 2012. http://blog.al.com/archiblog/2012/06/why_no_protest_in_birmingham.html.

Arruebarrena, James. Telephone interview with author, 3 May 2013.

Associated Press. "Layoffs Announced at Easton *Express-Times*, Newark *Star-Ledger*." PennLive.com, 16 January 2013, updated 16 January 2013. http://www.pennlive.com/midstate/index.ssf/2013/01/easton_express_times_layoffs.html.

Astor, Dave. "Newhouse News Service to Close." *Editor & Publisher*, 30 July 2008. http://www.editorandpublisher.com/Article/UPDATED-Newhouse-News-Service-to-Close (subscription required).

Bacon-Blood, Littice, and Kevin Gill. "Paper's New Owner to Beef Up New Orleans Edition." Associated Press report via CNBC.com, 2 May 2013. http://www.cnbc.com/id/100700843.

Beaujon, Andrew. "Critics Ask if *Times-Picayune*, Other Advance Papers Are Ready for Their New Digital Focus." Poynter.org, 25 May 2012. http://www.poynter.org/latest-news/mediawire/175209/critics-ask-if-times-picayune-other-advance-papers-are-ready-for-their-new-digital-focus/.

———. "*Press-Register* Editor on 'Exciting Changes' Headline: 'Perhaps I Got Carried Away,'" Poynter.org, 25 May 2012. http://www.poynter.org/latest-news/mediawire/175225/press-register-editor-on-exciting-changes-headline-perhaps-i-got-carried-away/.

———. "Newhouse on New Orleans Changes: 'There's Every Reason to Be Upset and Angry, but . . .'" Poynter.org, 3 August 2010. http://www.poynter.org/latest-news/mediawire/183922/newhouse-theres-every-reason-to-be-upset-and-angry-but/.

Beller, Peter C. "Building the Great Newspaper Paywall." News Hook, 5 July 2012. http://ebyline.biz/2012/07/building-the-great-newspaper-paywall/.

"Benjamin C. Bradlee Editor of the Year Award." National Press Foundation, n.d. http://nationalpress.org/awards/detail/benjamin_bradlee_editor_of_the_year_award/archives/.

Benson, Tom. "Tom Benson's Letter of Support for a Daily Newspaper in New Orleans." New Orleans Saints Official Website, 27 May 2012 posted 29 May 2012. http://www.neworleanssaints.com/news-and-events/article-1/Tom-Bensons-Letter-of-Support-for-a-Daily-Newspaper-in-New-Orleans/8a88a5e1-2d35-408c-840d-3c447d283c91.

———. Letter to Steven Newhouse, 25 July 2012. http://images.bimedia.net/documents/BENSON+LETTER.pdf.

Bentley, Jules. "The Murder of the *Times-Picayune*: Part One." NOLA Anarcha, 9 July - 4 August 2012. http://nolaanarcha.blogspot.com/2012/07/murder-of-times-picayune-part-one.html.

Boone, Timothy. "John Georges 'Extremely Proud' to Own the *Advocate*." *Advocate*, 2 May 2013. http://theadvocate.com/home/5860899-125/georges-extremely-proud-to-own.

———. "The *Advocate* Names N.O. Sales, Marketing Director," *Advocate*, 28 May 2013, http://theadvocate.com/news/business/6039161-123/the-advocate-names-no-sales.

Bond, Michaelle. "The Embattled Editor." *American Journalism Review* | AJR.org, June/July 2012. http://ajr.org/Article.asp?id=5367.

Braden-Capone, Megan. Interview with author, 12 March 2013.

———. Facebook interview with author, 4 May 2013

Bradley, Jeff. "How about Thursday? I'm Just Not Sure." Jeff-Bradley.com, 23 January 2013. http://jeffbradleyblog.blogspot.com/2013/01/how-about-thursday-im-not-so-sure.html.

Brainard, Curtis. "Calling Katrina: New Orleans *Times-Picayune*'s 2005 Hurricane Coverage Included in NYU's 'Top 10 Works of the Decade.'" *Columbia Journalism Review*, 6 April 2010. http://www.cjr.org/the_observatory/calling_katrina.php?page=all.

Brighthouse.com. "Brighthouse Networks: Property Solutions." Brighthouse.com, n.d.http://properties.brighthouse.com/BottomNav/AboutUs.aspx.

Brylski, Cheron. Telephone interview with author, 21 May 2013.

Buffett, Warren. 2012 Shareholders' Letter for Berkshire Hathaway, Inc., 1 March 2013. http://www.berkshirehathaway.com/letters/2012ltr.pdf.

Bureau of Labor Statistics. "BLS Spotlight on Statistics: Media and Information." US Department of Labor, January 2013. http://www.bls.gov/spotlight/2013/media/data_cew_establishments.htm.

Byers, Dylan. "Newhouse: 'No' on *Times-Picayune* Sale." Politico.com, 10 July 2012. http://www.politico.com/blogs/media/2012/07/newhouse-spurns-request-to-sell-timespicayune-128512.html.

Calmes, Maggie. "What Is the *Black and Gold Report*, and How Can I Get It?" NOLA.com | *Times-Picayune*, 26 September 2012, updated 28 September 2012. http://blog.nola.com/faq/2012/09/what_is_the_black_and_gold_rep.html.

Carmody, Deirdre. "At Condé Nast, Newhouse Maintains Loose Reins With a Tight Grip." *New York Times*, 27 July 1992.

Carr, David. "A Flood Begets a Paper Ark." *New York Times*, 30 April 2007. http://www.nytimes.com/2007/04/30/business/media/30carr.html.

———. "*Portfolio* Magazine Shut, a Victim of Recession." *New York Times*, 27 April 2009. http://www.nytimes.com/2009/04/28/business/media/28mag.html.

———. "New Orleans Paper Said to Face Deep Cuts and May Cut Back Publication." Media Decoder, *New York Times*, 23 May 2012. http://

mediadecoder.blogs.nytimes.com/2012/05/23/new-orleans-paper-said-to-face-deep-cuts-and-may-cut-back-on-publication/?smid=pl-share.

———. "Audio: Veteran *Times-Picayune* Reporter on How Staff Heard the News." Media Decoder, *New York Times*, 25 May 2012. http://mediadecoder.blogs.nytimes.com/2012/05/25/audio-veteran-times-picayune-reporter-on-how-staff-heard-the-news/.

———. "A Doomed Romance With a New Orleans Newspaper." *New York Times,* 27 May 2012. http://www.nytimes.com/2012/05/28/business/media/the-times-picayune-new-orleans-and-a-doomed-romance.html?smid=pl-share.

———. "The Fissures Are Growing for Papers." *New York Times*, 8 July 2012. http://www.nytimes.com/2012/07/09/business/media/newspapers-are-running-out-of-time-to-adapt-to-digital-future.html?pagewanted=all&_r=0.

———. "Pay Wall Push: Why Newspapers Are Hopping Over the Picket Fence." Media Decoder, *New York Times*, 7 December 2012. http://mediadecoder.blogs.nytimes.com/2012/12/07/pay-wall-push-why-newspapers-are-hopping-over-the-picket-fence/?smid=pl-share.

———. "Newspaper Monopoly That Lost Its Grip." *New York Times*, 12 May 2013. http://www.nytimes.com/2013/05/13/business/media/in-new-orleans-times-picayunes-monopoly-crumbles.html?smid=pl-share.

———. Telephone interview with author, 20 May 2013.

Carr, David and Jim Amoss. "*Times-Picayune* Editor on Commitment. Accountability Amid Cutbacks." Interviewed by Judy Woodruff, *PBS NewsHour*, 13 June 2012. http://www.pbs.org/newshour/bb/media/jan-june12/nolapaper_06-13.html.

Champion, Laurel. "Letter from *Ann Arbor News* Publisher Laurel Champion." MLive.com, 23 March 2009. http://www.mlive.com/news/ann-arbor/index.ssf/2009/03/letter_from_ann_arbor_news_pub.html.

Chittum, Ryan. "New Orleans Meets the Hamster Wheel," CJR.org, 14 June 2012. http://www.cjr.org/the_audit/new_orleans_meets_the_hamster.php?page=all.

———. "The Louisiana Newspaper War." Audit, CJR.org, 21 December 2012. http://www.cjr.org/the_audit/the_louisiana_newspaper_war.php.

———. "An Eye on the *Times-Picayune's* Numbers." Audit, CJR.org, 22 February 2013. http://www.cjr.org/the_audit/an_eye_on_the_times-picayunes.php?page=all.

———. "The Battle of New Orleans: Is Advance Publications Securing the Future of Local News—or Needlessly Sacrificing It?" *Columbia Journalism Review*, 1 March 2013. http://www.cjr.org/feature/the_battle_of_new_orleans.php?page=all.

———. Email interview with author, 13 May 2013.

Clifford, Stephanie. "Condé Nast's Executive on Why the Company Closed Four Magazines." Media Decoder, *New York Times*, 5 October 2009. http://

mediadecoder.blogs.nytimes.com/2009/10/05/conde-nasts-townsend-on-why-the-company-closed-four-magazines/.

Columbia University Office of Communications and Public Affairs. "Three Journalism Leaders Elected to Head Pulitzer Prize Board." Columbia News, 12 May 2011. http://www.pulitzer.org/2011_board_chairs.

Costanza, Rusty. Interview with author, 15 March 2013.

Courtade, Ana. Telephone interviews with author, 25 March, 31 May, and 30 June.

Dabney, Thomas Ewing. *One Hundred Great Years: The Story of The* Times-Picayune *From Its Founding to 1940*. Baton Rouge: Louisiana State University Press, 1944.

DeBerry, Jarvis. "A Forceful Voice About the City's Survival." *Nieman Reports: Nieman Foundation for Journalism at Harvard*, Fall 2007. http://www.nieman.harvard.edu/reports/article/100154/A-Forceful-Voice-About-a-Citys-Survival.aspx.

DeLatte, Cass and Lisa. Interview with author, 16 March 2013.

DeLatte, Lisa. Telephone interview with author, 3 June 2013.

Descant, Skip. "Advocate Plans Localized Edition for New Orleans." *Advocate*, 28 July 2012. http://theadvocate.com/news/business/3423596-123/advocate-laying-plans-for-new.

Deutsch, Linda. "New Orleans *Times-Picayune* Trying to Report, Survive." Associated Press, 16 January 2006. http://www.editorandpublisher.com/Article/New-Orleans-Times-Picayune-Trying-to-Report-Survive (subscription required).

Doctor, Ken. "The Newsonomics of Advance's New Orleans Strategy." Nieman Journalism Lab, 4 October 2012. http://www.niemanlab.org/2012/10/the-newsonomics-of-advances-new-orleans-strategy/.

———. Telephone interview with author, 10 May 2013.

Dreussi, Rollie. Telephone interview with author, 3 May 2013.

Eastlow International Center for Journalism and New Media, "Previous Anvil of Freedom Winners." n.d., http://www.estlow.org/index.php?option=com_content&task=view&id=93&Itemid=91.

Economist. "News Adventures: After Years of Bad Headlines the Industry Finally Has Some Good News." *Economist*, 8 December 2012. http://www.economist.com/news/business/21567934-after-years-bad-headlines-industry-finally-has-some-good-news-news-adventures.

Edmonds, Rick. "Cutting Print Is a Money-Loser for *Times-Picayune*, But Cutting Staff Makes Changes Slightly Profitable." Poynter.org, 18 June 2012. http://www.poynter.org/latest-news/business-news/the-biz-blog/177005/cutting-print-is-a-money-loser-for-times-picayune-but-cutting-staff-makes-changes-slightly-profitable/.

———. "The Business Case for and Against Advance's Strategy for the Future of

News." Poynter.org, 7 August 2012, updated 10 August 2012. http://www. poynter.org/latest-news/business-news/the-biz-blog/184002/the-business-case-for-and-against-advances-strategy-for-the-future-of-news/.

———. Telephone interview with author, 7 May 2013.

Eggers, Terry. Interview with Tom Beres, Mary Anne Sharkey, and Dennis Eckart. *Between the Lines*, WKYC-TV, 23 December 2012. http://www.wkyc. com/news/article/274465/45/Between-the-Lines-PD-publisher-discusses-papers-futureough.

Elbers, Christina. "Paper Is Better for New Orleans Community: A Letter to the Editor." NOLA.com | *Times-Picayune*, 27 June 2012. http://www.nola.com/ opinions/index.ssf/2012/06/paper_is_better_for_new_orlean.html.

Eng, Bernie. "Remember to Pick Up Your Great Lakes Bay Edition Tuesday Newspaper at a Nearby Newsstand." MLive.com, 28 March 2010, updated 7 April 2010, http://www.mlive.com/news/saginaw/index.ssf/2010/03/ remember_to_pick_up_your_great.html.

Feeney, Susan. "The Friends of The *Times-Picayune* Relief Fund." *Nieman Reports: Nieman Foundation for Journalism at Harvard,* Fall 2007. http://www.nieman. harvard.edu/reports/article/100201/The-Friends-of-The-Times-Picayune-Relief-Fund.aspx.

Felsenthal, Carol. *Citizen Newhouse: Portrait of a Media Merchant.* New York: Seven Stories Press, 1998.

Fenton, Jacob. "Broadband Adoption Map: South Lags Behind, Rural Areas Improve." Investigative reporting workshop at American University School of Communication, 23 March 2012. http://investigativereportingworkshop. org/investigations/broadband-adoption/htmlmulti/broadband-adoption-map/.

Ferguson, Charlie. Interview with author, 18 March 2013.

Fishman, Steve. "Si Newhouse's Dream Factory." *New York Magazine*, 31 May 2009. http://nymag.com/news/media/57076/.

Fitzgerald, Mark. Email interview with author, 21 May 2013.

Frassinelli, Bruce. "The End of the *Post-Standard* as We Know It." *Oswego County Business Magazine,* 5 September 2012. http://oswegocountybusiness.com/ index.php?a=3832.

Gambit | BestOfNewOrleans.com. "Mr. Newhouse's Noise." *Gambit* | BestOfNewOrleans.com, 18 June 2013. http://www.bestofneworleans.com/ gambit/mr-newhouses-noise/Content?oid=2024458.

Gaydou, Dan. "Letter from Publisher Dan Gaydou: Announcing the MLive Media Group." MLive.com, 2 November 2011. http://blog.mlive.com/ updates/2011/11/letter_from_our_publisher_anno.html.

Georges, John. Interview with author, 28 May 2013.

Gissler, Sig. Telephone interview with author, 3 May 2013.

Glaser, Mark. "NOLA.com Blogs and Forums Help Save Lives After Katrina."

Online Journalism Review, 13 September 2005. http://www.ojr.org/ojr/stories/050913glaser/.

Gould, Izzy. "April 27, 2011 Storms: Restored Piano Symbolizes Second Chance for Tuscaloosa Resident." Video, 6 November 2011. http://blog.al.com/live/2011/11/april_27_2011_storms_refurbish.html.

Greater Baton Rouge Business Report staff. "*Advocate* Deal Up to Georges, Publisher Says." *Greater Baton Rouge Business Report*, 21 February 2013. http://businessreport.com/daily-report/PM/2212013/Advocate_deal_up_to_Georges_publisher_says.

Greenberg, Paul. "Exciting Changes, or: How Not to Report the News." Tribune Media Services, 31 May 2012. http://articles.chicagotribune.com/2012-05-31/opinion/sns-201205311830--tms--pgreenbgtp--u-a20120531-20120531_1_newspaper-bad-news-front-page.

Griffin-Nolan, Ed. "When Newspapers Are the News."*Syracuse New Times*, 20 February 2013. http://www.syracusenewtimes.com/newyork/article-6454-when-newspapers-are-the-news.html.

———. "Post-Mortem." *Syracuse New Times*, 13 February 2013. http://www.syracusenewtimes.com/newyork/article-6446-post-mortem.html.

Gritter, Kim. Telephone interview with author, 21 May 2013.

Guernsey, Lisa. "Hurricane Forces New Orleans Newspaper to Face a Daunting Set of Obstacles." *New York Times*, 5 September 2005. http://www.nytimes.com/2005/09/05/business/media/05picayune.html.

Hagey, Keach. "*Times-Picayune* Is Singing the Blues to Angry Readers." *Wall Street Journal*, 9 September 2012. http://online.wsj.com/article/SB1000087239639044358930457763802326261 6192.html?mg=id-wsj#articleTabs%3Darticle.

Hammer, David. "John Georges Is a Big Spender Searching for His Voice in Mayoral Race." *Times-Picayune*, 14 January 2010. http://www.nola.com/politics/index.ssf/2010/01/post_261.html.

———. Email interview with author, 21 April 2013.

Harvey, Christine. Facebook interview with author, 26 May 2013.

Haughney, Christine. "Asset Sales Help Lift Profit at New York Times Company, but Ad Revenue Declines." *New York Times*, 7 February 2013. http://www.nytimes.com/2013/02/08/business/asset-sales-help-quarterly-profit-at-times-company.html?smid=pl-share.

———. "*Times-Picayune* Plans a New Print Tabloid." *New York Times*, 30 April 2013. http://www.nytimes.com/2013/05/01/business/media/times-picayune-plans-a-new-print-tabloid.html.

Hinton, Matthew. Email interview with author, 2 April 2013.

Hogh, Joey. Telephone interview with the author. 13 March 2013.

Holan, Mark. "'Newhouse Pledge,' Job Security, Now Relics of Once-Thriving Newspaper Industry." Poynter.org, 23 September 2009. http://www.poynter.org/latest-news/top-stories/98490/newhouse-pledge-job-security-now-relics-of-once-thriving-newspaper-industry/.

Holbert, Rob. "Bronson Takes on *P-R*." *Lagniappe*, 22 September 2009. http:// classic.lagniappemobile.com/article.asp?articleID=2642&sid=18.

———. "Testimony Ends in Bronson Suit." *Lagniappe*, 8 April 2011. http://classic. lagniappemobile.com/article.asp?articleID=4395&sid=1.

———. "Damn the Torpedoes by Rob Holbert." *Lagniappe*, 29 May 2012. http:// classic.lagniappemobile.com/article.asp?articleID=5483&SID=3.

———, and Peter Teske. "Defense Witnesses Called in Bronson Suit." *Lagniappe*, 7 April 2011. http://classic.lagniappemobile.com/article. asp?articleID=4391&sid=1.

Hoss, Mike, and Dominic Massa. "Benson Offers to Buy *Times-Picayune*; Paper Not for Sale, Say Advance Officials." WWL-TV, 26 July 2012. http://www. wwltv.com/news/Benson-Times-Picayune-163863846.html.

Hughes, Cathy. Interview with author, 17 March 2013.

Ives, Nat. "What Print Cuts at *Times-Picayune* Mean for Papers." *Advertising Age*, 28 May 2012. http://adage.com/article/media/print-cuts-times-picayune-papers/235006/.

Kalter, Lindsay. "The Ann Arbor Precedent." *American Journalism Review*, August/September 2012. http://ajr.org/Article.asp?id=5377.

Kaplan, Joel. Telephone interview with author, 23 May 2013.

Kennedy, Sam. "Express-Times Will No Longer Print in Easton." *Morning Call*, 24 April 2013. http://articles.mcall.com/2013-04-24/news/mc-easton-express-times-moves-printing-20130424_1_express-times-website-publisher-lou-stancampiano-other-advance-newspapers.

Kent, Dawn. "Prices for *Birmingham News* and Mobile *Press-Register* Buildings Top $21 Million." AL.com, 25 January 2013. http://blog.al.com/wire/2013/01/birmingham_news_building_price.html.

Key Executives Mega-Conference. Conference program. New Orleans, Louisiana, 17-20 February 2013. http://www.mega-conference.com/Program.pdf.

Knauss, Tim. "Syracuse Media Group's Move Signals Shift to Digital-First Focus for News and Ads." Syracuse.com | *Post-Standard*, 20 January 2013. http:// www.syracuse.com/news/index.ssf/2013/01/digital-first_syracuse_media_g.html.

Kurtz, Howard. "Why Warren Buffett Still Buys Newspapers as the Industry Sinks." *Daily Beast*, 4 June 2012. http://www.thedailybeast.com/articles/2012/06/04/why-warren-buffett-still-buys-newspapers-as-the-industry-sinks.html.

Kwon, Wade. "*Birmingham News* Fires More than 100 Employees." *Media of Birmingham*, 12 June 2012. http://mediaofbirmingham.com/2012/06/12/birmingham-news-fires-more-than-100-employees/.

Laborde, Errol. Interview with author, 13 March 2013.

Langeveld, Martin. "The Coming Death of Seven-Day Publication." Nieman

Journalism Lab, 21 December 2012. http://www.niemanlab.org/2012/12/the-coming-death-of-seven-day-publication/.

Larcom, Geoff. Interview with author, 4 March 2013.

Lassman, David. "New Headquarters of Syracuse Media Group." Syracuse.com | *Post-Standard*, 14 May 2013. http://photos.syracuse.com/post-standard/2013/05/new_headquarters_of_syracuse_m_64.html.

Lisheron, Mark. "Big Time in the Big Easy." *American Journalism Review*, July/August 1997. http://www.ajr.org/article.asp?id=682.

Louisiana Economic Development. "Digital Interactive Media and Software Development Incentive." n.d., http://www.louisianaeconomicdevelopment.com/incentives/digital-interactive-media-and-software-development-incentive.aspx.

Lyons, Lori. Interview with author, 21 April 2013.

Maier, Thomas. *Newhouse: All the Glitter, Power, & Glory of America's Richest Media Empire & the Secretive Man Behind It.* Boulder, Colorado: Johnson Books, 1997.

Massett, Ray, general manager, *Times-Picayune*, to Greg A. Anders, state rapid response coordinator, Louisiana Workforce Commission, New Orleans, 15 June 2012.

Mathews, Ricky. "A Sea of Destruction: Recovery Will Be a Marathon, Not a Sprint (Ricky Mathews)." AL.com | *Press-Register*, 8 May 2011. http://blog.al.com/press-register-commentary/2011/05/a_sea_of_destruction_recovery.html.

———. "NOLA.com and the *Times-Picayune* Are Here to Stay." NOLA.com | *Times-Picayune*, 17 June 2013. http://www.nola.com/opinions/index.ssf/2012/06/the_times-picayune_and_nolacom.html.

Mayer III, Emmett. Email interview with author, 22 April 2013.

Maynard, Micheline. "What New Orleans Can Expect When Its Newspaper Goes Away," Forbes.com, 24 May 2012. http://www.forbes.com/sites/michelinemaynard/2012/05/24/what-new-orleans-can-expect-when-its-newspaper-goes-away/.

———. "3 Numbers in the Battle to Save the New Orleans *Times-Picayune*." Forbes.com, 25 May 2012. http://www.forbes.com/sites/michelinemaynard/2012/05/25/3-numbers-in-the-battle-to-save-the-new-orleans-times-picayune/.

McClemore, Dylan. "Mass Layoffs or 'Job Notifications'? Advance's Attempt to Spin Its Deep South Newspaper Guttings." DylanMcClemore.com, 13 June 2012. http://dylanmclemore.com/2012/06/13/mass-layoffs-or-job-notifications-advances-attempt-to-spin-its-deep-south-newspaper-guttings/.

McCollam, Douglas. "Up and Down on the Bayou: A Snapshot of the *Times-Picayune* Five Years After Katrina." *Columbia Journalism Review,* 1 July 2010. http://www.cjr.org/behind_the_news/timespicayune_five_years_later.php?page=all.

McCusker, John. Interview with author, 18 March 2013.

McHugh, Bill. "Is the *Times-Picayune* Brand Being Killed Off?" Dump the *Picayune*.com, 12 November 2012. http://www.dumpthepicayune.com/is-the-times-picayune-brand-being-killed-off/.

———. Email interview with author, 21 February 2013.

McQuaid, John. "Why a Weak Website Can't Replace a Daily Newspaper in New Orleans." Atlantic.com, 12 June 2012. http://www.theatlantic.com/national/archive/2012/06/why-a-weak-website-cant-replace-a-daily-newspaper-in-new-orleans/258393/.

———. Twitter post. 30 April 2013, 12:31 p.m. https://twitter.com/johnmcquaid.

Meeker, Richard H. *Newspaperman: S.I. Newhouse and the Business of News.* New York and New Haven: Ticknor & Fields, 1983.

———. Interview with author, 16 April 2013.

Meeks, David. "Lessons in Rebuilding: A House and a Newspaper." *Nieman Reports: Nieman Foundation for Journalism at Harvard,* Fall 2007. http://www.nieman.harvard.edu/reports/article/100155/Lessons-in-Rebuilding-A-House-and-a-Newspaper.aspx.

Mesh, Aaron. "Stop the Presses: The *Oregonian* May Not Be a Daily Newspaper Much Longer." *Willamette Weekly,* 8 August 2012. http://www.wweek.com/portland/article-19535-stop_the_presses.html.

Milling, Anne. Interview with author, 15 March 2013.

Mitchell, Dan. "Profits Aren't the Only Consideration for Newspapers." A Service of CNN, *Fortune, & Money,* 7 June 2012. http://tech.fortune.cnn.com/2012/06/07/profits-arent-the-only-consideration-for-newspapers/.

Moos, Julie. "Cleveland *Plain Dealer* Union Gets New Deal That Protects Staff from Future Layoffs, Raises Pay 8%." Poynter.org, 7 December 2012. http://www.poynter.org/latest-news/mediawire/197469/cleveland-plain-dealer-union-gets-new-deal-that-protects-staff-from-future-layoffs-raises-pay-8/.

Moos, Julie, and Steve Myers. "How *Times-Picayune,* Alabama Newspaper Changes Played on Their Front Pages." Poynter.org, 25 May 2012, updated 28 May 2012. http://www.poynter.org/latest-news/mediawire/175181/how-times-picayune-alabama-newspaper-changes-played-on-their-front-pages/.

[MORE]. 4, no. 5 (May 1974).

Morton, John. Telephone interview with author, 8 May 2013.

———. Email interview with author, 10 May 2013.

Murphy, Paul. "Citizens' Group Forms to Save Daily *Times-Picayune* Newspaper." WWL-TV, 4 June 2012. http://www.wwltv.com/news/Times-Picayune-Citizens-Group-Forms-To-Save-Daily-Newspaper-157059965.html.

Mutter, Alan D. "What's Next For Newspapers?" Reflections of a Newsosaur.com. 12 July 2012. http://newsosaur.blogspot.com/2012/07/whats-next-for-newspapers.html.

———. Telephone interview with author, 30 April 2013.

Nelson, Jack. "New Orleans *Times-Picayune* Series on Racism." Pew Research Center's Project for Excellence in Journalism Case Studies, 15 February 2003. http://www.journalism.org/node/1784 and http://www.unc.edu/~pmeyer/racism.html.

Nelson, Kelly. Email to Catherine Hughes, 11 December 2012.

New York Times. "Samuel I. Newhouse, Publisher, Dies at 84." *New York Times*, 30 August 1979. http://select.nytimes.com/gst/abstract.html?res=F50711F6345 D12728DDDA90B94D0405B898BF1D3 (subscription required).

———. "Ashton Phelps, 69, Is Dead; New Orleans News Executive." *New York Times*, 22 March 1983. http://www.nytimes.com/1983/03/22/obituaries/ashton-phelps-69-is-dead-new-orleans-news-executive.html.

New Orleans bureau. "*Advocate* to Publish N.O. Area Obituaries." *Advocate*, 31 May 2013. http://theadvocate.com/news/neworleans/6117065-148/advocate-to-publish-no-areaobituaries.

———. "Award-Winning Reporter John Simerman to Join the *Advocate's* New Orleans Staff." *Advocate*, 31 May 2013. http://theadvocate.com/news/neworleans/6128563-148/award-winning-reporter-john-simerman-to

Newhouse, Steve. "Steve Newhouse Explains Michigan Transition, *Times-Picayune* Future." Poynter.org, 3 August 2012, updated 6 August 2012. http://www.poynter.org/latest-news/business-news/183948/steve-newhouse-explains-michigan-transition-times-picayune-future/.

Newspaper Association of America. "The American Newspaper Media Industry Revenue Profile 2012." Newspaper Association of America, 8 April 2013. http://www.naa.org/Trends-and-Numbers/Newspaper-Revenue/Newspaper-Media-Industry-Revenue-Profile-2012.aspx.

The Newspaper Guild, Local 1. "TNG Local 1: the Northeast Ohio Newspaper Guild," n.d., http://tnglocal1.org/mainpages/home.htm.

Niles, Robert. "NOLA.com Blogs and Forums Help Save Lives After Katrina." *Online Journalism Review*, 13 September 2005. http://www.ojr.org/050913glaser/.

NOLA.com | *Times-Picayune*. "T-P Resumes Printing." NOLA.com | *Times-Picayune*. 1 September 2005, updated 8 July 2010. http://www.nola.com/katrina/index.ssf/2005/09/t-p_resumes_printing.html.

———. "City Not Safe for Anyone." NOLA.com | *Times-Picayune*. 1 September 2005, updated 13 August 2010. http://www.nola.com/katrina/index.ssf/2005/09/city_not_safe_for_anyone.html.

———. "1980: New Orleans' Two Major Newspapers Merge." NOLA.com | *Times-Picayune*. 23 December 2011. http://www.nola.com/175years/index.ssf/2011/12/1980_new_orleans_becomes_a_sin.html.

———. "New Digitally Focused Company Launches this Fall with Beefed Up Online Coverage; the *Times-Picayune* Will Move this Fall to Three Printed Papers a Week." NOLA.com | *Times-Picayune*. 24 May 2012, updated 5 June

2012. http://www.nola.com/business/index.ssf/2012/05/nolamediagroup. html.

———. "Brett Anderson Invited to Return after Nieman Fellowship." NOLA.com | *Times-Picayune*. 15 June 2012. http://www.nola.com/dining/index. ssf/2012/06/brett_anderson_invited_to_retu.html.

———. "The *Times-Picayune* Will Print and Deliver New Orleans Saints Coverage After Every Game this Year." NOLA.com | *Times-Picayune*. 26 July 2012, updated 27 July 2012. http://www.nola.com/saints/index.ssf/2012/07/ the_times-picayune_will_print.html.

———. "NOLA Media Group Launches $500,000 Effort to Boost Community Access to Digital Technology, Information." NOLA.com | *Times-Picayune*. 24 September 2012. http://www.nola.com/business/index.ssf/2012/09/nola_ media_group_launches_5000.html

———. "NOLA Media Group Signs Long-Term Lease in Downtown Baton Rouge." NOLA.com | *Times-Picayune*. 3 October 2012. http://www.nola. com/business/index.ssf/2012/10/nola_media_group_signs_long-te.html.

———. "Early Sunday Edition to Hit Newsstands Saturday Mornings Beginning Oct. 6." NOLA.com | *Times-Picayune*, 5 October 2012. http://www.nola. com/business/index.ssf/2012/10/early_sunday_edition_to_hit_ne.html.

———. "Meet the *Times-Picayune*/NOLA.com Community Roundtable: Editorial." NOLA.com | *Times-Picayune*, 9 December 2012; updated 20 December 2012. http://www.nola.com/opinions/index.ssf/2012/12/meet_ the_times-picayunenolacom.html.

———. "Nola Access Initiative Chooses Columbia Parc for $20,000 Technology Grant." NOLA.com | *Times-Picayune*. 21 May 2013. http://www.nola.com/ business/index.ssf/2013/05/nola_access_initiative_chooses.html.

Nolan, Bruce. "*Times-Picayune* Publisher Ashton Phelps Jr. to Retire This Year." NOLA.com | *Times-Picayune*, 27 March 2012. http://www.nola.com/ business/index.ssf/2012/03/times-picayune_publisher_ashto.html.

———. "I Had a License to Be There," JimRomenesko.com. 28 September 2012, http://jimromenesko.com/2012/09/28/a-times-picayune-veterans-farewell/.

———. Interview with author, 19 March 2013.

O'Byrne, James. "Bicycling Into the Heart of the Flood: A Hurricane Katrina Remembrance." NOLA.com | *Times-Picayune*, 28 August 2010, updated 29 Aug. 2011. http://www.nola.com/katrina/index.ssf/2010/08/bicycling_ into_the_heart_of_th.html.

———. "*BR*, a Free Weekly Publication from NOLA.com, Launches Wednesday." NOLA.com | *Times-Picayune*, 24 April 2013, http://www.nola.com/ business/baton-rouge/index.ssf/2013/04/br_a_free_weekly_publication_f. html.

———, Mark Schleifstein, and Susan Feeney. "Journalism Driven By Passion." *Nieman Reports*, Fall 2007. http://www.nieman.harvard.edu/reports/

article/100149/Journalism-Driven-By-Passion.aspx.

Peck, Renée. "Viewpoint: 'We Are One City.'" NolaVie.com, 18 June 2013. http://nolavie.com/2012/06/viewpoint-we-are-one-city-95567.html.

Perlstein, Michael. "Covering Katrina: On Taking it Personally." In *The Mind of a Journalist*, edited by Jim Willis. Los Angeles: Sage, 2010.

Pew Research Center's Project for Excellence in Journalism. "The State of the News Media 2013: An Annual Report on American Journalism." Pew Research Center's Project for Excellence in Journalism, 18 March 2013. http://stateofthemedia.org/.

Phelps, Ashton, Jr. Memo to employees, 23 June 2008.

——. Memo to employees, 26 December 2008.

——. Letter to employees, 5 August 2009.

——. Letter to employees, 7 December 2009.

——. Memo to employees, 16 November 2011.

——. Memo to employees, 19 January 2012.

Pitt, Patti. Telephone interview with author, 7 May 2013.

Plyer, Allison. "Facts for Features: Hurricane Katrina Impact." Greater New Orleans Community Data Center, 10 August 2012. http://www.gnocdc.org/Factsforfeatures/HurricaneKatrinaImpact/index.html.

——. "Facts for Features: Hurricane Katrina Recovery." Greater New Orleans Community Data Center, 3 February 2013. http://www.gnocdc.org/Factsforfeatures/HurricaneKatrinaRecovery/index.html.

Pope, John. "Personal Circumstances Intersect with Professional Obligations." *Nieman Reports: Nieman Foundation for Journalism at Harvard*, Fall 2007. http://www.nieman.harvard.edu/reports/article/100153/Personal-Circumstances-Intersect-With-Professional-Obligations.aspx.

——. "Johanna Schindler, Director of Communications at UNO, Dies at 53." NOLA.com | *Times-Picayune*, 8 March 2010. http://www.nola.com/news/index.ssf/2010/03/johanna_schindler_director_of.html.

——. "NOLA Media Group Announces Ad Sales Leadership Team." Nola.com | *Times-Picayune*, 5 August 2012. http://www.nola.com/business/index.ssf/2012/08/nola_media_group_announces_ad.html.

Pulitzer.org. "The 2006 Pulitzer Prize Winners: Commentary." Pulitzer.org, n.d. http://www.pulitzer.org/citation/2006-Commentary.

Rawls, Alex. "The *T-P* Rally & America's Petri Dish." MySplitMilk.com, 11 June 2012. http://myspiltmilk.com/t-p-rally-americas-petri-dish.

Riegel, Stephanie. "News Alert: John Georges Potential Advocate Buyer," *Greater Baton Rouge Business Report*, 26 January 2013, http://www.businessreport.com/daily-report/1262013/News_alert-John_Georges_potential_Advocate_buyer#ixzz2UeclMFhw.

Riegel, Stephanie. "Baton Rouge's New Power Broker: John Georges," *Greater Baton Rouge Business Report*, 13 May 2013. http://www.businessreport.com/

article/20130513/BUSINESSREPORT0401/130519966.

Robertson, Campbell. "New Orleans Struggles With Latest Storm, Newspaper Layoffs." *New York Times*, 12 June 2013. http://www.nytimes. com/2012/06/13/us/new-orleans-struggles-with-latest-storm-newspaper-layoffs.html?smid=pl-share.

Romenesko, Jim. "Warren Buffett Buys Media General Papers for $142 Million." JimRomenesko.com, 17 May 2012. http://jimromenesko.com/2012/05/17/warren-buffet-buys-media-general-papers-for-142m.

Roop, Lee. "Alabama Media Group Signs Lease to Move *Huntsville Times* Offices Downtown in Early 2013." *Alabama Business News*, 5 December 2012. http://bamabusinessnews.com/alabama-media-group-signs-lease-to-move-huntsville-times-offices-downtown-in-early-2013-updated-2/.

Rose, Chris. *One Dead in Attic*. New Orleans: Chris Rose Books, 2005.

———. Interview with author, 31 May 2013.

———. "Stop the Presses: Life and Death at the *Times-Picayune*." *Oxford American*, 27 August 2012. http://www.oxfordamerican.org/articles/2012/aug/27/new-south-journalism-sometimes-picayune/.

Rosenstiel, Tom, Mark Jurkowitz, and Hong Ji. "The Search for a New Business Model: How Newspapers are Faring Trying to Build Digital Revenue." Pew Research Center's Project for Excellence in Journalism, 5 March 2012. http://www.journalism.org/analysis_report/industry_looking_ahead.

Saba, Jennifer. "*Times-Picayune* Circ Down Nearly 30% Over Four Years." *Editor & Publisher*, 28 April 2008. http://www.editorandpublisher.com/Article/-Times-Picayune-Circ-Down-Nearly-30-Over-Four-years (subscription required).

———. "New Study Charts Readership Reach—Guess Who's No. 1?" *Editor & Publisher*, 2 June 2009. http://www.editorandpublisher.com/Article/New-Study-Charts-Readership-Reach-Guess-Who-s-No-1- (subscription required).

Saulny, Susan. "After Long Stress, Newsman in New Orleans Unravels." *New York Times*, 10 August 2006. http://www.nytimes.com/2006/08/10/us/10orleans.html?_r=0.

Schleifstein, Mark. "Covering the Coast." *GW Magazine*, Fall 2010. http://www.gwu.edu/~magazine/archive/2010_fall/feature2.html.

———. Interview with author, 15 March 2013.

Serna, Joseph. "Hurricane Sandy Death Toll Climbs Above 110, N.Y. Hardest Hit." *Los Angeles Times*, 3 November 2012. http://articles.latimes.com/2012/nov/03/nation/la-na-nn-hurricane-sandy-deaths-climb-20121103.

Shafer, Jack. "The Great Newspaper Liquidation." Reuters.com. 5 June 2012. http://blogs.reuters.com/jackshafer/2012/06/05/the-great-newspaper-liquidation/.

Shea, Dan. Interview with author, 14 March 2013.

———. Email interview with author, 9 May 2013.

———. "Former *T-P* Editor: The *Advocate* Will Give the City a Daily Newspaper." Interviewed by Melanie Hebert. *The 504*, WUPL-TV and WWL-TV, 16 May 2013. http://www.wwltv.com/on-tv/wupl/Former-T-P-editor-The-Advocate-will-give-the-city-a-daily-newspaper-207810411.html?ref=prev

Shearer, Harry. "The Sometimes Picayune: Want to Damage New Orleans (again)? Decimate its Newspaper." *Columbia Journalism Review*, 6 June 2012. http://www.cjr.org/behind_the_news/the_sometimes_picayune.php?page=all.

Sherman, G. "Newhouses Right *Times-Picayune* As It Bails Water." *New York Observer*, 12 September 2005. http://observer.com/2005/09/newhouses-right-itimespicayunei-as-it-bails-water.

Sherman, Ted. "*Star-Ledger* Publisher Says Newspaper Will Close if Unions Don't Give Concessions." *Star-Ledger*, 26 June 2013. http://www.nj.com/sussex-county/index.ssf/2013/06/star-ledger.html#incart_river.

———, and Kelly Heyboer. "*Star-Ledger* Announces Layoffs of 34 Employees, Including 18 Newsroom Staff." *Star-Ledger*, 17 January 2013. http://www.nj.com/news/index.ssf/2013/01/star-ledger_announces_layoffs.html.

Sirigos, Constantine S. "50th Wealthiest Greeks in America," *National Herald*, 27 March 2012. https://s3.amazonaws.com/2013backup/tnhcontent/pdf/inserts/2012/Insert_3_2012_5516.pdf.

Smith, Robert L. "*Plain Dealer* Staff Launches Campaign to Save the Daily Paper." Cleveland.com | *Plain Dealer*, 9 November 2012. http://www.cleveland.com/business/index.ssf/2012/11/plain_dealer_staff_launch_a_ca.html.

Smith, Robert L. "*Plain Dealer* to Remain Daily, but 7-Day Home-Delivery Will End: Newsroom Briefed about *PD* Changes." Cleveland.com | *Plain Dealer*, 4 April 2013, updated 5 April 2013. http://www.cleveland.com/business/index.ssf/2013/04/plain_dealer_to_remain_daily_b.html#incart_m-rpt-2

Spicer, Beverly. "The Ordeal of Ted Jackson and the New Orleans *Times Picayune*." Digital Journalist, December 2005. http://digitaljournalist.org/issue0512/jackson_intro.html.

Stevenson, A.E. "Possible Sale in the Works for the *Advocate*." WBRZ-TV, 25 January 2013. http://www.wbrz.com/news/possible-sale-in-the-works-for-the-advocate-.

Stoeffel, Kat. "The Sunset of Si." *New York Observer*, 1 August 2012. http://observer.com/2012/08/the-sunset-of-si-as-the-conde-nast-chairman-fades-away-his-glossy-kingdom-is-losing-some-sparkle/?show=all.

Strupp, Joe. "Advance Announces Company-wide Furloughs." *Editor & Publisher*. 23 March 2009. http://www.editorandpublisher.com/Article/Advance (subscription required).

Talbot, George. "Ricky Mathews Named President, Publisher of *Press-Register*." AL.com | *Press-Register*, 18 August 2009. http://www.al.com/news/press-register/metro.ssf?/base/news/1250586943198880.xml&coll=3.

Taylor, Brett Will. "Hello? Steve Newhouse? It's WTF calling." NolaVie.org, 14 June 2012. http://nolavie.com/2012/06/love-nola-hello-steve-newhouse-its-wtf-calling-78390.html.

Theim, Rebecca. "NOLA Media Group Reps Paint Glowing Picture of *Times-Picayune* Digital Transition." DashTHIRTYdash.org, 10 December 2012. http://dashthirtydash.org/2012/12/10/out-to-lunch.

———. "NOLA.com Editor on Messy Digital Announcement: 'Arrogant to Think We Could Keep a Secret in a Newsroom.'" DashTHIRTYdash.org, 12 December 2012. http://dashthirtydash.org/2012/12/12/arrogant/.

———. "New Orleans' 2013 Mardi Gras Parades Take Aim at Radical Changes, Layoffs at *Times-Picayune*." DashTHIRTYdash.org, 8 February 2013, http://dashthirtydash.org/2013/02/08/2013-mardi-gras-tp-satire/.

Thevenot, Brian. "Apocalypse in New Orleans." *American Journalism Review*, October/November 2005. http://www.ajr.org/article.asp?id=3959.

———. "To Love This City Back to Life." *American Journalism Review*, August/September 2006. http://www.ajr.org/article.asp?id=4155.

Time. "The Newspaper Collector." 27 July 1962.

Times-Picayune. "From A to Z: *The Times-Picayune* Employee Benefits for Permanent and Term Full-Time Employees." New Orleans: 1991.

———. "Editorial: Faster, Faster–Please." 2 September 2005. http://www.nola.com/katrina/index.ssf/2005/09/editorial_faster_faster_--please.html.

———. "An Open Letter to the President." 4 September 2005. http://www.nola.com/katrina/pages/090405/a15.pdf.

———. "Yes, We Are Worth It." 2 September 2005. http://www.nola.com/katrina/pages/090205/a15.pdf.

———. "Exhibit A: The *Times-Picayune*. Department, Title, Age, Selected for Layoff?" 12 June 2012.

———. PDF of the front page. *Times-Picayune*. 13 June 2013. http://media.nola.com/pages/other/MetroA1June132012.pdf.

Tisserand, Michael. Email interview with author, 21 April 2013.

Trickey, Erick. "*Plain Dealer* Union Members Drink 7-Day Lager, Mull Bitter Agreement." *Cleveland Magazine*, 7 December 2012. http://www.clevelandmagazine.blogspot.com/2012/12/plain-dealer-union-members-drink-7-day.html.

Troeh, Eve. "Two Newspapers Battle It Out For The New Orleans Market." National Public Radio, 29 May 2013. http://www.npr.org/2013/05/29/186900885/two-newspapers-battle-it-out-for-the-new-orleans-market.

Vega, Tanzina. "Small Gain in Newspaper Circulations, Aided by Digital Subscriptions." Media Decoder, *New York Times*, 1 May 2012. http://mediadecoder.blogs.nytimes.com/2012/05/01/newspaper-circulations-hold-steady-aided-by-digital-subscriptions/?smid=pl-share.

Vitter, David. "Vitter Urges Newhouse to Sell the *Times Picayune*." Official website of US Sen. David Vitter, 26 July 2012. http://www.vitter.senate.gov/newsroom/press/vitter-urges-newhouse-to-sell-the-times-picayune.

Vorkapic, Rudy Matthew. "The Future of the *Times-Picayune* Newspaper." *New Orleans Levee*, 13 July 2012. http://nolevee.com/?p=1894.

———. "Daily *Times-Picayune* Newspaper Dead at 175." *New Orleans Levee*, 8 October 2012. http://nolevee.com/?p=2263.

Wagner, Cheryl. *Plenty Enough Suck to Go Around: A Memoir of Floods, Fires, Parades and Plywood.* New York: Citadel Press, 2009.

Waterbury Republican-American. "Is New Orleans Worth Reclaiming?" 31 August 2005. http://www.freerepublic.com/focus/f-news/1474336/posts.

WDSU.com. "Jindal Laments Changes at *Times-Picayune.*"1 July 2012. http://www.wdsu.com/news/politics/Jindal-laments-changes-at-Times-Picayune/-/9853324/15364302/-/146jm0q/-/index.html#ixzz2PLRY89UQ

Weld for Birmingham. "Death by 400 Cuts." 19 June 2012. http://weldbham.com/blog/2012/06/19/death-of-400-cuts-advances-retreat-the-lifelines-of-those-bylines/.

Wells, Carlie Kollath. "*Times-Picayune* Publisher: 'This Is Chapter Two.'" Poynter.org, 19 February 2013, updated 20 February 2013. http://www.poynter.org/latest-news/top-stories/204743/times-picayune-publisher-this-is-chapter-two/.

———. "New *Times-Picayune*'s Newsroom Features 'Hotel Seating.'" BusinessJournalism.org, 19 February 2013. http://businessjournalism.org/2013/02/19/new-times-picayunes-newsroom-features-hotel-seating/.

Wemple, Erik. "*Times-Picayune* Publisher Spews Standard Workforce-Reduction Garbage." A Reported Opinion Blog on News Media, *Washington Post*, 24 May 2012. http://www.washingtonpost.com/blogs/erik-wemple/post/times-picayune-publisher-spews-standard-workforce-reduction-garbage/2012/05/24/gJQAfy4FnU_blog.html.

———. "*Times-Picayune* Food Critic Says Nieman Fellowship Prompted His Layoff." A Reported Opinion Blog on News Media, *Washington Post*, 12 June 2012. http://www.washingtonpost.com/blogs/erik-wemple/post/times-picayune-restaurant-critic-laid-off/2012/06/12/gJQA3dywXV_blog.html.

White, Jaquetta. "*Times-Picayune* Lays Off Nearly One-Third of Its Staff." NOLA.com | *Times-Picayune*, 12 June 2012. http://www.nola.com/business/index.ssf/2012/06/times_picayune_employees_to_le.html.

———. "Most *Times-Picayune* Workers Accept Offer to Work for Successor Companies." NOLA.com | *Times-Picayune*, 29 June 2012. http://www.nola.com/business/index.ssf/2012/06/many_times-picayune_workers_ac.html.

Whitmire, Kyle. "New Orleans Rallies around *Times-Picayune*, but Where's the Outrage in Birmingham?" *Weld for Birmingham*, 5 June 2012. http://weldbham.com/secondfront/2012/06/05/new-orleans-rallies-around-times-picayune-but-wheres-the-outrage-in-birmingham/.

Wilson, Grace. Facebook post. 6 May 2013, 10:13 a.m. https://www.facebook.
    com/iLoveNewOrleans/activity/861696251845?og_perm_src=OPEN_
    GRAPH_SINGLE_STORY.
Yeoman, Barry. "The Redemption of Chris Rose." *Columbia Journalism Review,*
    January/February 2008. http://barryyeoman.com/2008/01/chris-rose/.

Index